The Internet FOR DUMMIES®

A Wiley Brand

14th Edition

by John R. Levine
Margaret Levine Young

The Internet For Dummies®, 14th Edition

Published by: **John Wiley & Sons, Inc.,** 111 River Street, Hoboken, NJ 07030-5774, www.wiley.com

Copyright © 2015 by John Wiley & Sons, Inc., Hoboken, New Jersey

Published simultaneously in Canada

No part of this publication may be reproduced, stored in a retrieval system or transmitted in any form or by any means, electronic, mechanical, photocopying, recording, scanning or otherwise, except as permitted under Sections 107 or 108 of the 1976 United States Copyright Act, without the prior written permission of the Publisher. Requests to the Publisher for permission should be addressed to the Permissions Department, John Wiley & Sons, Inc., 111 River Street, Hoboken, NJ 07030, (201) 748-6011, fax (201) 748-6008, or online at http://www.wiley.com/go/permissions.

Trademarks: Wiley, For Dummies, the Dummies Man logo, Dummies.com, Making Everything Easier, and related trade dress are trademarks or registered trademarks of John Wiley & Sons, Inc. and may not be used without written permission. All other trademarks are the property of their respective owners. John Wiley & Sons, Inc. is not associated with any product or vendor mentioned in this book.

LIMIT OF LIABILITY/DISCLAIMER OF WARRANTY: THE PUBLISHER AND THE AUTHOR MAKE NO REPRESENTATIONS OR WARRANTIES WITH RESPECT TO THE ACCURACY OR COMPLETENESS OF THE CONTENTS OF THIS WORK AND SPECIFICALLY DISCLAIM ALL WARRANTIES, INCLUDING WITHOUT LIMITATION WARRANTIES OF FITNESS FOR A PARTICULAR PURPOSE. NO WARRANTY MAY BE CREATED OR EXTENDED BY SALES OR PROMOTIONAL MATERIALS. THE ADVICE AND STRATEGIES CONTAINED HEREIN MAY NOT BE SUITABLE FOR EVERY SITUATION. THIS WORK IS SOLD WITH THE UNDERSTANDING THAT THE PUBLISHER IS NOT ENGAGED IN RENDERING LEGAL, ACCOUNTING, OR OTHER PROFESSIONAL SERVICES. IF PROFESSIONAL ASSISTANCE IS REQUIRED, THE SERVICES OF A COMPETENT PROFESSIONAL PERSON SHOULD BE SOUGHT. NEITHER THE PUBLISHER NOR THE AUTHOR SHALL BE LIABLE FOR DAMAGES ARISING HEREFROM. THE FACT THAT AN ORGANIZATION OR WEBSITE IS REFERRED TO IN THIS WORK AS A CITATION AND/OR A POTENTIAL SOURCE OF FURTHER INFORMATION DOES NOT MEAN THAT THE AUTHOR OR THE PUBLISHER ENDORSES THE INFORMATION THE ORGANIZATION OR WEBSITE MAY PROVIDE OR RECOMMENDATIONS IT MAY MAKE. FURTHER, READERS SHOULD BE AWARE THAT INTERNET WEBSITES LISTED IN THIS WORK MAY HAVE CHANGED OR DISAPPEARED BETWEEN WHEN THIS WORK WAS WRITTEN AND WHEN IT IS READ.

For general information on our other products and services, please contact our Customer Care Department within the U.S. at 877-762-2974, outside the U.S. at 317-572-3993, or fax 317-572-4002. For technical support, please visit www.wiley.com/techsupport.

Wiley publishes in a variety of print and electronic formats and by print-on-demand. Some material included with standard print versions of this book may not be included in e-books or in print-on-demand. If this book refers to media such as a CD or DVD that is not included in the version you purchased, you may download this material at http://booksupport.wiley.com. For more information about Wiley products, visit www.wiley.com.

Library of Congress Control Number is available from the publisher.

ISBN 978-1-118-96769-0 (pbk); ISBN 978-1-118-96775-1 (ePub); ISBN 978-1-118-96773-7 (ePDF)

Manufactured in the United States of America

10 9 8 7 6 5 4 3 2

Contents at a Glance

Table of Contents

Introduction

*W*elcome to *The Internet For Dummies,* 14th Edition. The Internet has become so interwoven in today's life — work, school, politics, and play — that ignoring it is no longer an option. This book describes what you do to become an *Internaut* (someone who navigates the Internet with skill) — how to get started, what you need to know, and where to go for help. And, we describe it in plain old English.

When we first wrote *The Internet For Dummies* 21 years ago (yikes!), a typical Internet user was a student who connected from college or a technical worker who had access at the office. The World Wide Web was so new that it had only a few hundred Web pages and we only mentioned it in one chapter of the book. The Internet has grown like crazy to include a billion (dare we say it?) normal people, connecting from computers at home or work, along with students ranging from elementary school to adult education. This 14th edition focuses on what's the most interesting to typical users — how to find things on the World Wide Web, download interesting things, send and receive electronic mail (email), and shop, invest, chat, and play games online.

About This Book

We don't flatter ourselves to think you're interested enough in the Internet to sit down and read the entire book (although it should be a fine book for the bathroom). When you run into a problem using the Internet ("Hmm, I *thought* that I knew how to find old TV shows online, but I don't seem to remember"), just dip into the book long enough to solve your problem.

Pertinent sections include

- Understanding what the Internet is
- Staying safe online
- Getting your computer (or tablet or phone or whatever) connected to the Internet
- Climbing around the World Wide Web
- Finding people, places, and things
- Communicating by email

- Hanging out with friends using Facebook, instant messaging, and other methods
- Watching movies, listening to radio shows, shopping, and other fun online activities
- Putting your own stuff online with websites and social networks

How to Use This Book

To begin, please read the first two chapters. They give you an overview of the Internet and some important safety tips. If you have children or grandchildren, read Chapter 3, too. When you're ready to get yourself on the Internet, turn to Part II and read Chapter 4. Chapter 6 describes how to use the web — you aren't truly online until you can see a web page. Parts III through VI egg you on and provide extra support — they describe the web and email and other stuff you can do on the Internet.

Because the Internet is ever-changing, we put additional information online, which we can update more often than this book can be republished. We authors have a website with updates and history and other interesting articles, at net.gurus.org.

When you have to follow a complicated procedure, we spell it out step by step wherever possible. When you have to type something, it appears in the book in **boldface.** Type it just as it appears. Use the same capitalization we do — a few systems care deeply about CAPITAL and lowercase (small) letters. Then press the Enter key. The book tells you what should happen when you give each command and what your options are.

When you have to choose commands from menus, we use the ⇨ symbol. For example, we write File⇨Exit when we want you to choose the File command from the menu bar and then choose the Exit command from the menu that appears.

Who Are You?

In writing this book, we made a few assumptions about you:

- You have or would like to have access to the Internet.
- You want to get some work done online. (We consider the term *work* to include the concepts *play* and *learn*.)
- You aren't interested in becoming the world's next great Internet expert, at least not this week.

How This Book Is Organized

This book has six parts, and the parts stand on their own. Although you can begin reading wherever you like, you should at least skim Parts I and II first to become acquainted with some unavoidable Internet jargon and find out how to get your computer on the Internet.

Here are the parts of the book:

In Part I, "Welcome to the Internet," you find out what the Internet is and why it's interesting (at least why we think it's interesting). Also, this part gives you vital terminology and explains concepts that help you as you read the later parts of the book. Part I discusses security and privacy issues and gives some thoughts about children's use of the Internet.

For the nuts and bolts of getting online, read Part II, "Internet, Here I Come!" For most users, by far the most difficult part of the Internet is getting to that first connection, with software loaded, configuration configured, and modem modeming or broadband banding broadly. After that, it's (relatively) smooth sailing. We also tell you how to use the World Wide Web, the most popular online application. You also get a briefing on avoiding and blocking online hazards, such as viruses and spam.

Part III, "Hanging Out with Friends Online," looks at the important communication services: sending and receiving email, swapping instant messages, and chatting. You find out how to exchange email with people down the hall or on other continents, how to make the most of Internet-based phone and video conferencing programs, how to use instant messaging programs to chat with your online pals, how to get going with Facebook and Twitter (the ultimate answers to free time), and how to use email mailing lists to keep in touch with people of similar interests.

Part IV, "The Web Is Full of Cool Stuff," dives into the web in more detail. We discuss how to get around on the web, how to find stuff (which isn't as easy as it should be), and how to shop online. We also include chapters on listening to music, watching videos, shopping, and managing your finances on the Internet.

Part V, "Putting Your Own Stuff on the Web," talks about how to post all kinds of material on the Internet. Putting your writing, photos, and videos online is easier than ever because of the range of free web services you can use, including blogs, which let anyone be an online journalist.

Part VI, "The Part of Tens," is a compendium of ready references and useful facts (which, we suppose, suggests that the rest of the book is full of useless facts).

This book's Cheat Sheet, which summarizes how to use the most important web browsers and email programs in the book, is online at www.dummies.com/cheatsheet/internet.

Icons Used in This Book

Lets you know that some particularly nerdy, technoid information is coming up so that you can skip it, if you want. (On the other hand, you may want to read it.)

Indicates that a nifty little shortcut or timesaver is explained.

Gaack! We found out about this information the hard way! Don't let it happen to you!

Indicates something to file away in your memory archives.

Beyond the Book

Understanding the Internet goes beyond these pages and onto the web, where you can access additional information. There's a handy-dandy cheat sheet that reiterates the basics and web extras.

- ✔ **Cheat Sheet:** You can find this book's online Cheat Sheet at www.dummies.com/cheatsheet/internet. See the Cheat Sheet for Internet survival tips.

- ✔ **Web Extras:** Companion articles to this book's content are available at www.dummies.com/extras/internet. The topics range from trading with villagers, building a dog army, and ten useful crafting recipes.

- ✔ **Updates:** If this book has any updates, they'll be posted at www.dummies.com/extras/internet.

If you want to contact the authors directly, send Internet email to internet14@gurus.org (our friendly robot usually answers immediately; the human authors read all the email and answer as much as they can) or visit the authors' website at net.gurus.org.

Part I
Getting Started with the Internet

In this part . . .

✔ Understand why the Internet is a big deal

✔ Be safe on the Internet

✔ Introduce your kids to the Internet

Chapter 1

What's So Great about the Internet?

In This Chapter

▶ What, really, is the Internet?

▶ For that matter, what is a network?

▶ What is the Internet good for?

It's huge, it's sprawling, it's globe spanning, and it has become part of our lives. It must be . . . the Internet. We all know something about it, and most of us have tried to use it, with more or less success. (If you've had less, you've come to the right place.) In this chapter, we look at what the Internet is and can do, before we dive into details in the rest of this book.

If you're new to the Internet, and especially if you don't have much computer experience, *be patient with yourself.* Many of the ideas here are completely new. Allow yourself some time to read and reread. The Internet is a different world with its own language, and it takes some getting used to.

Even experienced computer users can find using the Internet more complex than other tasks they've tackled. The Internet isn't a single software package and doesn't easily lend itself to the kind of step-by-step instructions we'd provide for a single, fixed program. This book is as step-by-step as we can make it, but the Internet resembles a living organism mutating at an astonishing rate more than it resembles Microsoft Word and Excel, which sit quietly on your computer. After you get set up and practice a little, using the Internet seems like second nature; in the beginning, however, it can be daunting.

So What Is the Internet?

The Internet — also known as the *Net* — is the world's largest computer network. "What is a network?" you may ask. Even if you already know, you may want to read the next couple of paragraphs to make sure that we're speaking the same language.

Where did the Internet come from?

The ancestor of the Internet is the *ARPANET,* a project funded by the Department of Defense (DoD) in 1969, as an experiment in reliable networking and to link DoD and military research contractors, including many universities doing military-funded research. (ARPA stands for Advanced Research Projects Administration, the branch of the DoD in charge of handing out grant money. For enhanced confusion, the agency is now known as *DARPA* — the added *D* is for *Defense,* in case anyone wondered where the money came from.) Although the ARPANET started small — connecting three computers in California with one in Utah — it quickly grew to span the continent and, via radio link, Europe.

In the early 1980s, the ARPANET grew into the early Internet, a group of interlinked networks connecting many educational and research sites funded by the National Science Foundation (NSF), along with the original military sites. By 1990, it was clear that the Internet was here to stay, and DARPA and the NSF bowed out in favor of the commercially run networks that make up today's Internet. (And, yes, although Al Gore didn't invent the Internet, he was instrumental in keeping it funded so that it could turn into the Internet we know now.) Familiar companies such as AT&T, Comcast, Sprint, and Verizon run some networks; others belong to specialty companies, such as Level3 and Cogent. No matter which one you're attached to, they all interconnect, so it's all one giant Internet. For more information, read our web page at net.gurus.org/history.

A computer *network* is a bunch of computers that communicate with each other, sort of like a radio or TV network connects a bunch of radio or TV stations so that they can share the latest episode of *The Big Bang Theory.*

Don't take the analogy too far. In *broadcast* networking, TV networks send the same information to all stations at the same time; in computer networking, each particular message is routed to a particular computer, so different computers can display different things. Unlike TV networks, computer networks are two-way: When computer A sends a message to computer B, B can send a reply back to A.

Some computer networks consist of a central computer and a bunch of remote stations that report to it (for example, a central airline-reservation computer with thousands of screens and keyboards in airports and travel agencies). Other networks, including the Internet, are more egalitarian and permit any computer on the network to communicate with any other computer. Many wireless devices — cellphones, tablets, and their ilk — expand the reach of the Internet right into our pockets. (Hands off our wallets!)

The Internet isn't simply one network — it's a network of networks, all freely exchanging information. The networks range from the big, corporate networks to tiny ones (such as the one John built in his back bedroom, made from a couple of old PCs he bought at an electronics parts store) and everything in between. College and university networks have long been part of the

Internet, and now high schools and elementary schools are joining in. Lately, the Internet has become so popular that many households have more than one computer, as well as portable devices like tablets and smart phones, and are creating their own little networks that connect to the Internet.

What's All the Hoopla?

Everywhere you turn, you can find traces of the Internet. Household products, business cards, radio shows, and movie credits list their website addresses (usually starting with *www* and ending with *.com*) and their email addresses. New people you meet would rather give you an email address than a phone number. Everyone seems to be "going online" and "googling it."

The Internet affects our lives on a scale as significant as the telephone and television. When it comes to spreading information, the Internet is the most significant invention since the printing press. If you use a telephone, write letters, read a newspaper or magazine, or do business or any kind of research, the Internet can radically alter your worldview.

On networks, size counts a great deal: The larger a network is, the more stuff it has to offer. Because the Internet is the world's largest interconnected group of computer networks, it has an amazing array of information to offer.

When people talk about the Internet, they usually talk about what they can do, what they have found, and whom they have met. The number of available services is too huge to list in this chapter, but here are the Big Three:

- ✔ **Electronic mail (email):** This service is certainly the most widely used — you can exchange email with millions of people all over the world. People use email for anything for which they might use paper (mail, faxes, special delivery of documents) or the telephone (gossip, recipes, love letters) to communicate — you name it. We hear that some people even use it for stuff related to work. Electronic *mailing lists* enable you to join group discussions with people who have similar interests and to meet people over the Net. Part III of this book has all the details.

- ✔ **The World Wide Web:** When people talk these days about surfing the Net, they often mean checking out sites on this (buzzword alert) global multimedia hyperlinked database. In fact, people are talking more about the web and less about the Internet. Are they the same thing? Technically, the answer is "No." But practically speaking, the answer for many people is "Pretty close." We tell you the truth, the whole truth, and nothing but the truth in Part II of this book.

  Websites can provide you with information ranging from travel information to how to raise chickens. You can also look at videos, listen to music, buy stuff, sell stuff, and play video games.

The software used to navigate the web is a *browser*. The most popular browsers now are Firefox, Google Chrome, Internet Explorer, and Safari. We tell you all about them in Chapter 6.

✔ **Instant messaging (IM'ing):** Programs such as Facebook Messenger and WhatsApp let you send messages that "pop up" on the recipient's screen. We hear tales of nimble-fingered youth carrying on upward of 13 IM sessions simultaneously. Some websites also provide messaging services. We tell you about IM programs in Chapter 12.

The Internet is unlike any other communications media we've ever encountered. People of all ages, colors, creeds, and countries freely share ideas, stories, data, opinions, and products.

Anybody can access it

One great thing about the Internet is that it's the most open network in the world. Thousands of computers provide facilities that are available to anyone who has Internet access. Although pay services exist (and more are added every day), most Internet services are free for the taking after you're online. If you don't already have access to the Internet by way of your company, your school, your library, or a friend, you can pay for access by using an Internet service provider (ISP). We talk about some ISPs in Chapter 4.

One significant change in Net use in the past few years has been the move to ever smaller, lighter, and cheaper equipment to connect to it. A *netbook* is a small, inexpensive computer, about the size and weight of this book, that's intended mainly for connecting to the Net. If a netbook is too big for you, a smartphone such as the Apple iPhone or one using Google Android puts a computer, and the Internet, in your pocket with an always-on connection. A *tablet* such as an Apple iPad, or an Android tablet from Samsung, Asus, and other vendors, has a bigger screen than a phone and is easier to use than a phone, while still fitting in a purse or a (large) pocket. Unfortunately named *phablets* are oversized phones that are closer in size to tablets while still being usable as phones.

It's politically, socially, and religiously correct

Another great thing about the Internet is that it is what one may call "socially unstratified." That is, one computer is no better than any other, and no person is any better than any other. Who you are on the Internet depends solely on how you present yourself when you're using your computer. If what you say makes you sound like an intelligent, interesting person, that's who you are. It doesn't matter how old you are or what you look like or whether you're a student, business executive, or construction worker. Physical disabilities don't matter — we correspond with deaf and blind people. If they hadn't felt like telling us, we never would have known. People become famous (and infamous) in the Internet community as a result of their own efforts.

The Net advantage

The Internet has become totally mainstream, and you're falling further behind the curve — and at a faster rate — if you haven't yet gotten started. Increasingly, news gets out on the Internet before it's available any other way, and the cyber deprived are losing ground.

Here are some of the ways people use the Internet:

✔ **Find information:** Many websites have information free for the taking. It ranges from IRS tax forms that you can print and use to help-wanted ads, real estate listings, and recipes. From U.S. Supreme Court decisions and library card catalogs to the text of old books, digitized pictures (many suitable for family audiences), and an enormous variety of software — from games to operating systems — you can find virtually anything on the Net. You can check the weather forecast, view movie listings, find your childhood sweetheart, browse catalogs, and see school closings for anywhere in the world, from anywhere in the world.

Special tools known as *search engines* help you find information (and people) on the web. See Chapter 13 to find out how to search for the information you need.

Does the Internet truly reach every continent?

Some skeptical readers, after reading the claim that the Internet spans every continent, may point out that Antarctica is a continent, even though its population consists largely of penguins, who (as far as we know) aren't interested in computer networks. Does the Internet go there? It does. A few machines at the Scott Base on McMurdo Sound in Antarctica are on the Internet, connected by radio link to New Zealand. The base at the South Pole has a link to the United States. See the polar webcam at www.usap.gov.

At the time we wrote this book, the largest Internet-free land mass in the world was probably an uninhabited island in the Canadian arctic — Devon Island, perhaps, when its simulated Martian outpost isn't in use. (You can look it up on the Internet.) Even there, a satellite connection can provide an Internet connection, so perhaps nowhere on the surface of the earth is truly Internet-free.

- ✔ **Stay in touch:** *Weblogs* (or *blogs*) let people and organizations distribute current information about themselves rapidly and easily. *Microblogs,* such as Twitter, combine the Net with mobile phone text messages to let people stay up to date anywhere, at any time.

- ✔ **Get an education:** School teachers coordinate projects with classrooms all over the globe. College students and their families exchange email to facilitate letter-writing and keep down the cost of phone calls. Students do research from their home computers. The latest encyclopedias are online.

- ✔ **Buy and sell stuff:** On the Internet, you can buy anything from books about beer-making to stock in microbreweries. And you can make some cash by cleaning out your closets and selling your old junk on eBay. Software companies sell software and provide updates on the Net. Most software distribution is migrating to the Internet, where a customer can download and install programs without waiting for a CD to arrive. We talk about the relevant issues in Chapter 15.

- ✔ **Travel:** Cities, towns, states, and countries are using the web to put up (or *post*) tourist and event information. Travelers find weather information, maps, and museum hours as well as plane, train, and bus schedules and tickets. While you're at it, you can rent a car and make hotel reservations.

- ✔ **Use intranets:** Businesses have figured out that this Internet concept is truly useful, and they create their own, private networks — like mini-Internets. On these *intranets,* companies use web pages for posting company information such as benefits, filing expense reports and time sheets, and ordering supplies. An intranet helps an organization provide information that employees can see from inside the company that folks on the outside can't see, including manuals, forms, videos of boring meetings, and, of course, endless memos. In some organizations, email and intranets reduce the amount of paper wasted on this stuff.

- ✔ **Play games:** Internet-based multiuser games can easily absorb all your waking hours and an alarming number of what would otherwise be your sleeping hours. You can challenge other players who can be anywhere in the world. Many kinds of games are available on the web, including such traditionally addictive games as bridge, hearts, chess, checkers, and go. In Chapter 20, we tell you where to find these games.

- ✔ **Find love:** People are finding romance on the Net. Singles ads and matchmaking sites vie for users. The Internet long ago grew beyond the original bunch of socially challenged, 22-year-old, nerdy guys and now has turned into the world's biggest matchmaker, for people of all ages, genders, preferences, and life situations.

✔ **Heal:** Patients and doctors keep up to date with the latest medical findings, share treatment experience, and support one another around medical problems. We even know of some practitioners who exchange email directly with their patients.

✔ **Invest:** People research financial information, buy stock, and invest money online, as we tell you about in Chapter 16. Some online companies trade their own shares. Investors are finding new ventures, and new ventures are finding capital.

✔ **Participate in nonprofits:** Churches, synagogues, mosques, schools, clubs, teen centers, and other community organizations post pages telling web users about themselves and inviting new people. The online church newsletter *always* arrives before Sunday.

Cloudy with a chance of servers

Computers these days are very, very fast — so fast that they have far more processor power than they can use. (Your computer is drawing shimmery, semi-translucent, animated borders around the windows on your screen because it has nothing better to do between keystrokes.) Computer servers turn out to have the same problem — it takes a large website to keep a server busy, and servers are often idle for most of the day.

It also turns out that it's much more efficient to run many computer servers in one place, where they can share mounting racks, power, air conditioning, and fast network connections, so for many years the standard way to run a web server has been to rent space for it in a data center. But those servers are still idle most of the time. The advanced, cutting-edge *virtualization* technology allows one superfast server to operate as though it were many independent, reasonably fast, *virtual* servers and, more importantly, to start and stop virtual servers as needed. So now, someone who before would have owned or rented a few physical computers can now ask a data center to start up virtual servers when they're needed and stop them when they aren't. Because different virtual servers are busy at different times, this situation tends to even out the load, particularly when a company is big enough to have data centers in several parts of the world; people in Europe are using their virtual servers while Californians are asleep, and vice versa. A name such as *demand-allocated, geographically distributed virtual servers* isn't snappy enough, so they call it *cloud computing* instead.

From a user's point of view, no difference exists between a website run in "the cloud" and one run any other way, but cloud computing enables website operators to run a substantial web operation and not have to buy server equipment or even know the exact locations of the servers they're using. Cloud providers tend to be big companies that already have big data centers — notably, Amazon and Microsoft. (John uses the Amazon cloud service and believes that his data is probably somewhere near Seattle. The website Margy manages, www.uua.org, lives in a cloud over Virginia and may move soon to one over Boston.)

Fun historical fact. Virtualization was invented by IBM researchers in 1967, and mainframe computers have used it for four decades, so maybe it's not all that cutting-edge. But don't tell cloud enthusiasts or else you'll hurt their feelings.

Okay, What Next?

If you're ready to jump on the Internet, first read Chapter 2 for some safety tips. If you have children (or grandchildren), read Chapter 3 about what kids should (and shouldn't) do online.

Done? Chapter 4 tells you how to get connected!

Turn off the computer now and then

We can tell you from experience that when you're on the Net, the hands on the clock slow down and stop and you can spend more time online than you can imagine. For some people, it's impossible to go ten minutes without checking email, dirty dishes are ignored while visiting "just one more" web page, and they reach the point of possibly having an Internet addiction. Remember that the Net is a fine adjunct to real life — not a substitute.

As our friend and longtime Net user Jean Polly regularly says: The Internet is closing! Go outside and play!

Chapter 2

Is the Internet Safe? Viruses, Spyware, Spam, and Other Yucky Stuff

● ●

In This Chapter

▶ Taking a look at the dangers that lurk on the Net

▶ Protecting your online privacy

▶ Understanding how viruses can infect your computer

▶ Preventing spyware-makers from installing unwanted software on your PC

▶ Controlling how much junk email you're stuck looking at

▶ Keeping yourself and your family safe online

● ●

*W*e like the Internet. It has been part of our lives — and livelihoods — for years. We'd love to tell you that all the stuff you may have read about the dangers of connecting a computer to the Internet is hype. We can't. The success of the Internet has attracted unsavory people who view you as a money tree ready to be plucked. (Nothing personal — they see everybody that way.) In a few countries, perpetrating Internet fraud is now a major part of the national economy.

Even if no one steals your money, people can collect information about your online activities, which results in a real loss of privacy. And, some people are trying to take over your computer so that they can use it for nefarious purposes. When a new computer is hooked up to the Internet, it isn't a question of *whether* it will come under cyberattack, but *when*. And not in months or days — but in hours or minutes.

When you combine the Internet with cellphones and global positioning systems (GPSs), privacy issues become even scarier. Cellphone providers can tell where you are whenever you have your phone with you. Phones or other online devices with a GPS can help you find your way around, but they can also report on your whereabouts.

Now that we've given you the bad news, relax: The Internet doesn't have to be a dangerous place. Using the Internet is like walking around a big city — yes, you need to be careful, use some protection, and stay out of dangerous areas, but you can also safely take advantage of the wonders that the Net has to offer.

This chapter describes the types of issues that abound on the Internet:

- ✔ **Privacy issues** involve how much people can find out about you over the Internet.

- ✔ **Security issues** have to do with keeping control over which programs are running on your computer.

- ✔ Just plain **annoyance issues** include ending up with a mailbox full of *spam* (junk email) or web browser windows popping up with advertisements.

Throughout the rest of this book, we include instructions for staying safe by using a firewall, a virus checker, a spyware scanner, and some common sense. Chapter 3 talks about rules for letting kids use the Internet, and most of the suggestions make sense for grown-ups, too.

Privacy: Who's Who and What They Can Tell about You

Advances in technology are eroding the privacy that most of us take for granted. Technology we use every day — credit cards, cellphones, electronic key cards, and automobile toll transponders — allow our every purchase and movement to be tracked. The Internet is an extension of this trend. Many of your online activities can be watched and recorded — sometimes for innocent reasons and sometimes not.

All this is further compounded by the amount of publicly available information that is now conveniently available to people all over the world via the Internet. When paper records were maintained by government officials and people had to visit the office and dig through files for the specific information they wanted, a lot less information abuse was possible. Now the potential exists for anyone anywhere to access information about people hitherto unknown, and to gather information from various sources, including online directories. No longer is a geographical or time deterrent enough.

Some people worry that snoops on the Net will intercept their private email or web pages. That's quite unlikely, actually, other than the specific case of public Wi-Fi networks; see the sidebar "The perils of free Wi-Fi," later in this chapter, or government surveillance, which is beyond the scope of this book. The more serious problem is that advertisers build profiles of the sites you visit and the stuff you buy. Most web ads are provided by a handful of companies, such as Google's DoubleClick, AOL's Advertising.com, and Microsoft's Razorfish, which can use their ads to determine that the same person (you) is visiting a lot of different websites. Using this information, these companies can create a profile. They say they don't create these personal profiles, but they don't say they won't in the future.

Several techniques for gathering information about you as you use the Internet, or tricking you into providing information, are described in the next few sections.

Who is the party to whom I am speaking?

Although the Internet seems completely anonymous, it isn't. People used to have Internet usernames that bore some resemblance to their true identities — their names or initials or some such combination in conjunction with their university or corporation names gave fairly traceable routes to real people. Creating a new email address now takes just a few minutes, so revealing your identity is definitely optional.

Depending on who you are and what you want to do on the Net, you may, in fact, want different names and different accounts. Here are some legitimate reasons for wanting them:

- ✔ You're a professional — a physician, for example — and you want to participate in a mailing list or newsgroup without being asked for your professional opinion.

- ✔ You want help with an area of concern that you feel is private and you don't want your problem known to people close to you who may find out if your name is associated with it.

- ✔ You do business on the Internet, and you socialize on the Net. You may want to keep these activities separate.

Most Net activities can be traced. If you start to abuse the anonymous nature of the Net, you'll find that you aren't so anonymous after all.

Safety first

The anonymous, faceless nature of the Internet has its downside, too. To protect you and your family, take these simple precautions:

- ✔ Before posting information on a social networking site like Facebook or Google Plus, carefully review your privacy settings. See Chapter 10 for details. These sites give the impression that the information you provide will be visible only to your close, personal friends, but it ain't necessarily so.

- ✔ When posting information that appears on a public website (other than your own, or your social networking sites) or in any discussion venue, don't use your full name unless you want to be identified as the author of the information. This advice doesn't apply if you're working in a business context, such as posting information on your company's website.

- ✔ Never provide your name, address, or phone number to someone you don't know.

- ✔ Never believe anyone who says that he's from "Facebook tech support," "eBay fraud prevention," "PayPal administration," or a similar-sounding authority and asks you for your password. No legitimate entity will ever ask you for your password.

- ✔ Be especially careful about disclosing information about kids. Don't fill out profiles that ask for a kid's name, hometown, school, age, address, or phone number, because they're invariably used for "targeted marketing" (also known as junk mail).

Although relatively rare, horrible things have happened to a few people who have taken their Internet encounters into real life. Many wonderful things have happened, too. We've met some of our best friends over the Net, and some people have met and subsequently married. We just want to encourage you to use common sense whenever you set up a meeting with a Net friend. A person you email or swap instant messages with is still largely a stranger, and if you want to meet in person, take the same precautions you would take on a first date with someone you don't know: Meet in a public place, perhaps with a friend along, and be sure that your family knows where you are and when you're planning to be back.

The Net is a wonderful place, and meeting new people and making new friends is one of the big attractions. We just want to make sure that you're as careful as you would be in the rest of your life.

Phishing for inphormation

Phishing is the fastest-growing Internet crime, and you're the target. The good news is that protecting yourself is easy when you and your family know how to spot the phish-hook.

Learn what phishing looks like. After you start using the Internet and receiving email (as described in Chapter 8), there's an excellent chance that you'll receive a message like this one:

```
Subject: Ebay Important Warning

From: eBay Billing Department! <Service@eBay.com>

eBay Fraud Mediation Request

You have recieved this email because you or someone
had used your account to make fake bids at eBay.

THE FRAUD ALERT ID CODE CONTAINED IN THIS MESSAGE
WILL BE ATTACHED IN OUR FRAUD MEDIATION REQUEST FORM,
IN ORDER TO VERIFY YOUR EBAY ACCOUNT REGISTRATION
INFORMATIONS.

Fraud Alert ID CODE: 00937614

Please access the following form to complete the
verification of your eBay account registration
informations:

http://www.eBay.com/cgi_bin/secure/Fraud Alert ID CODE:
        00937614

If we do not receive the appropriate verification within
48 hours, then we will assume this eBay account is
fraudulent and will be suspended.

Regards, Safeharbor Department (Trust and Safety
Department), eBay Inc.
```

Sounds authentic and scary, doesn't it? Think you had better deal with this message right away? Better think again. You are the phish, and this message is the bait. The underlined text in the middle is the hook. Click it and soon an official-looking page appears that looks just like an eBay sign-in page. After you enter your username and password, another official-looking page asks for your credit card number, PIN, billing address, checking account details (complete with a helpful graphic so that you can find the right numbers on your personal checks), Social Security number, date of birth, mother's maiden name, and driver's license number. The page is smart enough to reject an invalid credit card number. If you fill in all the information and press Continue, you see a valid eBay page that says you've logged out. Then, who knows? The bad guys know enough about you to do anything from making a small purchase paid for by your credit card to full-scale identity theft that can take months or years to straighten out.

This message *did not* come from eBay. Millions of these types of messages are sent over the Internet every day.

Certain clues might alert you. The misspelled words *recieved* and *informa-tions* suggest that the author is someone whose English skills are limited. And, if you take the trouble to save the email to a file and then print it, the underlined link in the middle of the message looks like this:

```
<a href="http://192.168.45.67/cgi_bin"> http://www.
       eBay.com/cgi_bin/secure/Fraud Alert ID CODE:
       00937614</a>
```

The text between the angle brackets (< and >) is where the link goes in real-ity, to a website with a numeric address. (When we tried clicking the link two days after we got the mail, the website had already been shut down. Those eBay security folks are on the ball.)

Don't take the bait

Phishers have gotten a lot more skillful since the earliest phishes a decade ago, and now often have good editors and use a spell checker, so you can't rely on spelling and grammar mistakes, although they're dead giveaways when you spot them. Here are a few additional tips:

- ✔ Assume that every email that leads you to a page seeking passwords or credit card numbers or other personal information is a phishing expedition.

- ✔ If the email purports to be from a company you've never heard of, ignore it.

- ✔ If the message says that it's from a company with whom you have an account, go to the company's website by typing the company's URL into your browser (see Chapter 7), *not* by clicking a link in the email. When you get to the company's website, look for the My Account link. If there's a problem, when you log in, you should see a notice. If there's no way to log in and you're still concerned, forward a copy of the email to the cus-tomer service department or pick up the phone and call the number on your card or monthly statement.

One trick phishers use to fool Internet users is *website spoofing* — tricking your browser into displaying one address when you're actually at another site. Some browsers allow a website to show only its main address so that it doesn't look so geeky. Phishers take advantage of this ability. Better web browsers offer protection against website spoofing — they always show the actual web address of the page you're on.

To summarize, make sure that your family knows this rule well: Never, *never,* **never** enter passwords, credit card numbers, or other personal information at a web page you opened by clicking a link in an email.

Web bugs track the ads you read

Ever since the World Wide Web became a household word (okay, three words), companies have increasingly viewed their Internet presence as a vital way to advertise their goods and services and conduct their business. They spend millions of dollars on their websites and advertising email (the legitimate kind you actually asked for) — and want very much to know just how people use them. It's a small wonder that when you visit a site, companies can keep track of your actions as you move from link to link within the site. But they *really* want to know what you were doing before you entered their sites — and even more they want to know whether you read their mail. To gather this intelligence, they insert tiny images in mail messages that they call *web beacons* and everyone else calls *web bugs* that report your actions back to the mailer.

Most mail programs offer the option not to fetch images in mail messages from unknown or untrusted senders, which stops web bugs and also makes your mail reading faster.

Cookies can be good

When you browse the web (as described in Chapter 6), the web server needs to know who you are if you want to do things that require logging in, collecting items in a virtual shopping cart, or completing any other process that requires that the website remember information about you as you move from page to page. The most commonly used trick that allows websites to track what you're doing is setting cookies. A *cookie* is a tiny file, stored on your computer, that contains the address of the website and codes that your browser sends back to the website every time you visit a page there. Cookies don't usually contain personal or dangerous information; they're mostly innocuous and — believe it or not — useful.

If you plan to shop on the web (described in Chapter 15) or use other web services, cookies make it all possible. When you're using an airline reservation site, for example, the site uses cookies to separate the flights you're reserving from the ones that other users are reserving at the same time. On the other hand, you might use your credit card to purchase an item or a service on a website and the site uses a cookie to remember the account with your credit card number. Suppose that you provide this information from a computer at work and the next person to visit that site uses the same computer. That person could, possibly, make purchases on your credit card. Oops.

Internet users have various feelings about cookies. Some of us don't care about them, and some of us view them as an unconscionable invasion of privacy. You get to decide for yourself. Contrary to rumor, cookie files cannot get other information from your hard disk, give you a bad haircut, or otherwise mess up your life. They collect only information that the browser tells them about. Your web browser lets you control whether and when cookies are stored on your computer; see Chapter 7 for details.

The web browser equivalents of web bugs are *tracking cookies*. If several websites show ads from the same advertising network, the ad network can use cookies to tell whenever you're looking at one of its ads. By piecing together the information from many websites, these tracking companies form a clear picture of where you go online — and what you look at when you get there. Many are careful to provide only statistical information to their clients, but the potential for abuse is there. It's worth noting that US courts set a lower standard of protection for "business records" gathered in this way than they do for personal papers stored in our homes. Fortunately, most web browsers provide an option to reject *third-party* cookies, or cookies from anyone other than the source of the web page itself; this makes tracking cookies go away.

Do not track, or maybe do

With the increasing awareness of online privacy issues have come proposals for do-not-track laws, analogous to telephone do-not-call laws. The idea is that whenever you visit a website, you can tell your web browser to send a do-not-track indicator that tells the website not to track you. (Many browsers, including Firefox, already have this feature.) We have mixed feelings about whether it's a good idea.

For one thing, it's not at all clear what *do not track* means. If you order from, say, Amazon, it uses cookies to remember your session and your shopping cart, and to recognize you when you return using the same browser. Most people agree that this strategy is acceptable because it's all the same company and you deliberately made the first visit to Amazon. Well, okay, lots of people have set up Google accounts to use Gmail (see Chapter 8) and other Google services. Because the DoubleClick ad network is part of Google, it's okay for DoubleClick to track you because it's all the same company, right? Uh, no. Privacy researchers have multiday conferences to deal with issues such as this one, and the questions are far from resolved.

The other, even more serious, problem is that *you can't tell whether a site is obeying do-not-track*. If a marketer ignores your do-not-call listing, you can tell because your phone rings, but if it ignores your do-not-track, how can you tell? Suspiciously relevant spam from companies you've never heard of?

The United States is the only advanced country without comprehensive privacy laws, and do-not-track is just a Band-Aid. Don't settle for less.

Google yourself

One big attraction of the Internet is *all the data out there* that's now easy to access. Some of that data is about you. If you have your own blog or have a personal website (see Chapters 17 and 18), expect that all the information you put up there is available for everyone to see — usually, forever. (We find stuff about ourselves from more than 25 years ago.) Other people also put up information — newsletters, event listings, pictures from events, and other pictures, for example. Your online data trail may be longer than you think. If you haven't done it before, search the web for your own name. Enter your name in quotes in either the Google or Bing search box and press Enter. If you have a common name, you may need to throw in your middle initial or add the name of your town or school. (If you do this often, you're *ego surfing*.)

We know where you are

Cellphones and GPS receivers make the privacy situation even more complicated. Anyone with a cellphone can take pictures or videos of you and email them to friends or post them to the web, which can be anywhere from innocent fun to citizen journalism to seriously creepy. (We've read news reports of people standing with their cellphones at the foot of stairwells and escalators and trying to take pictures up girls' skirts. Ewww.) Modern cellphones have built-in GPS receivers, primarily intended to provide your location if you call 911, but also potentially usable to track your location whenever the phone is on.

Lots of cellphone users *want* to be tracked. Travel apps (programs) like Yelp and Facebook can tell you about restaurants and attractions near you, but only if they know where you are.

Security: How People Can Take Over Your PC

You can download and install software directly over the Internet, which is a useful feature. If you need a viewer program to display and print a tax form or when you want to install a free upgrade to a program that you purchased earlier, it just takes a few clicks. How convenient!

However, other people can also install programs on your computer without your permission. Hey, wait a minute — whose computer is it, anyway? These programs can arrive in a number of ways, mainly by email or your web browser.

Viruses arrive by email

Computer *viruses* are programs that jump from computer to computer, just as real viruses jump from person to person. Computer viruses can spread using any mechanism that computers use to talk to each other, such as networks, data CDs, and DVDs. Viruses have been around computers for a long time. Originally, viruses lived in program files that people downloaded using a file transfer program or their web browsers. Now most viruses are spread by opening files that are sent by email, as attachments to mail messages.

There was a time long ago when people in the know (like we thought we were) laughed at newcomers to the Internet who worried about getting viruses by email. Email messages back then consisted only of text files and could not contain programs. Then email attachments were introduced. People could then send computer software — including those sneaky viruses — by email. Isn't progress wonderful?

What viruses do

When a virus lands on your computer, it has to manage somehow to get executed. Getting *executed* in computer jargon means being brought to life; a virus is a program, and programs have to be run in order to start doing their nefarious work. After a virus is running, it does two things:

1. Looks around and tries to find your address book, which it uses to courteously send copies of itself to all your friends and acquaintances, often wrapped up in authentic-sounding messages ("Hey, enjoyed the other night, thought this file would amuse you!").

2. Executes its payload, which is the reason that virus writers go to all that trouble and assume the risk. (They do occasionally end up in jail.)

The *payload* is the illegal activity that the virus is running from your machine. A payload can record your every keystroke (including your passwords). It can launch an attack at specific or random targets over the Internet. It frequently sends spam from your computer. Whatever it's doing, you don't want it to do. Trust us: If your computer starts to act quirky or extremely sluggish, chances are good that you've contracted a virus or 20.

In the good old days, virus writers were content just to see their viruses spread, but like everything else about the Internet, virus writing is now a big business, in many cases controlled by organized crime syndicates.

What you can do about viruses

Don't worry *too* much about viruses — excellent virus-checking programs are available that check all incoming mail before the viruses can attack. In Chapter 4, which describes connecting to the Internet, we recommend installing a virus checker. After you install it, be sure to update it regularly so that you're always protected against the latest viruses. You can subscribe to receive updates automatically.

Worms come right over the Net

A *worm* is like a virus, except that it doesn't need to hitch a ride on an email message. A worm simply jumps directly from one computer to another over the Net, entering your computer by way of security flaws in its network software. Unfortunately, the most popular type of network software on the Net, the kind in Microsoft Windows, is riddled with security holes — so many that if you attach a nice, fresh Windows machine to a broadband Net connection, the machine is overrun with worms in less than a minute.

If you rigorously apply all security updates from Microsoft, they fix most of the known security flaws, but it takes a lot longer than a minute to apply them all. Hence, we strongly encourage anyone using a broadband connection to use a hardware *firewall,* a box that sits between the Net and your computer and keeps the worms out. If you have a broadband connection, you probably should use an inexpensive *router* to hook up your computers, anyway, and all these devices include a firewall as a standard feature. See Chapter 4 for more information.

Spyware arrives via websites

Spyware (which includes *adware*) is similar to a virus, except that your computer catches it in a different way. Rather than arrive by email, spyware is downloaded by your browser. Generally, you need to click something on a web page to download and install spyware, but many people have been easily misled into installing spyware that purports to be a graphics viewer or another type of program they think they might want.

Know what spyware does

Spyware got its name from being frequently used for sneaky purposes, such as spying on whatever you're typing. Sometimes, spyware gathers information about you and sends it off to another site without your knowledge or consent. A common use for spyware is finding out which sites you're visiting so that advertisers can display pop-up ads (described later in this chapter) that are targeted to your interests.

Targeted advertising isn't inherently evil. The Google AdSense program, for example, places ads on participating web pages based on the contents of those pages. Targeted ads are worth more to advertisers because you're more likely to respond to an ad about something you're already reading about.

Spyware can also send spam from your computer, capture every keystroke you type and send it to a malefactor over the Net, and do all the other Bad Things that worms and viruses do.

Don't voluntarily install spyware

Lots of cute little free programs are available for download, but don't install them unless you've checked to see that they're safe *and* useful. Most free toolbars, screen savers, news tickers, and other utilities are spyware in disguise. Besides, the more programs you run on your computer, the slower all your other programs run. Check with friends before downloading the latest program. Or, search the web for the program's name (see Chapter 13) to find positive or negative reviews. Download programs only from reputable websites. Keep your computer free from software clutter.

Are Macs the solution?

We hear you Apple Macintosh users gloating as you read this chapter: "We don't have these problems. Why don't people just use Macs?" Mac users still have to put up with phishing and other forms of junk email, and spyware has started to appear on Macs. But to date, almost none of the viruses or worms affects Macs, and the threat of spyware is lower than for PCs. Although this situation can change, we think that Mac users will always have an easier time on the Net. First, Macs are so scarce (compared to Windows machines) that it isn't worth a virus writer's time to attack them — partly because this scarcity also makes it hard to spread Mac viruses. Most email addresses in a Mac user's address book belong to Windows users anyway, so if a Mac virus makes copies of itself, the copies it mails out don't find nice,

vulnerable homes. (Designing a virus that runs on *both* Windows and Macs is difficult, even now.) Finally, the Mac OS X is designed to be more secure than Windows and is difficult to infect.

Current Intel-based Macs can run Windows programs, or can even be set up to run native Windows, for applications that are Windows-only. We know of companies whose support staffs run *everything* on Macs — because they don't get infected. When employees need to run something on a PC, they do it in a window on the Mac screen. Cool.

But don't be silly. All our advice about not clicking on unknown links or downloading untrusted software also applies to *you*, Mac users.

This advice is particularly important on your mobile device. Some free apps are free because the programmer wrote them for fun, or they provide access to a commercial site, or they hope they can get you to upgrade to a more capable paid version. But some are free because they show ads and report back to headquarters. On Android devices, when you install an app it tells you what system facilities the app uses, and you should always do a sanity check. If you find a cool pinball app, and it wants access to your address book, huh, what does pinball have to do with your friends' addresses? It's probably spyware that will steal the addresses.

Protect your computer from spyware

Spyware programs are often designed to be hard to remove — which can mess up your operating system. Rather than wait until you contract a bad case of spyware and then try to uninstall it, a better idea is to inoculate your computer against spyware. To block spyware, be careful about the screen elements you click. Install a spyware checking program that can scan your system periodically, such as the free Microsoft Windows Defender. See Chapter 4 for details.

Spyware can attack Macs and even phones

Macintosh computers aren't immune to spyware. (See the nearby sidebar, "Are Macs the solution?") The Macintosh operating system is by design more secure than Windows, so few viruses and little spyware attack it. But a Mac user is just as likely as a PC user to be fooled into clicking a link to a free porn site that downloads spyware to your computer along with that sexy video. Even smartphones (such as the iPhone or Android phones) can be infected with spyware, and although most spyware targets Windows, it also targets other kinds of computers and phones, so think before you click on any of these devices.

Adware: Just another kind of spyware

Adware, a controversial type of software that many people consider to be spyware, is installed as part of certain programs that are distributed for free. It watches what you do on your computer and displays targeted ads — even when you run other programs. We think that no users in their right minds would knowingly install a program that peppers them with ads — and we want laws to ban the practice, pointing out that adware often behaves like a parasite, by obscuring or replacing ads from competing websites.

Before downloading a free program, make sure that you understand what the deal is. If you aren't sure, don't download it. Make sure that your kids know not to download free games, song lyrics, and the like — most are infested with adware. If you don't, before you know it, you'll have so many pop-up ads that you'll have to unplug your computer to shut it up.

Pop-up browser windows pop up all over the place

One of the worst innovations in recent decades is the *pop-up* window that appears on your screen unbidden (by you) when you visit certain websites. Some pop-ups appear immediately, and others are *pop-unders,* which are hidden under your main window until you close it. The pop-ups you're most likely to see are ads for mortgages and airline tickets. (No, we don't give their names here; they have plenty of publicity already.)

Several mechanisms can make pop-ups appear on your computer:

- ✔ A website can open a new browser window. Sometimes this new window displays an ad or other annoying information. But sometimes the new window has useful information — some websites use pop-up windows as a sort of Help system for using the site.

- ✔ Spyware or other programs can display pop-up windows.

Luckily, web browsers now can prevent most websites from opening unwanted new browser windows. See Chapter 7 to find out how to tell your browser how to display fewer pop-ups.

What's the secret word, Harry?

Everywhere you go these days, someone wants you to enter a password or pass code. Even Harry Potter has to tell his password to a magic portrait just to enter the Gryffindor dormitory (although there's apparently no security between the boys' and girls' wings). Security experts are nearly unanimous in telling us how we should protect all our passwords:

- ✔ Pick complex passwords that are long enough that no one can guess them.

  Never use as a password a word that occurs in the dictionary. Consider sticking a number or two into your password.

- ✔ Never use the same password for different accounts.

- ✔ Memorize your passwords and never write them down.

- ✔ Change your passwords frequently.

- ✔ Find out how hard a hacker would have to work to guess your password. Microsoft has a site that tells you, at microsoft.com/protect/yourself/ password/checker.mspx.

The perils of free Wi-Fi

Wi-Fi, the wireless way that your laptop can connect to the Internet, is available in many public places, including airports and coffee shops. As explained in Chapter 4, when you use Wi-Fi to connect your computer to the Internet, you locate the network and click Connect and then start using the Internet. One of the first things you'll probably do is use your web browser to check your email or connect to your company's network, And, in the process, you type a password or two.

Can you trust the Wi-Fi network? How do you know that the Wi-Fi network isn't listening to what you type, including your passwords? Well, you don't.

Wi-Fi snooping is surprisingly easy. A thief sets up a computer in an airport lounge or a coffee shop with a computer listening to all the radio traffic on the local Wi-Fi network. She monitors what you type and uses your passwords to send spam or empty your bank account or perform other nefarious deeds.

What's a traveling Internet user to do? You can significantly decrease the likelihood of snooping by using secure https websites (which show a lock icon in the browser) rather than unsecured http websites. A secure site encrypts the traffic between your browser and the website so that even if someone is listening in, all they see is the meaningless encrypted traffic. If you use a mail program such as Thunderbird or Outlook to check your mail (see Chapter 8), set your incoming and outgoing mail connections to use encryption (often called *SSL* or *TLS*), which offers the same benefits.

If you absolutely must use public Wi-Fi to check your email while you're on the road and you don't have an https or SSL connection (which you should, all popular webmail systems offer them), here's what to do, advice courtesy of our friend Mark Steinwinter:

1. Before you leave on your trip, change your email password (and any other password you plan to use).

2. While on your trip, limit your public Wi-Fi use to the accounts whose passwords you changed before leaving. Go ahead and use websites that don't require a password.

3. As soon as you return home, change your email password again. You can change it back to the one you used before your trip, or to another password. Just assume that a Bad Guy has the password you used on your trip, and never use this password again.

This sound advice is intended for everyone — except ordinary human beings. Most of us have far too many passwords to keep track of and too little brain to store them in.

One common-sense approach is to use a single password for accounts where you have little risk of loss, such as the one you need in order to read an online newspaper. Use separate, stronger passwords for the accounts that truly matter (such as your online banking account). If you feel you can't remember them all, write them down and keep them in a safe place, not on a Post-It note stuck to your monitor.

Our warning about not using a password that's in the dictionary — take that one seriously! Hackers managed to find a hole in our firewall one day, and we had stupidly left one password set to a normal English word (*weather*, if you must know). It took the hackers less than two hours to break into our computer, by simply having their computer generate every English word until they found one that worked.

When making up a password, stick numbers and punctuation into words or glue two words together with some numbers, or spell things backward. Use both capital and lowercase letters, too. If your kids are Fred and Susie and your house number is 426, how about Fred426susiE? Or Susie426dreF? Using the first letters of every word in a phrase is a good method, too. If your favorite song is "I Wanna Hold Your Hand," by The Beatles, it wouldn't be that difficult to remember a password like Iwhyh1963. You get the idea!

Over the years, we've ended up with so many passwords that we started storing them in a text file — which anyone with access to our PC could read! This isn't a horrible idea, as long as your PC has a password to keep random people from logging in, but you can do better. If you have a lot of passwords and no way to remember them, consider using a password manager, which is designed to store your passwords in a safe place. Of course, you have to remember one password — for your password manager. We use KeePass, a freeware, open source program that you can download from `www.keepass.info` for PCs and Macs.

Be careful with password hints

Website operators are tired of dealing with customers who forget their passwords, so a new computer tool has emerged in the past few years — the password hint. When you create a new account, the friendly identity manager software asks for your username and new password. It then makes you select and answer a couple of security questions, such as "What's your favorite color?" or "What's your pet's name?"

Sometime in the future, you try to log in to that account — and find that you forgot its pesky password. No problemo! You're asked the security questions you picked; if you type the right answer, you're in. The problem is that a thief pretending to be you sees the same challenge.

Rather than guess your password, all he has to guess is your favorite color (blue, maybe?) and figure out your pet's name (and did your kid post captioned photos of Rover on the school website as part of his third grade computer literacy project?).

If you encounter one of these password hints when you sign up for an important account, pick questions whose answers an attacker can't glean by researching you. And, there's no rule that says you have to answer the security questions truthfully. You can pick a friend's pet, for example, or a color you detest, or you can say that your favorite color is Rover and your pet's name is Purple. You just have to remember your less-than-truthful answers to these questions.

Spam, Bacon, Spam, Eggs, and Spam

Pink tender morsel,
Glistening with salty gel.
What the hell is it?

Hawaiian lunch meat?
Someone else's old shoe heels?
We may never know.

— SPAM haikus, found on the Internet, sometimes credited to Christopher James Hume and Reber Clark

More and more often, we receive unsolicited bulk email (abbreviated UBE but usually called *spam*) from organizations or people we don't know. Spam is the online version of junk mail. Offline, junk mailers have to pay postage. Unfortunately, online, the cost of sending out a bazillion pieces of junk mail is virtually zilch.

Email spam (not to be confused with SPAM, the meat-related product from Minnesota that's quite popular in Hawaii) means that thousands of copies of an unwanted message are sent to email accounts and even to instant message programs. The message usually consists of unsavory advertising for get-rich-quick schemes or dubious drugs — something that you might not want to see and that you definitely don't want your children to see. Many spam messages tout worthless stocks that the spammers have bought and hope you'll buy at inflated prices. The message is *spam,* the practice is *spamming,* and the person sending the spam is a *spammer.* Phishing often involves spam, too.

Spam, unfortunately, is a major problem on the Internet because it's extremely cheap for sleazy advertisers to send. We receive hundreds or thousands of pieces of spam a day, and the number continues to increase. Spam doesn't have to be commercial (we've seen religious and political spam), but it has to be unsolicited; if you asked for it, it isn't spam.

Why it's called spam

The meat? SPAM might be short for *spiced ham.* Oh, you mean the unwanted email? It came from the Monty Python skit in which a group of Vikings sing the word *spam* repeatedly in a march tempo, drowning out all other discourse. (Search for *Monty Python spam* at your favorite search engine and you'll find plenty of sites where you can listen to it.) Spam can drown out all other mail because some people receive so much spam that they stop using email entirely.

Why it's so bad

You may think that spam, like postal junk mail, is just a nuisance we have to live with. But it's worse than junk mail, in several ways. Spam costs you money. Email recipients pay much more than the sender does to deliver a message. Sending email is cheap: A spammer can send thousands of messages an hour from a PC. After that, it costs you time to download, read (at least the subject line), and dispose of the mail. The amount of spam is now about 20 times the amount of real email, and if spam volume continues to grow at its alarming pace, pretty soon real email will prove to be useless because it's buried under the junk. Another problem is that spam filters, which are supposed to discard only spam, can throw away good messages by mistake.

Not only do spam recipients have to bear a cost, but all this volume of email also strains the resources of the email servers and the entire Internet. ISPs have to pass along the added costs to its users. Spam volume doubled or tripled for many years, and is still growing, although not as fast. Large ISPs we know have estimated that more than 95 percent of their incoming email is spam, and many ISPs have told us that as much as $2 of the monthly fee goes to handling and cleaning up after spam. Spammers send 100 *billion* spam messages *every day*. And, as ISPs try harder to filter out spam, more and more legitimate mail is being mistaken for spam and bounced.

Many spam messages include a line that instructs you how to get off their lists, something like "Send us a message with the word REMOVE in it." Reply to messages or click links to unsubscribe *only* if the messages are from lists that you remember subscribing to or from companies you have done business with. Anyone else will either ignore you or add you to other spam lists.

What you can do about it

You don't have to put up with a lot of spam. Spam filters can weed out most of the spam you receive. See Chapter 9 to see how to use the spam filter that may already be built into your email program or how to install a separate spam filtering program. Also visit www.cauce.org, the Coalition Against Unsolicited Commercial Email, which is the major grass roots antispam organization.

Safety: How to Keep Yourself and Your Family Safe

Viruses, spyware, phishing, pop-ups, spam — is the Internet worth all this trouble? No, you don't have to give up on the Internet in despair or disgust. You just have to put in a little extra effort to use it safely. In addition to the technological fixes we suggest (virus checkers, spyware scanners, and pop-up blockers), you need to develop some smarts about online security. Here's a quick checklist:

✔ **Develop healthy skepticism.** If it sounds too good to be true, it isn't true. No one in Africa has $25 million to share with you if you help them move it out of the country, nor did you win a sweepstakes you never entered. As the old saying goes, there's a fool born every minute. Today's sucker doesn't have to be you.

✔ **Keep your computer's software up-to-date.** Both Microsoft and Apple have features that make this process more or less painless. Use them. The latest software updates usually fix exploitable security flaws.

✔ **Use a firewall and keep it updated.** Your computer probably has firewall software built in. Make sure that your firewall is turned on. Some malware programs know how to turn off protective software, so check it every week or so. We recommend using a router — a device that lets you share Internet connections among several computers (whether wired or wireless) — because routers include built-in firewall programs that malware programs cannot disable or bypass. These units are so cheap that you should get one even if you have only one computer. (See Chapter 5 for details.)

✔ **Install virus-protection and spyware-protection software and keep it current.** You can get either free or paid software. Use it. Chapter 4 tells you how to install virus checkers and spyware scanners.

You must keep the virus description files in your antivirus software updated — automatically if possible, and every week at least. (New viruses are launched every day.) Your antivirus software should automatically download the updates; check your documentation.

✔ **Don't open an email attachment unless it's from someone you know** *and* **you're expecting it.** Contact the sender if you aren't sure.

✔ **Don't click links in email messages unless you're sure that you know where they lead.** If you click one and the site you end up at wants your password or credit card number or dog's name, close your browser window. Don't even think about giving out any information.

✔ **Pick passwords that are hard to guess, and never give them to anyone else**. Don't give them to the nice lady who says she's from the Help desk or to the bogus FBI special agent who claims to need it for tracking down a kidnapped child. No one.

✔ **Be consistent.** If you share your computer with several family members or housemates, make sure that every person understands these rules and agrees to follow them.

For more tips about staying safe online, the US government runs the OnGuard Online site at www.onguardonline.gov.

Chapter 3

Kids and the Internet

*F*ace it: Most kids are way more comfortable on the Internet than their parents (and grandparents) are. Schools assign kids to do research on the web and email information to other students or their teachers. Online games are designed for kids of all ages. Forbidding your kids from using the Net altogether is hopeless (unless they're younger than about 6), but you want to keep your kids safe. This chapter talks about what's great — and what's scary — about children and youth using the Internet.

With millions of kids online, a discussion about family Internet use is critical. (Obviously, if this isn't your concern, just skip this chapter and go to another one.)

Really Cool Ways Kids Use the Net

The Net is amazing. It can help kids do the things they *have* to do (like homework) as well as what they *want* to do:

> ✔ **Research homework assignments:** The Internet is an incredible way to expand the walls of a school. The Net can connect kids to libraries, research resources, museums, other schools, and other people. Kids can visit the American Museum of Natural History for information about anthropology and other natural sciences (at www.amnh.org) and the

Sistine Chapel (`w2.vatican.va/content/vatican/en.html` as of when we wrote this chapter, although web pages can move at any time); they can watch spotted newts in their native habitat; they can hear new music and make new friends; or they can learn about the history of computing (as shown in Figure 3-1). These days, many schools assume that kids have access to the web, so parents had better be ready.

Figure 3-1:
Many museums have useful information online.

✔ **Make friends in other countries:** School projects such as the Global Schoolhouse (GSH) connect kids around the world by working collaboratively on all types of projects. Its annual cyber fairs have brought together more than 500,000 students from hundreds of schools in at least 37 countries! Kids can find out more at the Global SchoolNet website, `www.globalschoolnet.org`.

✔ **Practice foreign languages:** Kids can visit online chat rooms, where they can try out their French, Spanish, Portuguese, Russian, Japanese, or even Esperanto.

✔ **Pay for downloaded music:** Kids love music, and they can buy music over the Internet in several ways. (Adults can too, as it turns out.) The Apple iTunes music store, at `www.apple.com/itunes`, sells songs for about 99 cents. Other sites, such as `www.pandora.com`, let you create your own "radio station" that plays music you like. See Chapter 14 for details.

- ✔ **Write an encyclopedia article:** Wikipedia, at `en.wikipedia.org`, is a free online encyclopedia that anyone can contribute to. It's a useful research tool, but, even better, kids can add the material they found while researching those term papers to make Wikipedia even better. A worldwide team of volunteer writers and editors updates the material continually, and you — or your child! — can be one of them. (See Chapter 20 to find out what wikis are.)

- ✔ **Put your own pictures, music, or other stuff on the web:** A website can be as clever or as stupid as you like. You and your kids can post your stories or artwork for family and friends to admire. We explain how to do these things in Part V.

When you or your kids search for a topic, you may see pages written by the world's greatest authority on that topic, some crackpot pushing a harebrained theory, a college kid's term paper, a guy on a bulletin board who thinks he's an expert, or, more likely, all of the above. Some websites are maintained by hate groups and push truly nasty venom. Learning how to identify all these types of information is one of the most valuable skills that children (or anyone else) can acquire.

So-So Ways Kids Use the Net

Here are some ideas that adults might consider a waste of time, but hey, we can't be serious all the time:

- ✔ **Play games:** Many popular games (both traditional — such as chess, bridge, hearts, and go — and video) have options that let kids compete against other players on the Internet. See the sidebar "Games on the web."

- ✔ **Hang out with friends:** The Facebook website (see Chapter 10) allows people to share their thoughts, photos, videos, and random comments. Many teenagers appear to live on Facebook.

- ✔ **Talk on a videophone:** Thanks to software such as Google Hangouts and Skype, kids can see their friends while talking to them (not recommended on bad hair days). Chapter 12 talks about free video programs.

- ✔ **Shop:** What can we say? Internet shopping is like shopping at the mall, except that the Internet is always open and you don't have to hunt for a parking place. Kids can sell stuff too. Chapter 15 gets you started.

Games on the web

You can find almost any game on the web, from classic solitaire to video games to games that secretly teach you something. Some run right in your web browser while others are programs you download and run. Here are a few places to look for single-player and multiplayer games:

✔ **AddictingGames:** One of the countless websites dedicated to solitary gaming is at `www.addictinggames.com`. A good search engine can help you find others, such as Miniclip (`www.miniclip.com`).

✔ **Angry Birds:** If you have never played Angry Birds (downloadable from `www.angrybirds.com`), you can join us as some of the very few people on the planet who have never done so. We've just never gotten around to it!

✔ **Game Show Network:** The GSN cable-television games network has a website where you can play along with the shows, at `www.gsn.com`. If you win, your name may even appear on TV!

✔ **Games.com:** The site `www.games.com` has numerous solitaire games available to anyone willing to create a free account. Free Internet Games (`www.friv.com`) does, too.

✔ **Merchandising advertising:** Many corporations advertise their products in downloadable games. If you like Legos, for example, try `play.lego.com`. The websites for certain action movies offer related games.

✔ **MSN Games:** Puzzle, card, word, trivia, and other types of games are available at the Microsoft site `zone.msn.com`. Yahoo! Games at `games.yahoo.com` is the same idea.

✔ **Steam:** You or your kids can download a wide variety of games from `store.steampowered.com`. They aren't cheap, but the graphics are terrific.

✔ **VirtualNES:** If you loved your old Nintendo game console, you'll love `www.virtualnes.com`, which offers classic Nintendo Entertainment System games for free. (It's legal because the games are now out of copyright.)

Not-So-Good Ways Kids Use the Net

Make sure that your kids or grandkids stay away from the following ideas, which will just get them into trouble, some of it serious:

✔ **Plagiarism:** That's the fancy word for passing off other people's work as your own. Plagiarizing from the Internet is just as wrong as plagiarizing from a book — and is (for that matter) a lot easier for teachers to catch because teachers can use search engines, too.

✔ **Bullying:** Your kids are undoubtedly hearing a lot about online bullying at school, and it's important. In the old days, unpopular kids could get away from their oppressors at home; now the Internet and kids making fun of them follow them everywhere.

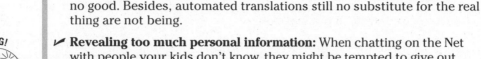

- ✔ **Cheating:** Using translating software to do language homework is also no good. Besides, automated translations still no substitute for the real thing are not being.

- ✔ **Revealing too much personal information:** When chatting on the Net with people your kids don't know, they might be tempted to give out identifying information about themselves or your family, but it's dangerous — doing so can get your kids stalked, ripped off, or worse. Even revealing their email addresses can invite unwanted junk mail. Some seemingly innocent questions that strangers ask online aren't so innocent, so we go into more detail later in this chapter about what to watch for.

- ✔ **Sharing commercial music and videos:** Now that kids can easily buy music online, they don't have much excuse for using file sharing software to trade music or videos without permission. The music and movie industries are getting better at finding people who do that — and are taking legal action against them. It can cost you a lot of money.

- ✔ **Visiting porn and hate sites:** This advice is between you and your kids. Parents should make clear rules about what types of websites are acceptable, post the rules near the computer, and stick to them.

- ✔ **Pretending to be someone else online:** Kids should make up pseudonyms so that they don't have to use their real names. (This strategy can be one way to limit how much any stranger finds out.) But, pretending that you're a talent agent for *American Idol* or the latest reality show looking for a date is a bad idea.

- ✔ **Hanging out in adult chat rooms:** If kids pretend to be older than they are, they can get themselves *and* the chat room hosts into trouble.

- ✔ **Letting the Internet take over your life:** If the only thing your kids want to do after school is get online, it's time to set some limits. (Ditto for you and your work!)

Truly Brain-Dead Things Kids Should Never Do

Here are some ideas that kids should *never* consider because they can lead directly into major trouble:

- ✔ **Meet online friends in person without telling a parent:** If a child or youth meets someone online and wants to meet that person face-to-face, it's fine — maybe. But parents need to take precautions! First, make sure that your kid tells you about the meeting so that you can decide together how to proceed. Second, no one (child, youth, or adult) should ever meet an online friend in a private place: Always arrange to meet in a public place, such as a restaurant. Finally, go to the meeting with your child, in case they have been completely misled. (You can lurk discreetly nearby, so bring a book.)

✔ **Do anything illegal — online or off:** The Internet feels totally anonymous, but it's not. If kids or adults commit a crime, the police can get the Internet connection records from your Internet service provider (ISP) and find out who was connected over which modem on which day and at what time with which numeric Internet (IP) address, and they'll find you.

✔ **Break into other computers or create viruses:** This little escapade might have been considered a prank back in the 1980s, but the authorities have long since lost their sense of humor about it. Kids *have* gone to jail for it.

The Internet and Little Kids

We are strong advocates of allowing kids to be kids, and we believe that humans are better teachers than computers are. Now that you know our predisposition, maybe you can guess what we're going to say next: We are not in favor of sticking a young child in front of a screen. How young is too young? We believe that younger than age 5 is too young. At young ages, kids benefit more from playing with trees, balls, clay, crayons, paint, mud, monkey bars, bicycles, other kids, and especially older siblings. Computers make lousy babysitters. If your young children use computers, choose their programs and websites carefully, and limit their screen time.

We think that Internet access is more appropriate for somewhat older kids (fourth or fifth grade and older), but your mileage may vary. Even so, we think it's a good idea to limit the amount of time that anyone, especially a kid, spends online. We (despite our good looks) have been playing with computers for over 40 years (each), and we know what happens to kids who are allowed to stay glued to their computers for unlimited lengths of time. Trust us: *It is not good.* Do you remember those old sayings "You are what you eat" and "Garbage in, garbage out"? What your brain devours makes a difference.

As human beings (what a concept), kids need to be able to communicate with other human beings. Too often, kids who have difficulty doing this prefer to get absorbed in computers — which doesn't help develop their social skills. Existing problems in this department grow worse, leading to more isolation. If you're starting to feel like your child is out of touch and you want to put the machine in its place (and maybe even encourage your child to get her life back), here are some quick self-defense tips:

✔ Keep a private log of all the time your child spends in front of the screen during one week. Then ask your child whether this is really how she wants to spend her life.

✔ Keep your kids' computers in public places, like living rooms and dens, so what kids do with them is visible to the family. Keep your kids' smartphones charging overnight in your bedroom, so they don't intrude on your children's sleep.

✔ Help your child find a hobby that doesn't involve a screen. Encourage him to join a team, form a band, or create some artwork.

✔ Have your child set aside one computer-free day every week.

✔ Make your child have meals and conversations with live human beings (that would be you and the rest of your family), face-to-face, in real time.

Surf Safe

Make sure your kids or grandkids know the safety rules for using the Net. Here are some basic guidelines for your kids to start with:

✔ **Never reveal exactly who you are.** Your child should use only his first name and shouldn't provide a last name, an address, a phone number, or the name of his school.

✔ **Never, *ever,* tell anyone your password.** No honest person or organization will ever ask you or your kid for it.

✔ **Be suspicious of strangers who seem to know a lot about you.** Maybe they say they're a friend of yours (the parent) who is supposed to pick up your kid after school or pick up a package from your house. Make sure your kid knows to never go with a stranger or let one into the house without asking a trusted (offline) adult first.

Here are a few more guidelines to help kids sidestep online trouble:

✔ **Think before you give your email address to anybody.** Many websites ask users to register, and many sites require users to provide working email addresses that they verify by sending confirmation messages. Before you let your child register with a website, make sure that it's run by a reputable company from which you won't mind getting junk mail.

✔ **Never agree to talk to someone on the phone or meet someone in person without checking it out with a parent first.** Most people a kid can meet online are okay, but a few creepy types out there have made the Internet their hunting ground.

✔ **Don't assume that people are telling you the truth.** That "kid" who says he's your kid's age and gender and seems to share your child's interests and hobbies may in reality be a lonely 40-year-old. If your kids have younger siblings, impress upon them how important it is to watch out for the safety of their younger "sibs." They may not understand what a stranger is and may believe that everything people tell them online is always true.

✔ **If someone is scaring you or making you uncomfortable — especially if the person says not to tell your parents —** *tell* **your parents.** If something bothers your child, make sure she knows to ask you to talk to your Internet service provider. Remind your kid that she can always turn off the computer.

Sell, Sell, Sell!

When you spend a lot of time online, you soon notice that everyone seems to be trying to sell you something. Kids, particularly those from middle- and upper-income families, are a lucrative target market, and the Net is being viewed as another way to capture this market.

Targeting kids for selling isn't new. Remember Joe Camel of the Camel cigarette campaign that was aimed at kids? Some schools make students watch Channel One, a system that brings advertising directly to the classroom. If you watch TV, you know how TV programs for kids push their own lines of toys and action figures.

Kids should know that big company marketing departments have designed kid-friendly, fascinating, captivating software to help them better market to you. Delightful, familiar cartoon characters deftly elicit strategic marketing information directly from the keyboard in your home.

You should be aware of this situation and know what to do when someone on the web is asking your kids for information. If your kids have access to credit cards, yours or their own, they can spend big bucks over the Internet. Beware of online stores where you have configured your web browser to remember your passwords, because your kids will be able to waltz right in and start buying. And, your kids should be aware that if they spend your money online without permission, they're going to get into big trouble for it.

The Children's Online Privacy Protection Act (COPPA) limits the information that companies can collect from children under 13 (or at least children who *admit* they're under 13) without explicit parental consent — which, by the way, we think parents should rarely give. We heard of one marketer who said he wanted to use the Net to create personal relationships with all the kids who use his product. Ugh. We have names for guys who want relationships with kids, and they're not nice names.

The FTC (www.onguardonline.gov/articles/0031-protecting-your-childs-privacy-online) has more useful information for teachers about COPPA and online privacy that is useful for parents, too.

Who's Online?

Lots of kids — and grown-ups — are putting up websites about themselves and their families. Social networking sites such as Facebook (see Chapter 10) make it easy. We think that creating websites is cool, but we strongly encourage families who use the Net for personal reasons (distinct from business-people who use the Net for business purposes) *not* to use their full or real names. We also advise you and your children never to disclose your address, phone number, Social Security number, or account passwords in online social situations to anyone who asks for this kind of information — online or off. This advice applies especially when people who claim to be in positions of authority ask for them— for example, instant messages or even phone calls from people claiming that they're from Microsoft tech support. They're not, as we detail in Chapter 2.

People with real authority *never* ask questions seeking highly personal information. For one thing, Internet service providers don't handle member accounts by using instant messages, and they never ask for credit card information by email. It all makes a solid case for knowing how your Internet service provider does its work.

More than ever, children need to develop critical-thinking skills. They have to be able to evaluate what they read and see — especially on the web.

Regrettably, almost anyone with an email address receives their share of junk email *(spam)*. This situation will only get worse until we have effective laws — as well as technology — against unwanted email. In the meantime, remember this important rule: If an email offer sounds too good to be true, it isn't true — and if an ad shows up from someone you don't know, it's also good evidence that it isn't true.

The Internet in Schools

Some schools and libraries use software to filter Internet access for kids. A variety of filtering systems are available, at a range of costs and installation hassles, that promise to filter out inappropriate and harmful websites. It sounds good, but many kids are smart enough to find ways around rules, and extremely smart kids can find ways around software systems designed to "protect" them.

Checking out colleges on the Net

Most colleges and universities have sites on the web. You can find a directory of online campus tours at www.campustours.com, with links to lots more info about the colleges and universities.

After you're a little more adept at using the Net, you can use it to take a closer look at classes and professors to gain a better idea of what colleges have to offer.

Not just for kids: School on the Net

Your child's education, as well as your own, isn't over when you finish high school or college or (for those of us seriously dedicated to avoiding real life) graduate school. There's always more to learn. Nothing's quite like learning directly from a first-rate teacher in a classroom, but learning over the Net can be the next best thing to being there — particularly for students who live far from school or have irregular schedules. You can now take everything online from high school equivalency exams to professional continuing education to college and graduate courses leading to degrees. Some courses are strictly online; others use a combination of classroom, lab, and online instruction.

We believe that Internet filtering in schools isn't a good approach. Kids are quicker and more highly motivated and have more time to spend breaking into and out of systems than most adults we know, and this method doesn't encourage them to do something more productive than electronic lock-picking.

Many institutions rely successfully on students' signed contracts that detail explicitly what is appropriate and what is inappropriate to use. Students who violate these contracts lose their Internet or computer privileges. We recommend the approach of contracts and consequences, from which kids can truly learn.

Many schools use the Internet to post information that students can use in their classes, including a summary of the curriculum, upcoming assignments, and links to websites with useful resources. One such system is Moodle (at www.moodle.org) — ask your kids whether their teachers post assignments and resources online.

Schools all over the world now offer online instruction, and some (such as MIT, at `web.mit.edu`) make all their course material available online for free. If the course is on the Net, it doesn't matter whether the school is across the street or across the ocean. You can find thousands of schools and courses in directories such as these:

```
www.petersons.com/college-search/distance-education.aspx
www.usnewsuniversitydirectory.com
www.onlineschools.org
```

A Few Useful Websites

Here are a few sites that may be useful for kids and parents (and grandparents).

These sites focus on education and parenting:

- ✔ **The Global Schoolhouse,** at `www.globalschoolnet.org`, is an online meeting place for teachers, students, and parents.

- ✔ **KidPub,** at `www.kidpub.com`, features book reviews and writing contests for and by kids.

- ✔ **Funbrain,** at `www.funbrain.com`, has educational games for kindergarten through eighth grade.

These sites are just plain fun:

- ✔ **Astronomy Picture of the Day, as in** `apod.nasa.gov/apod`, displays a different gorgeous picture of the cosmos every day. Your tax dollars at work!

- ✔ **The Yuckiest Site on the Internet,** at `www.cyberbee.com/yucky`, is just what it sounds like — the yuckier, the better!

- ✔ At the **CIA Kids' Page,** at `https://www.cia.gov/kids-page`, you have to type the https:// part (it's a secure site — that's what the *s* means) because it's, you know, the CIA.

- ✔ **Pattern Maker** at `www.zefrank.com/dtoy_vs_byokal` is a fun little drawing programs.

- ✔ *Sports Illustrated* **for Kids,** at `www.sikids.com`, features sports news and games, but no swimsuits.

Part II
Internet, Here I Come!

In this part . . .

- ✔ Gathering your equipment and connecting to the Internet
- ✔ Set up your network or Wi-Fi hotspot
- ✔ Choose a browser and explore web pages
- ✔ Get the most from your favorite browser

Chapter 4

Assembling Your Gear and Climbing on the Net

"**G**reat!" you say, "How do I connect my device to the Internet?" The answer is, "It depends." (You'll hear that answer perhaps more often than you'd like.) The Internet isn't one network — it's 100,000 separate networks hooked together, each with its own rules and procedures, and you can get to the Net from any one of them. Readers of previous editions of this book pleaded (they said other things too, but this is a family-oriented book) for step-by-step directions on how to get on, so we made this chapter as "step-tual" as possible.

Here (drumroll, please) are the basic steps:

1. **Figure out which type of device you have or can use.**

2. **Figure out which types of Internet connections are available where you are.**

3. **Sign up for your connection, if it requires an account.**

4. **Set up your device to use your new connection, and decide whether you like it.**

5. **Install the software you need to protect your device from viruses and spyware, for some kinds of devices.**

   See Chapter 2 for scary descriptions of the types of Internet dangers you need to protect yourself from.

If you have more than one device to connect to the Internet, see Chapter 5. For example, you might want to be able to access the Net from a computer and a tablet or two at your home or office.

Internet accounts are easy to use, but they can be tricky to set up. In fact, connecting for the first time can be the most difficult part of your Internet experience. Installing and setting up Internet connection software used to require that you type lots of scary-looking numerical Internet addresses, hostnames, communications-port numbers — you name it. These days, making the connection is much easier, partly because Internet software can now figure out most of the details itself, but mostly because all recent versions of Windows, Macs, and Linux and all tablets and smartphones include setup software that can step you through the process.

What Kind of Device Do You Need?

Because the Internet is a computer network, the only way to hook up to it is to use some kind of computer. But computers appear in all sorts of disguises — including phones, tablets, MP3 music players, and toasters (okay, not really) — and they may well already be in your home, whether you know it or not.

Hey, I don't even have a computer!

If you don't have a computer and aren't ready or able to buy one, you still have options.

A likely place to find Internet access is in your public library. Most libraries have added Internet access centers, with clusters of Internet-connected computers among the bookshelves. These computers tend to be popular, so call ahead to reserve time or find out which hours are less crowded.

Another option is your local cybercafé or restaurant. You can surf the Net while sipping your favorite beverage and sharing your cyber experience. If you want to check out the Internet, a cybercafé is a great place to try before you buy. Some have computers ready for you to use, whereas others require you to bring your own laptop. (See Chapter 5 for laptop safety tips.)

If you want to use the Internet from your very own home, you're stuck getting some kind of computer, tablet, smartphone, or other device. Luckily, almost any newish computer can connect to the Internet, and you can get perfectly usable ones for less than $300. Tablets and smartphones can be even cheaper.

Yup, I have this old, beige box in the closet

Almost any personal computer made since 1980 is adequate for *some* type of connection to the Internet. But unless you have a really good friend who is a computer geek and wants to spend a lot of time at your house helping you get online, don't bother fooling with that old clunker — unless, of course, you're looking for a reason for the geek to spend a lot of time at your house, but that's your business.

If you can afford it, we strongly encourage you to buy a new computer or at least one that isn't more than two or three years old. Old computers tend to run old versions of software. New computers come with Internet software already installed and are configured for the latest in web technology. Any version of Windows older than Windows Vista or any Mac system older than OS X is more hassle than it's worth to try to use.

Yup, I got a brand-new BitBucket 2015

Ah, you *have* a computer, either desktop or laptop. (Or maybe you're thinking about buying one.) Most Internet users connect by way of a broadband connection, Wi-Fi (a wireless connection described in the section "Getting Wi-Fi with Your Latté"), or in a few areas where broadband isn't available, by the computer dialing over the phone line. When you first turn on your new computer, or when you run one of the Internet programs that comes installed, your computer offers to attempt to connect right then and there. First read the rest of this chapter, starting with the section "The Types of Internet Connections." We have some warnings and some options we think you ought to consider first.

Yup, I'm getting a tablet such as an iPad

If you don't care about having a real keyboard, you can also consider a *tablet computer,* such as the iPad, Nexus, Surface, Kindle Fire, or Galaxy Tab. These flat, magazine-size computers look like oversized cellphones. The screens are about the size of a book, so they're convenient for reading and watching videos, but not so helpful for typing. We were initially skeptical about tablets, but now we take ours everywhere. *Phablets* are somewhere between a phone and a tablet in size – small enough to fit in a large pocket. If you expect to do a lot of typing, you can even get add-on keyboards that connect to your tablet. Unless you have large fingers, they work pretty well.

Some tablets (and phablets) can connect to the cellular phone network. All can connect using Wi-Fi, described in the section "Getting Wi-Fi with Your Latté" later in this chapter. The advantage of a cellular tablet is that you can get online anywhere there's cell service, but you have to pay a monthly connection fee. Wi-Fi works only where there's a Wi-Fi signal, but there's no monthly charge.

Yup, I got this little smartphone

The newfangled, Internet-enabled *smartphone* is a tiny computer that happens to have a phone antenna, a microphone, and speakers built in. They have smaller screens and smaller, onscreen keyboards, so industry groups devised a way to show web pages on those screens and navigate around them. When you leave the phone store, your smartphone will be set up to connect to the Internet. Read "Internet via Smartphones and Tablets" later in this chapter.

Like computers, which come primarily in Windows, Mac, and Linux varieties, smartphones come in several flavors. The major types of smartphones are:

- ✔ **Android:** This system is *open source* (anyone can see the code and create compatible software). Because it's sponsored by Google, you can use your Google Apps (such as Gmail, Google Calendar, and Google Maps) on these phones. Android phones are available from a number of manufacturers and work on most cellphone networks.

- ✔ **iPhone:** The iPhone is a beautiful thing, and its sleek design created a huge sensation when it debuted in 2007. All iPhones are made by Apple. Figure 4-1 shows an iPhone displaying email.

- ✔ **Windows Mobile:** A variety of phones use a version of Windows designed for phones and other handheld devices. Windows Mobile phones are available from several manufacturers.

For each of these smartphone operating systems, you can buy a variety of different phones in different shapes and sizes. Some have little keyboards, some flip open, some have larger screens, some are bigger or heavier, some can connect to the Internet by way of Wi-Fi as well as by using the cellphone system, some allow you to use an external keyboard — you get the idea. Shop around. New smartphone models are available every month.

Figure 4-1:
Smart-
phones
(such as this
iPhone) can
read and
send email,
browse the
web, and
use other
Internet
services.

The Types of Internet Connections

If you use a computer at a library, at work, at a cybercafé (generically known as a *Wi-Fi hotspot*, a place where you can connect to Wi-Fi), or at someone else's house, you don't need to worry about how it connects to the Internet, because someone else has already done the work. But if you want to use your computer, tablet, phone, or other device at home, you have several ways to connect:

- ✔ Using **cellular data** from a smartphone or a tablet with cellular data
- ✔ Using **Wi-Fi**
- ✔ Using a fast phone line (**DSL line**)
- ✔ Using your **cable** TV company
- ✔ Using a regular phone line (a.k.a. **dial-up**)

(If you're truly in the boondocks, you can also use a satellite to connect, usually via the same company from which you get satellite television.) Each of these connections is described in this chapter.

Table 4-1 shows what kind of device can device how.

Table 4-1	Devices and How They Connect to the Internet
Gizmo	How It Can Connect
Desktop computer	DSL line, cable, dial-up
Laptop computer	Wi-Fi, DSL line, cable
Tablet with cellular plan	Wi-Fi, cellular
Tablet without cellular plan	Wi-Fi
Smartphone	Wi-Fi, cellular

Chapter 5 describes how to set up your own Wi-Fi hotspot using your own DSL line or cable connection.

Internet via Smartphones and Tablets

You pay a lot extra for a smartphone. The phone itself can cost several hundred dollars, and you also pay for Internet use with something called a *data plan*, which costs $15 to $50 per month for a set amount of Internet usage. Email and audio uses very little of your data plan, while streaming video can max out the plan and cost you extra. With some smartphones (including the iPhone), you're forced to buy a monthly data plan. Nearly all smartphones can also use Wi-Fi (see the section "Getting Wi-Fi with Your Latté") when they're within range of a Wi-Fi hotspot. Wi-Fi is usually faster than mobile data, and isn't charged against your mobile data plan.

In most cases, each smartphone is available from and will work with only one carrier, so if you have preferences among carriers, you limit your choice of phones. Be sure you understand the monthly plan that comes with the phone and that the monthly data quota matches your usage. If you simply check email a few times a day, an itty-bitty plan is enough, but if you plan to stream video an hour each way on your commute, you need an all-you-can-eat plan.

All smartphones come with a web browser and an email program. (Otherwise, what's smart about them?) Most allow you to download additional application programs *(apps)* from a website. Some applications are free and others cost a few bucks. You can download maps (Google Maps has a smartphone version), instant messaging, and Internet games. Most can also play Internet audio and video files, so you can watch YouTube during your commute, preferably if someone else is driving.

The great thing about a smartphone, or a tablet that includes a cellular connection, is that when you buy one, the store sets up your Internet connection for you. Don't walk out of the store until you've set up your phone or tablet for email (described in Chapter 8) and know how to use the web browser (which we talk about in Chapter 6).

For much more information on the mobile Internet, see _Mobile Internet for Dummies_, written and published by people you know and trust. For more details on smartphones, go to www.dummies.com and search for specific phone models.

Getting Wi-Fi with Your Latté

In olden days, people would visit a coffee shop and order cups of coffee, of which there was a maximum of two kinds, regular and decaf, and then chat with people sitting _right next to them_. Now, of course, that situation is hopelessly 20th century. We cruise into the coffee shop with our laptop, tablet, or smartphone, order a half-caf single-shot mocha cappuccino grande with 2 percent milk and cocoa drizzle, hold the sprinkles, put on our Bluetooth earpiece, and talk or exchange messages with people thousands of miles away, utterly ignoring the losers at the next table. The magic of Wi-Fi makes this possible, as coffee shops install Wi-Fi _hotspots_ (public areas with Wi-Fi Internet access) to which customers can connect.

The amount of effort needed to get online using Wi-Fi varies from none to way too much. At some coffee shops, airports, and other places, Wi-Fi is free, while others require you to whip out a credit card to use it. You can set up your own Wi-Fi hotspot, too; see Chapter 5.

Watch out for bogus hotspots: see the sidebar "Snoops at the coffee shop."

Wi-Fi can be free, or not

More and more store and restaurants provide free Wi-Fi to attract your business. Some hotspots put a password on their Wi-Fi, to deter freeloaders outside on the sidewalk. In that case, there's usually a note next to the counter with the password, or you can just ask the barista. Or they may limit the amount of time you can use the Wi-Fi. We think it's rude to use the Wi-Fi without buying something, especially for small, locally-owned spots.

> ## Snoops at the coffee shop
>
> Although we think that a lot of concerns about Internet network security are overblown, one place where it's a real issue is on public Wi-Fi networks, like the ones in hotels and coffee shops. These networks frequently have no passwords, which means that *anyone on that network can snoop on your network connection.* Even if everyone in the coffee shop seems nice, a snoop might be sitting in a car out by the curb. And in a hotel, of course, you have no idea who's in all the nearby rooms.
>
> Fortunately, taking a few simple precautions will keep you safe. When visiting websites, make sure that any site where you type a password or other private information uses *SSL encryption:* The address starts with `https://`, and the little lock in the corner is locked. If the site has no SSL encryption, wait until you return home. For advice on securing your mail program, see the section "Wi-Fi and email don't mix," a little later in this chapter. If you see a network named Free Public Wi-Fi or something like that, do *not* use it, because it is a password-stealing virus running on a nearby infected computer by someone waiting to use your credit card to buy real estate in rural Iceland. Connect to Wi-Fi only when you are sure that it is a real, aboveboard Wi-Fi network.

Other places make you pay by the hour or the day. This fee adds an extra, annoying step to the connection process, the one where you pay. After your device is turned on, fire up your web browser. No matter what your home page is, the network is set up so that your browser shows *its* home page, which allows you to make payment arrangements.

There are about as many ways to pay for Wi-Fi access as there are flavors of coffee. Maybe you buy or are given a ticket at the counter with a code number to enter. More likely, the coffee shop made a deal with one of the large, national mobile phone providers, T-Mobile or AT&T, which makes a sideline of Wi-Fi. In this case, you pay with a credit card, either by the hour (at about $6 per hour) or by buying a package of hours. You sign up via your web browser — the Wi-Fi network lets you connect to the sign-up page for free, but you have to sign up and pay to do anything else.

Connecting to Wi-Fi from a tablet or phone

All mobile devices connect in more or less the same way.

1. **Open the Settings app.**

   On Androids, it's a blue gear icon. On iPhones and iPads, the gear is gray. On Windows Mobile, it's a red gear. (Who decides these things?)

2. **On iPhones and iPads, tap Wi-Fi.**

   It's already displayed on other the systems.

3. **If Wi-Fi is turned off, turn it on by sliding its slider to On.**

4. **When you see the list of networks, tap the one you want.**

5. **If the Wi-Fi hotspot requires a password, your device asks you for it.**

   Your phone or tablet should remember this Wi-Fi network in future, including its password.

Connecting to Wi-Fi from a laptop

To get your computer connected to Wi-Fi, follow these steps:

1. **Turn on or wake up your computer.**

   If your computer doesn't look for a Wi-Fi network by itself, tell it to connect.

2. **In Windows 8 or 8.1, display the Charms bar by swiping in from the right side of the screen or moving your mouse to the upper right-hand corner, click Settings, and click the Wireless Network icon (a set of five bars).**

   In Windows 7 or Vista, Click the Networking icon on the task bar or choose the Start⇨Connect To command to see the list of available Wi-Fi networks.

   On a Mac, click the Wi-Fi icon (a set of concentric curves) at the top of your screen, near the clock.

3. **Click the name of the network when it appears.**

   If you see a Connect Automatically checkbox, leave it checked if this is a network you want to connect to whenever you are in its vicinity

4. **If you are prompted for a password, enter it.**

5. **Click Connect.**

The next time you come back, your computer remembers the network and connects automatically.

Airports, hotels, and beyond

Coffee shops are hardly the only places that offer Wi-Fi. If you spend much time in airports (John does because he's on a lot of advisory boards), you find lots of Wi-Fi — with about the same options as in the coffee shops. The same two providers dominate, with a lot of little local ones as well. After a while, frequent travelers learn Wi-Fi folklore — say that there's free Wi-Fi in the airline club on the mezzanine in Terminal C of Newark airport, and you can use it from the food court downstairs.

Large cable providers, notably Comcast and Time-Warner (who may be one company by the time you read this), also have networks of hotspots for the benefit of their customers while they're on the road. Even better, their hotspots are *federated*, which means that anyone with an account on one cable provider can use the other cable providers' hotspots at no charge. If you have a cable account, and you see a hotspot with a cable provider's name such as Comcast's Xfinity, try connecting and logging in with email address and password you use for your email account at your cable provider.

Hotels, like cafés, treat Wi-Fi as either a service — like the ice machine on each floor — or a profit center, like your room's minibar full of overpriced beer. Some hotels still offer wired Internet connections (in which case a cable on the desk in your room plugs into your computer), and others go Wi-Fi. If you're at an ice-machine-style hotel, you may just be able to turn on your computer and go online with no fuss, or you may have to sign in through your browser, even though you don't have to pay. Some hotels with Wi-Fi give you a slip of paper with a login code when you register, to deter visitors who would otherwise sit in the lobby and use it for free. In minibar-style hotels, you have to log in through your browser. Most hotels put the charge on the room bill; some want your credit card number so that they can bill you separately. The typical charge is $10 per day, from noon to noon, but we've seen hourly rates, lower rates, and higher rates. Some hotels bundle the rate in a business package with long-distance phone calls and other goodies.

If you encounter a problem with a hotel's Internet service, rarely does anyone at the hotel know anything about it, though they should be able to give you an 800 number you can call to talk to someone at the company that provides the service.

Wi-Fi and email don't mix

Wi-Fi connections in coffee shops, airports, and hotels sure are convenient, but remember: *They aren't private.* This situation is a particular problem when you send and receive email, because you usually want your mail to be private *and* because your computer needs to send your network login and password over the Internet back to your mail server to pick up your mail. With a modest amount of advance planning, it shouldn't be hard to get your mail working securely on the road.

The simplest approach is *webmail* — a secure website where you can log in to read and send mail. Check to see whether your mail system offers optional webmail. If so, even if you don't use it at home, you might want to use it on the road, particularly if the webmail offers a secure server. See the section "The Web Is a Fine Place to Read Your Email" in Chapter 8 to find out how webmail works. Normally, we don't worry about secure websites (`https://` versus `http://`), but public Wi-Fi is one of the few cases where people might actually be snooping and the https security helps.

If you want to be *truly* paranoid, create an account at Gmail, Hotmail, Yahoo! Mail, or another webmail site, use it during your trip, and then close the account when you return home. Be sure not to use the same password you use for other sites or accounts.

Speedy Connections: DSL and Cable Internet

The most popular way to connect your computer to the Internet, available almost but not quite everywhere, is a *broadband* (high-speed) connection. This type of connection can be fast, with downloads often exceeding 10 million bits per second. Broadband connections are now available and affordable by mere mortals in all but the most rural locations in the United States and Canada. (Even rural locations can connect using the same satellite that provides satellite TV.)

If you want to connect a computer, or a couple of computers, to the Internet, or you want to set up your own Wi-Fi hotspot in your home or office (as described in Chapter 5), you'll want a broadband connection.

What is broadband, anyway?

There are two types of broadband Internet connections — DSL and cable:

✔ A *Digital Subscriber Line* (DSL) is a phone line that you order from your local telephone company, usually shared with the same line that connects your regular phones.

✔ A *cable* Internet account is provided by your local cable TV company, using the same cable connection that brings you 250 brain-numbing TV channels. Many cable companies also offer phone service, as part of a package.

DSL and cable Internet accounts have a lot in common: They're fast and they don't tie up your regular phone line. Some broadband accounts have a permanent connection that works a lot like a connection to a local network in an office. Others require you to log on every time you want to use the Internet. The Internet Service Provider (or ISP — your phone or cable company) provides most of the equipment — for example, the modem — and sometimes sends an installer to set it up with your computer. Ask your cable company about its Internet access and ask your phone company about its DSL. Then get one or the other.

Basic high-speed cable or DSL costs $30 per month depending on your location, plus installation and the cost of the special modem you need, minus whatever discount you receive for buying a package of broadband and other types of services the provider supplies. You usually get the best price with a package combining Internet with some or all of its phone, cable TV, and mobile phone services. Most providers offer faster service at higher prices, often a lot higher, like $100 per month for the fastest cable options.

A hidden cost in getting either cable or DSL Internet access is having to take a day off from work to wait for the installers, unless you feel brave enough to install it yourself. Sometimes the installers must make two trips to get things working. Try to make the first appointment in the morning. Also, the cable company or phone company is usually also your ISP unless you pay extra, so you don't have a choice of ISPs. In theory, the phone company provides DSL access on equal terms to all ISPs — but, in practice, its own ISP somehow always seems to be more equal than the others.

What's in an account?

An Internet account — DLS or cable — comes with

- ✔ **That all-important username and password:** You have to be able to connect, after all.

- ✔ **One or more email addresses, each with its own mailbox:** Most accounts have from one to five email addresses. If you have a family, every family member can have a separate address.

- ✔ **Webmail (a website where you can read your mail):** Webmail is useful when you want to check your mail and you're not at your own computer with your own email program. You can use a web browser to display your messages from any computer. See Chapter 8.

Your account should also come with a toll free or local number you can call for support. Every ISP has a website showing prices, sign-up instructions, and support information.

Cable and DSL modems

To connect to a DSL or cable account, you use a DSL or a cable modem. The phone or cable company often provides it (usually for a fee). Don't buy a DSL modem yourself — you need a modem compatible with your provider's equipment, but cable modems are now well enough standardized that you'll save money in the long run if you buy a $90 cable modem rather than renting one for $5/mo. When the cable installer comes, she should hook up the modem whether it's one you're renting or one you've bought.

A word about usernames and passwords

More than a billion people are on the Internet. Because only one of them is you, it would be nice if the rest of them couldn't go snooping through your files and email messages. For that reason — no matter which type of Internet account you have — your account has a username and a secret password associated with it.

Your *username* (or *user ID, login name, logon name,* or *screen name*) is unique among all the names assigned to your provider's users. It's usually also your email address, so don't pick a name like *snickerdoodle123* unless that's what

you want to tell your friends and put on your business cards.

Your password is secret and is the main thing that keeps bad guys from borrowing an account. Don't use a real word or a name. See the section "What's the secret word, Harry?" in Chapter 2 for ideas for passwords that you have some hope of remembering.

Never tell anyone else your password. Particularly don't tell people who claim to be from your ISP or your bank — they aren't.

If you live in a part of the country that gets thunderstorms, a nearby lightning strike will often blow out your modem. (You can probably guess how we learned about this.) If you buy a modem, ask if there's an extended warranty that covers failures due to electrical surges. Normally extended warranties are a bad deal, but in this specific case, they aren't.

How your computer connects to the modem

DSL and cable modems connect to your computer in one of 2 ½ ways:

- ✔ **Network adapter:** A *network adapter* (or *LAN adapter* or *Ethernet adapter* or *network interface card*) was originally designed for connecting computers into networks. If you have more than one computer in your home or office, you can use network adapters to connect the computers into a local-area network (LAN), as described in Chapter 5. A network adapter has an RJ-45 jack, which looks like a regular phone jack but is a little bigger, into which you plug your modem or network cable. Check the back and sides of your computer for holes that look like overgrown phone jacks. All modern PCs (and all Macs other than Macbook Air) have network adapters built in.

- ✔ **Wireless network adapter:** If your computer isn't located close to a phone or cable outlet or you have a laptop you carry around the house, you can create a wireless network, often called Wi-Fi. It works much the same as a wired network, only without the wires (duh!). All laptops, tablets, and smartphones built in the past five years have built-in Wi-Fi.

✔ **USB:** Almost all computers come with one or more *USB* (*Universal Serial Bus,* if you care) connectors, which are used for connecting all kinds of stuff to your computer, from mice to cameras to printers. A USB port on a computer looks like a small, narrow, rectangular hole. On tablets and phones, there's a micro-USB slot shaped like a flat trapezoid.

Getting your cable Internet hooked up

To sign up for a cable account, call your local cable company to open one. Unless you decide to install it yourself (which isn't all that hard), a technician comes and installs a network-connection doozus (technical term) where your TV cable comes into your house, brings a cable modem (which can look like a junior laptop computer with a spike hairdo) and/or router if you haven't bought your own, and hooks them together. Magic.

If you have cable television, the cable is split and one segment goes to your cable modem. If you don't have cable television, the cable company may have to install the actual cable before it can wire up your computer network. When the technician goes away, however, you have a permanent, high-speed connection to the Internet (as long as you pay your bill, about $30 to $200 a month, depending on speed and how many other services you get).

Getting your DSL hooked up

DSL service is supposed to use your existing phone line and in-house wiring. But DSL often works better if the phone company runs a new wire from the place where your phone line enters your building to wherever you use your computer. (Phone companies call this situation a *home run.*) For most kinds of DSL to work, you have to live within a couple of miles of your telephone central office, so DSL is unavailable in many rural areas.

DSL is available at different speeds. The higher speeds cost more (surprise, surprise!). The lowest speed, usually 640 Kbps or more, is adequate for most users although not very satisfactory for watching video.

If DSL service is available in your area, call your phone company to arrange for DSL service. Either it ships you the equipment to install yourself or a phone installer comes with a network connection box that you or the installer hook to your computer. Some DSL modems connect to a network adapter or USB connector, and most include a router (described in more detail later) that can also provide a Wi-Fi connection. And be sure to read the nearby sidebar, "Avoiding the DSL buzz."

Avoiding the DSL buzz

One clever thing about DSL is that the DSL connection shares the same phone wires with your phone without tying up the phone line. You can tell that this is the case because on all phones on the line with DSL, you may hear a loud buzz of Data Hornets swarming up and down your phone line. (Well, not really, but it can sound like it.)

To get rid of the buzz, you install a *DSL filter,* which filters out the buzz, between the phone line and all your phones. Filters are available from your DSL ISP, but you can probably find them cheaper at stores like Best Buy or RadioShack. The ideal way to install a filter is to run a separate wire from the box where the phone line enters your house to the DSL

modem, and to install one DSL filter in that box into which you plug the wire leading to all the phones. But life is rarely ideal, so most of us install a filter for every phone.

For the phone plug where your DSL modem is connected, you want a *splitter* filter with a filtered jack into which you plug a phone (the one you use to call tech support when your computer doesn't work) and a data-filtered jack for the DSL modem. For all other phones, the filter simply plugs into the phone jack and the phone cord plugs into the filter. For that tidy look, you can also get wall-phone filters (which fit between the phone and the wall plate that the phone is mounted on) and baseboard phone jacks with filters built in.

Wires galore!

Once your broadband connection is set up should look something like the one shown in Figure 4-2. The details may vary a little — John's DSL came with filters that include the two-for-one splitter, and the modem includes a Wi-Fi router, so there's no cable to the computer. For a cable setup, the phone wire comes from the modem rather than to the wall.

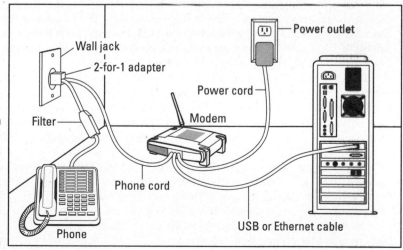

Figure 4-2: Your Windows computer, connected to a DSL line.

Fast, fibrous FiOS

Cable and DSL network speeds are limited by the old-fashioned copper wire they use. Fiber optics are much faster, and large telephone companies have been making and breaking promises to wire us up with fiber for about 30 years. According to Teletruth, a phone consumers' advocate, if Verizon had kept the promises that its predecessor Bell of Pennsylvania made in 1994, most Pennsylvania homes would be wired with 45-megabits-per-second fiber by now.

Verizon is finally sort of making good on its promises with *FiOS,* a fiber optic package that combines fairly fast Internet (not 45 megabits, though) with home Wi-Fi, phone, and TV. If you want fast Internet and high-definition TV and you're willing to sign up for at least a full year, it's not a bad deal and it costs $45 a month and more. But you might want to consider a few issues before signing up:

✔ **Verizon has some odd rules about the connections it supports.** In particular, it doesn't officially support wireless connections to Macs, only wired, although wireless works fine in practice.

✔ **There's no going back.** The person who hooks up the fiber often physically rips out your old copper phone line so that you can't switch back without paying for a full new installation.

✔ **It depends on your house power.** Regular phone service powers your phone from the central office, so the phone company's large batteries and professionally maintained backup generators keep the phones working if the power fails. FiOS uses your house power to run your phones as well as your Internet and TV connections. FiOS provides a battery that's supposed to keep your phone going for four hours if the power fails, but the battery lasts only two or three years, and if you don't remember to replace it (Verizon won't), you'll have an unpleasant surprise when the power fails and you want to use the phone.

After the DSL or cable Internet installer

The installer configures your computer to communicate with the Internet. Follow the instructions to connect to your account the first time; some DSL and cable modems come with a software CD you may need to use. Don't let the installer leave until you've gotten online and you know the connection works.

Even if you plan to use your computer via Wi-Fi (described in Chapter 5), it's easier to do the initial setup by plugging your computer into the router or modem with an Ethernet or USB cable. Wi-Fi has issues, like which of several networks in your neighborhood is the right one to use, while with a cable, there's no choice, it's the one at the other end of the cable.

Chances are good, at this point, that you're on the Internet. You should be able to start up a web browser, such as Internet Explorer, and type the name of a website in the Address bar at the top. (Try our net.gurus.org.) The web page should appear momentarily. If you have a connection with a username, it may ask you whether to connect. (Well, yeah, that's the idea, but sarcasm is lost on machinery.)

If you still can't connect, you can try configuring Windows yourself.

Configuring Windows 8.1 to connect

Windows 8.1 detects an Internet connection if one exists, so you may not have to do a thing. It spots Wi-Fi or a connected DSL or cable modem and does the right thing. If you have to set the connection up yourself, or fiddle with it afterwards, follow these steps:

1. **Press the Windows key until you see the Windows 8.1 Start screen. (That's the screen entitled "Start" with the multicolored boxes.) If you've installed a Windows 7–style menu, press the Windows key once and you'll see a menu with a search box in the lower left corner of the screen.**

   Either way, you are ready to search for the Network and Sharing Center, the application that enables you to see and configure your network setup.

2. **Type** network sharing.

   If you are on the Windows 8.1 Start screen, a Search box appears for you to type into, along with one search result: The Network and Sharing Center. If you use a Windows 7–style menu, it should also appear as a search result.

3. **Choose Network and Sharing Center.**

   The Network and Sharing Center displays a number of options, depending on what kind of connection you have. We cover some of the other options for dialup and wireless later in this chapter and in Chapter 5.

4. **Click Set Up a New Connection or Network, and then click Connect to the Internet, and then click Next.**

5. **Enter the information provided by your ISP.**

   In particular, enter the login name and password that your ISP gave you.

Configuring Windows 7 to connect

Windows 7 also detects an Internet connection if one exists. If you need to do it yourself, choose Start⇨Control Panel⇨Network and Internet⇨Network and Sharing Center. Then follow steps 2–4 for Windows 8.1.

Configuring Windows Vista to connect

If your network connects with a wired LAN connection and doesn't require a login or password (this includes most cable modems), Vista normally configures itself automagically. For connections that require a login, follow these steps:

1. **Choose Start⇨Connect To and then click the little Set Up a Connection or Network link.**

2. **For the Network Connection type, choose Connect to the Internet and click Next.**

3. **Select Broadband (PPPoE).**

4. **Enter the required information in the boxes.**

Configuring a Mac to connect

To set up a connection from Mac running OS X, click the Apple icon in the upper left corner of the screen, choose System Preferences, and click the Network icon. You see the Network window shown in Figure 4-3.

Either the USB Ethernet or Ethernet entry in the left-hand column should be green if your Mac is connected via cable to your modem. Click USB Ethernet to see its settings and follow the instructions from your ISP.

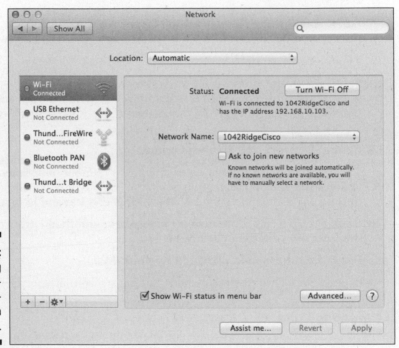

Figure 4-3:
Configuring your network connection on a Mac.

Checking your DSL or cable connection

After you're connected, you can check the status of your connection:

✔ **Windows 8 or 8.1:** Display the Network and Sharing Center by pressing the Windows key until you see the Windows 8.1 Start screen, typing "network sharing", and choosing `Network and Sharing Center`. (If you use a Windows 7–style menu, press the Windows key to display a search box.) You see an informational screen similar to Figure 4-4.

Dialing — the old-fashioned way

A *dialup modem* connects to a normal, everyday phone line — using the same little plug (an RJ-11 jack) and phone wire. You can unplug a phone and plug in a dialup modem in its place. The problems with dialup are that the connection is s-l-o-w and that your phone line is tied up while you're online.

Computers used to come with built-in dialup modems — examine your computer carefully for a phone jack and if you find one, plug a phone wire into it. Don't confuse the phone jack with a wired Ethernet jack, which looks quite similar but is wider. If your computer doesn't have a phone modem, get a USB modem that plugs into a USB jack on your computer.

To use a dialup Internet connection, you sign up with an ISP (your phone company or another company) for an Internet account. The features and services that one ISP offers are much like those of another. If you don't know what your local ISPs are, check the phone book or ads in the business section of your local paper.

If you aren't careful, you can end up paying more for the phone call than you do for your Internet account. *Use an ISP whose number is a free or untimed local call* (that is, you aren't paying by the minute). Nearly the entire continent is within a local call of an ISP; if you're one of the unlucky few, see whether your phone company has an unlimited long-distance plan.

Your ISP should give you information to set up your account: your username and password, its dialup phone number, and your email address if it's different from your username. Here's how to set up your computer to dial up your ISP, depending on your version of Windows:

- **Windows 8.1**: Press the Windows key until you see the Windows 8.1 Start screen, type **network sharing** and choose `Network and Sharing Center` from the list. (If you use a Windows 7–style menu, press the Windows key to display a search box.)

- **Windows 7**: Choose Start⇨Control Panel⇨Network and Internet⇨Network and Sharing Center⇨Set Up a New Connection or Network.

- **Windows Vista**: Choose Start⇨Connect To. In the window that opens, click the little Set Up a Connection or Network link. Click Set Up a Dial-Up Connection.

- **Macs**: Choose System Preferences from the Apple menu and click the Network icon. Click Assist Me and then click Assistant. Give your connection a name ("Home"? "Dialup"?), click Continue, and choose I Use a Telephone Modem to Dial My ISP.

Enter the phone number as you would dial it on your phone, as 7, 10, or 11 digits. Unless you share your computer with someone you don't trust, select the check box to remember your password.

After your dialup account is set up, your computer should connect automatically whenever you use your web browser or email program. You can also connect at any time. In Windows 8.1 or 7, click the Networking icon on the taskbar (it looks like the connection bars on a cellphone). In Windows Vista, choose Start⇨Connect To and then click the dialup connection and the Connect button. If you see a dialog box that asks for your ISP username and password, type them and then click Connect.

✔ **Windows 7:** Display the Network and Sharing Center by choosing
Start➪Control Panel➪Network and Internet➪Network and Sharing
Center. Look in the View Your Active Networks section, shown in
Figure 4-4.

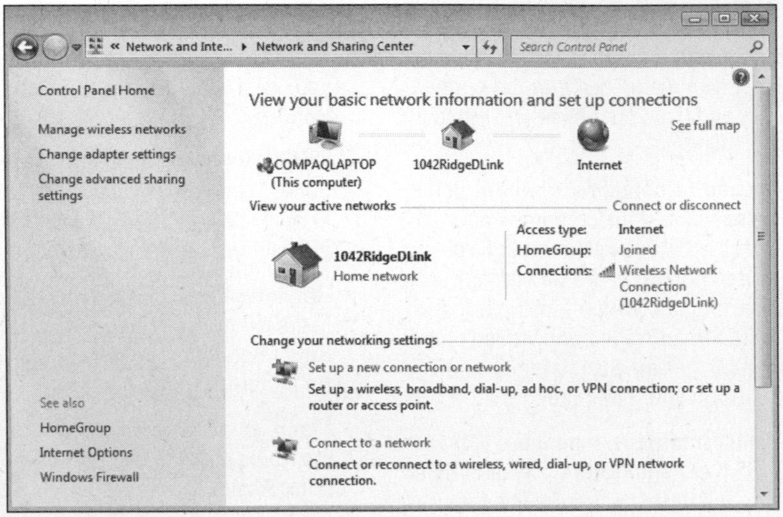

Figure 4-4:
The
Network
and Sharing
Center in
Windows 7
or 8 shows
how your
computer
connects to
the Internet.

✔ **Windows Vista:** Choose Start➪Control Panel➪Network and Sharing
Center. Broadband connections appear in the upper part of the window.

✔ **Macs:** Choose System Preferences from the Apple menu and click the
Network icon.

I'm In!

When you're connected to the Internet, you can monitor your connection or
reconnect or disconnect. There's a Networking icon on the Windows taskbar; it's in the lower right corner of the screen, to the left of the digital clock.
Here's where it is and what it does:

✔ **Windows 8.1:** A mobile-phone-connection-bars Networking icon appears
in the lower right corner of the screen. Hover over it to see the active
connections. When you click, the Network "charm" slides out from the
right-hand side of the screen with more networking options, including
choosing a Wi-Fi network and turning airplane mode on and off.

✔ **Windows 7:** The same Networking icon appears in the lower right corner
of the screen. Click it to see what you're connected to. Click Open Network
and Sharing Center at the bottom of its window to see more information
(refer to Figure 4-4).

✔ **Windows Vista:** A two-computer-screen icon appears in the lower right corner of the screen. Right-click the icon to see options.

Mac users see a Wi-Fi icon in the upper right of the screen. If you need information about a wired connection, choose System Preferences from the Apple menu and click the Network icon.

If you use a broadband account, you never need to disconnect. We love being able to saunter up to our computers at any time to check the weather, our email, a good buttermilk waffle recipe, or which movies Joe E. Brown was in, without having to wait for our computer to reconnect.

If you dial in to the Internet, you eventually want to disconnect (hang up) so that you can use your phone line to talk to actual human beings. You can leave the rest of your programs (such as your web browser and email program) running even when you aren't connected to the Net. To disconnect a dialup connection, double-click or right-click the Networking icon, which we just described, and choose Disconnect.

Essential Software to Keep Your System Safe

Okay, you're connected. Before you start surfing the web and emailing, you need to protect your computer from the Terrors of the Internet: viruses and spyware. Chapter 2 describes the concepts behind them, and now is the time to use protection.

Walling out the bad guys

A *firewall* is a barrier between your computer (or computers) and the Internet. In big companies, the firewall may consist of a computer that does nothing but monitor the incoming and outgoing traffic, checking for bad stuff. At your home or office, you have two good options:

Use firewall software you already have

Here's how to find it on a Windows:

✔ **Windows 8 or 8.1:** Press the Windows key until you see the Windows 8.1 Start screen, type **firewall**, and choose Windows Firewall (not the one "with Advanced Security," which takes you deep into geekland). (If you use a Windows 7–style menu, press the Windows key to display a search box.) You see a screen that looks like Figure 4-5.

✔ **Windows 7:** Choose Start⇨Control Panel⇨System and Security⇨Windows Firewall.

✔ **Windows Vista:** Click the little Security Center shield in the notification area at the bottom of the screen and then click Windows Firewall.

Figure 4-5: Windows 8.1, 7, and Vista come with built-in firewalls, which should be turned on.

Look for the "Windows Firewall state" and make sure it is "On." If not, click "Turns Windows Firewall on or off." When that's done, your computers have basic protection from hackers.

On a Mac, choose System Preferences from the Apple menu and click Security & Privacy. Then click the Firewall tab and click the Turn On Firewall button.

Use a router

A *router* is a small box that sits between your computer (or computers) and your broadband modem. Your modem may have a router built in; ask your installer. A router has one plug for a cable to your DSL or cable modem, several plugs (usually four) to which you can connect computers, and usually an antenna for wireless Wi-Fi connections. The router has firewall software running all the time. See Chapter 5 for how to use a router to connect more than one computer to one Internet account. As often as not, your DSL or cable modem includes a router, so you're all set. (If it has a Wi-Fi antenna, or at least four sockets on the back, it's a router.)

Even if you have only one computer that connects to the Internet, we recommend using a router. If your broadband provider didn't give you one, it costs about $40 and we're sure that you'll want to hook a second computer to the Internet before long. The firewall programs included in Windows 8.1, 7, Vista, and XP work fine, too. Hey, why not use both?

A router is a particularly good idea if you have a broadband connection that is always on (that is, always connected). The router is always on, too.

No viruses need apply

Viruses are sneaky programs that arrive by way of email or in downloaded programs, and immediately get up to no good. (See Chapter 2 for details.) You need to run a virus checker program all the time, and you need to update its list of viruses regularly so that the program can detect the latest viruses.

Many virus checkers are available. The free AVG from the `free.avg.com` website isn't bad, particularly at the price. Microsoft also has a good virus checker, named Windows Defender that comes preinstalled with Windows 8.1. If you use Windows 7 or earlier, download Microsoft Security Essentials for free from `windows.microsoft.com/en-us/windows/security-essentials-download`. Mac user should get ClamXAV from `www.clamxav.com`.

There are third party anti-virus programs available by paid subscription, but we don't find them to be any better than the free Windows Defender or Microsoft Security Essentials. Many PCs come with one preinstalled, with a free trial after which you see increasingly hysterical warnings that you need to buy a paid subscription NOW NOW NOW! Just un-install the other anti-virus and use these Microsoft programs.

Be sure that your virus checker is set to automatically download updates, which it should do at least several times a week.

Detecting spyware

Spyware is a class of programs that sneak onto your computer, usually when you're browsing the web, and run unbeknownst to you, doing God-knows-what. (See Chapter 2 for details.) A number of antispyware programs are available for free, although no single program seems to spot all types of spyware. We recommend that you run several antispyware programs from time to time, to sweep your hard disk and look for bad stuff.

Along with Windows Defender, which is built into Windows 8.1, and Microsoft Security Essentials for Windows 7 and Vista, the three free programs we use are:

- **Malwarebytes Anti-Malware,** at www.malwarebytes.org: Another competent anti-malware package, with a basic free version and a fancier paid version.

- **Spybot Search & Destroy,** at www.safer-networking.org: It's shareware; donations are appreciated. Note that several unscrupulous programs have started using the word *spybot* in their names, so don't just use a search engine to find the program; from your web browser, type the address shown in this paragraph.

- **Ad-Aware Personal Edition,** at www.lavasoft.com: It's also free, although the developer wants you to buy the fancier, paid version.

For help with downloading and installing a spyware-checking program, see Chapter 2. Macs host very little spyware, but if you are worried and don't mind paying for a program, you can download and install MacScan from macscan.securemac.com.

In addition, follow a few basic rules, which will make more sense after you read the later chapters of this book. (Don't worry: We mention the rules again in those later chapters, too.) Here they are:

- **Don't use Internet Explorer as your browser.** Most spyware is designed to use features of Internet Explorer to worm its way onto your computer. Instead, use Firefox or Chrome, as described in Chapter 6.

- **Don't use Internet Explorer within other applications.** For example, some email programs have an option to use Internet Explorer to display messages that contain HTML (web formatting). Turn off these options.

- **If you use Windows, turn on Automatic Updates and download and install the updates it suggests.** Microsoft issues security fixes to Windows about once a week. Windows 8.1, 7, and Vista download and install updates automatically unless you turn off this feature. In Windows 8 or 8.1, press the Windows key until you see the Windows 8 or 8.1 Start screen, type **update,** and choose Windows Update to check whether this feature is on. (If you use a Windows 7–style menu, press the Windows key to display a search box.) In Windows 7, you can ensure that Automatic Updates are on by choosing Start⇨Control Panel⇨System and Security⇨Windows Update. In Windows Vista, choose Start⇨Control Panel⇨Security⇨Windows Update. In the System Properties dialog box that appears, click the Automatic Updates tab. Choose the first or second option so that Windows lets you know when updates are available.

Get rid of your Dell or Gateway software

Many computers come with Internet software created by the hardware manufacturers, designed to give you an easier Internet experience. Unfortunately, we find that these programs only give you a more *confusing* Internet experience because each program is renamed to add the name of the hardware manufacturer. (AOL used to do this, too.) If your Dell or Gateway or other new computer comes with Dell or Gateway or other Internet programs, we recommend that you ignore them and use the standard Windows programs described in this book. The polite name for this stuff is *shovelware.* Columnist Walt Mossberg has a more descriptive name — craplets.

Our Favorite Internet Setup

You're probably wondering, "The authors of this book have used the Internet forever. What do they recommend as the very best way to connect to it?" Okay, you're probably not wondering that, but we wish you were. And we've got the answer.

The best Internet setup (in our humble opinions) is this:

- A computer (Windows, Mac, or Linux — they're all fine).
- A DSL or cable Internet account — broadband rocks! FiOS would be even better, but they don't offer it where we live.
- A *router,* to provide a firewall between your computer (or computers) and the Internet. Our routers also do Wi-Fi, so we can connect wirelessly (as described in Chapter 5).

You're Connected — Now What?

When you connect to your ISP, your computer becomes part of the Internet. You type stuff or click in programs running on your computer and those programs communicate over the Net to do whatever it is they do for you.

You can run several Internet programs at a time, which can be quite handy. You may be reading your email, for example, and receive a message describing a cool, new site on the World Wide Web. You can switch immediately to your web browser program (usually Chrome, Firefox, Internet Explorer, or Safari), look at the web page and then return to the mail program and pick up where you left off. Most email programs highlight *URLs* (web addresses) and enable you to go straight to your browser by clicking the URL in your email message.

You aren't limited to running programs that your Internet provider gives you. You can download a new Internet application from the Net and begin using it immediately — your ISP just acts as a data conduit between your computer and the rest of the Net.

To find out more about using the web, see Chapter 6. If you want to start off with email, read Chapter 8. Or, just flip through the rest of this book to see what looks interesting!

Chapter 5

Setting Up Your Own Network or Wi-Fi Hotspot

In This Chapter

▶ Setting up a network at home

▶ Creating your own Wi-Fi hotspot

These days, lots of families have more than one computer — perhaps one in the office, one in the family room, and one in their teenager's bedroom. Hey, one of us has one in the kitchen for our family's calendar and address book. And that's not to mention the road warrior laptop.

Luckily, you don't need a separate Internet connection for every computer. Instead, you can connect the computers into a network — with cables or through thin air with wireless Wi-Fi connections — and then set them up to share one Internet connection. This chapter shows you to set up both types of networks.

Just One Computer for Internet Access? Naah

Many years ago, back when computers were large, hulking things found only in glass-walled computer rooms, a wild-eyed visionary friend of ours claimed (to great skepticism) that computers would be everywhere, and would be so small and cheap that they would show up as prizes in cereal boxes. We're not sure about the cereal boxes, but it's certainly true that the last time we went to put an old computer in the closet, we didn't have room because of all the other old computers in there. Rather than let them rust in *your* closet, you may as well get some use out of them by connecting them all to the Internet.

With a broadband connection, it turns out to be pretty easy. No more arguing about who uses the phone line next! No more pouting from the computer users who didn't get the cable or DSL hookup! Everyone can send email, receive email, chat, and browse the web — all at the same time.

To share an Internet connection, you connect your computers to each other in a local-area network and then you connect the LAN (rather than an individual computer) to the Internet. A *local-area network* (or *LAN*) is — drumroll, please! — a network entirely contained in one local area, such as one building, and is connected by way of wires or wireless connections, with no phone lines within the LAN. Once the exclusive tool of businesses, LANs have become so cheap that they're showing up in homes. As long as your home is in one building, if you have some computers connected to each other, you have a LAN.

Figure 5-1 shows a typical home network: A cable or DSL modem connects to a *hardware router,* a device that connects your LAN to your Internet connection. Normally, you would connect your computer to a network hub (for a wired network) or an access point (for wireless) — but a hardware router has a hub or an access point built in. Then you connect the LAN to the rest of the computers around the house.

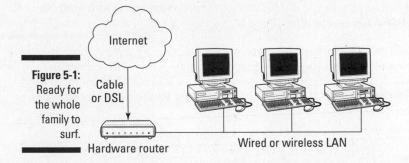

Figure 5-1: Ready for the whole family to surf.

Not all computers on your LAN all have to be running the same version of Windows — or even running Windows. You can connect PCs, Macs, and Linux computers as well as tablet computers, smartphones, and even devices like printers on the same LAN because they all speak the same networking protocol, the same protocol that the Internet itself uses (TCP/IP, if you were wondering).

First, Make a LAN

LANs come in two basic varieties: wired and wireless. In a wired network, a cable runs from each computer to a central box, whereas a wireless network uses radio signals rather than wires. Either way, you need a central box, which we talk about in a minute. If all your computers are in one room and you don't move them (or you're good at playing home electrician), a wired network is for you; otherwise, wireless is far easier to set up, although the resulting network runs slower. Combos are also possible; most wireless equipment has a few jacks for wires to connect to the computers that are close enough to run cables.

The box in the middle — a hub, switch, or router

For any variety of current LAN, you need a special box that connects everything. Here are the main kinds of boxes you have to choose from:

- ✔ A *hub* or *switch* is a book-size box with a bunch of jacks for network cables. It serves as a wired connection point that links all your computers into a LAN. A switch has a little extra circuitry to speed things up.

- ✔ An *access point* is the wireless equivalent of a hub, with a radio antenna or two and only one jack to connect to a wired network.

- ✔ A *router* is similar to a hub or an access point (or both) with the addition of Internet-connection smarts, like a firewall (as described in Chapter 4, in the section about walling out the bad guys).

- ✔ Some providers give you a combined modem and router. If they do, you're all set, no more equipment needed.

Our advice is to go for a router if your provider didn't give you one; it's cheap ($40 to $80), and it saves you days of hair-tearing grief because it keeps most worms out of your network. With a router, none of your computers needs to worry about connecting to the Internet — the router handles it.

Routers come in both wired and wireless versions. The wired versions have varying numbers of jacks, the wireless ones have one jack for the cable to the modem, an antenna for the wireless network, and usually a few jacks for running wires to computers in the same room. For some perverse reason, wireless routers are usually cheaper than wired, even though the wireless ones include everything the wired ones do plus the wireless radio. So get a wireless router. If you need more jacks than your router has, also get a cheap switch; run a cable from one of its jacks to one of the jacks on your router and it'll all be one big happy network.

Rent or buy?

Many providers will offer to rent you a modem, a router, or both, typically for the low, low price of $5/month each. This is rarely a good deal. You can buy your own router or modem at a big box store for about $75, and a little arithmetic reveals that you'll be saving money after a year and a half. Modem and router technology changes slowly, and the ones you get now should serve you for five years or more.

If you have DSL service from the phone company, they will invariably provide the modem at no extra charge because it has to match whatever DSL equipment they use at their end. Cable modems, on the other hand, are totally standardized using a spec called DOCSIS. The only question is whether to get DOCSIS version 2 or 3, with the answer being 3 because it's faster.

If you get your own router, setting it up is the same as if you got one from your provider, as we describe in "Setting up a router." If you buy your own cable modem, the cable company needs to know its MAC address, a 12 character identifier that's printed on a sticker on the modem. If you buy a modem before you get your service installed, the installer will plug in the modem and call in the MAC address. If you replace the modem yourself, it's not much harder. The modem has three connectors, a screw connector for the cable, an RJ-45 multi-pin connector for the Ethernet to your router, and a power connector of some sort, probably a thin wire to a power adapter. Just disconnect the old modem, connect the new modem the same way (use the new power adapter that comes with the new modem), then call your cable company to give them the new MAC address. The whole process shouldn't take more than 10 minutes, give or take how long they keep you on hold.

Setting up a Router

A router invariably comes with a short Ethernet cable to connect the router to the cable or DSL modem, so connect your router to your modem, plug in both devices, and turn them on. An *Ethernet cable* (also known as *Category 5,* or *Cat 5*) looks like a fat phone cable, with little plastic connectors that look just like phone plugs but a little larger. (Even their technical names are a little larger; a phone connector is an *RJ-11 jack,* whereas an Ethernet connector is an *RJ-45 jack.*) Some DSL ISPs provide a combined router and DSL modem, which has an RJ-11 jack for the DSL phone line rather than an incoming Ethernet jack.

Configuring routers for DSL connections that require a username and password

For the most part, routers take care of themselves, but if you have the kind of DSL connection that requires a username and password, you need to put those into the router. If your DSL connection doesn't require a username and password, you can probably just skip this section, although you can come back later if a program you're installing requires you to change the router's configuration. Setup instructions for routers are all the same in concept, but they differ in detail from one router to another — so you may have to (gaack!) glance at the instructions that came with the router.

Because the router has no screen or keyboard that would enable you to configure it, you use a computer connected to the router instead, by way of a web browser. The router has its own web address, accessible only from the computers on your LAN; the address is usually a strange-looking, all-numeric creation. Even if you plan to have an entirely wireless LAN, the initial setup is a lot easier if you connect a computer to the router by using an Ethernet cable, at least for now, so that the router can figure out which computer it's supposed to be talking to. ("Hey, there it is, at the other end of that wire!") Follow these steps:

1. **Turn off the router and the computer.**

   Computers are usually happier if you plug and unplug stuff while they're turned off.

2. **Plug an Ethernet cable into the network adapter on your computer and plug the other end into one of the jacks on the router.**

3. **Turn on the router and then turn on the computer.**

4. **Fire up your web browser and type the address of the router's control page — its home page, with configuration settings.**

   Usually, this page is at 192.168.0.1 or 192.168.0.254 or maybe 10.0.0.1 (special web addresses reserved by the Internet powers that be for private networks such as yours). If those web addresses don't work, check the router's instructions.

5. **If your router's configuration page requires a username and password, check your router's manual to find out what it is and then type it.**

   If you lost the manual, don't panic: Often, the username and password are printed on the bottom of the router. You see the configuration page for your router, similar to Figure 5-2.

6. **If you have a broadband connection that uses a login and password, find the text box or field to enter your login name and password for your broadband connection.**

   Either follow the instructions in your router manual or try clicking the tabs or links on the page until you find boxes with names such as Username and Password. Connections that use passwords may be named *PPPoE* (Point-to-Point over Ethernet, if you must know). Type them in.

7. **If you see a button or link named Save, Done, or OK, click it to make sure that the router saves your changes.**

   If you see no such button or link, don't worry.

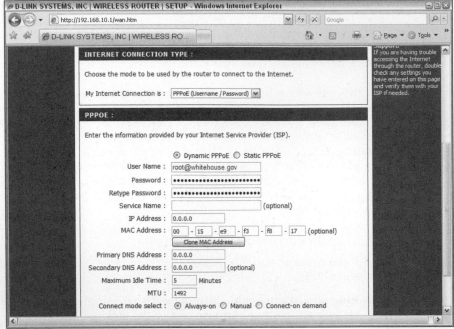

Figure 5-2:
Your router
has no
screen, so
you talk with
it by using
your web
browser.

Now your router knows how to log in to your DSL account. (If you will use the router as a Wi-Fi access point, you have more configuring to do, including setting a password. See the section "Forget the Wires — Go Wi-Fi!" later in this chapter.)

Connecting your LAN to the modem

Plug the router into your DSL or cable modem, turn on the modem (if it isn't on yet), restart the router (by unplugging the power cord and plugging it back in), and verify that you can connect to the outside Internet. If you have a combined DSL modem and router, plug the phone line into its DSL jack. (Try a visit to our home page at net.gurus.org.) If that doesn't work, check the modem cable and ensure that both the username and password setup are correct if your Internet connection needs them. Most routers have reset switches that you can use to return them to their factory settings. It can take a long time, several minutes, for a DSL or cable modem to start the connection, so you might check the little lights to see whether the one that says WAN (for wide-area network) is lit yet.

You can configure a bunch of other router settings that you shouldn't need to worry about unless you're planning to do something exotic. The firewall part of the router watches the Internet traffic as it passes through and blocks the traffic it doesn't like. Routers let through web pages, email, instant messages, and other standard types of Internet communication, but if you're doing something special, like playing certain types of online games, you may need to tell your router to allow additional types of data. If an online game or another program indicates that you need to "open a port" on your router, you need to return to this router configuration web page to make some changes.

Wiring Your Computers into a LAN

After you have the router set up, if you want to create a wired LAN, you need wires. (Okay, you already knew that.) Specifically, LANs use Cat 5 Ethernet cable with RJ-45 connectors — it looks the same as the cable you use to connect your router to your modem. Cat 5 cables are available at any office supply store, electrical supply store, computer store, or even the occasional drugstore or supermarket, and you can find them in varying lengths, from 3 feet to 50 feet or more. You need one cable to run from the router to each computer. It doesn't hurt to use a longer cable than you need, but it looks messy.

For every computer, plug one end of a Cat 5 cable into the computer's network adapter jack. (See the section in Chapter 4 about your computer connecting to the modem.) Plug the other end of the cable into the router.

After your computers are connected to the router and, indirectly, to each other, tell every computer about the LAN. Windows 8, 7, and Vista make it easy — as soon as you plug in your network cable, Windows contacts the router and sets up your connection. (The most common problem: The cable isn't plugged in all the way at one end or the other.)

If your computer doesn't connect automatically, try these steps in Windows 8.1:

1. **Open the Charms bar and click Search.**

2. **Enter network in the Search box.**

3. **Choose Network and Sharing Center to see which networks Windows thinks you're connected to.**

4. **Click Troubleshoot Problems.**

   Clicking this option usually walks you through the solution.

In Windows 7, try this:

1. **Choose Start➪Computer➪Network.**

   You see a window showing the computers and networks that Windows thinks you're connected to.

2. **Click Network and Sharing Center.**

   You see the window shown in Figure 4-4, over in Chapter 4.

3. **Click Set Up a New Connection or Network if this is the first time, or Connect to a Network to connect to a network that already exists (such as someone else's LAN).**

In Windows Vista, try this:

1. **Choose Start⇨Network.**

2. **Click Network and Sharing Center.**

3. **Click the Diagnose and Repair link to help fix the most common problems.**

If you connect a Mac to your LAN, it can probably see the LAN and work without your lifting a finger as soon as you connect the cable. If you want (or need) to configure your network connection, try this:

1. **Choose System Preferences from the Apple menu and click Network.**

   You see the Network window, which is shown in Figure 4-3 in Chapter 4. Either the Ethernet or USB Ethernet entry should have a green light to indicate that a cable of that type is connected.

2. **Click the Ethernet or USB Ethernet entry (whichever has the green light) to see the details of that connection.**

For more details on setting up your LAN, see *Home Networking Do-It-Yourself For Dummies* or *Home Networking All-in-One Desk Reference For Dummies*.

Forget the Wires — Go Wi-Fi!

If you have computers in more than one room in the house, using Wi-Fi is easier than snaking wires through the walls or basement. And Wi-Fi is absolutely required if you want to get online from a tablet or book-reader.

All recent laptops have Wi-Fi built in. For computers that don't, you can get Wi-Fi doozits with USB connectors and (less often) Wi-Fi add-in cards for desktop computers or older laptops. Wi-Fi makers do a remarkably good job of adhering to industry standards, so you can expect anyone's 11b or 11g or 11n Wi-Fi equipment to work with anyone else's.

The main practical difference among Wi-Fi equipment is range. Wi-Fi components have one standard feature in common: laughably optimistic estimates of how far away they can be from other Wi-Fi equipment and still work. Bigger antennas bring you more range — as does more expensive equipment. Wi-Fi radio waves use the same band as 2.4GHz cordless phones, so you can expect roughly the same range — like a cordless phone, your Wi-Fi connection will probably work in most parts of your house but not down to the end of your driveway. If your house is a normal size, normal Wi-Fi works fine. If you live in a $900,000 mansion, you might have to spring for the $100 Wi-Fi card rather than the $30 one.

Set a password, for Pete's sake!

You would probably notice if a random stranger walked into your house and plugged into your wired network. (At least, we like to think *we* would notice.) However, if you have a Wi-Fi network and a stranger is out on the street with a laptop scanning the area for unprotected wireless access points (a practice known as *wardriving*), he can connect to your Wi-Fi network and you can't easily tell. Some people don't care — at least until they realize that wardrivers can see *all* the shared files and printers on your LAN, and can send spam (and worse) over your network connection. You may well be able to hop on to your neighbors' Wi-Fi networks, and they on yours, which may or may not be okay, depending on how much you like your neighbors.

Fortunately, all Wi-Fi systems have optional passwords. Cryptographers laugh derisively at the poor security of Wi-Fi passwords, but they're adequate to make wardrivers and nosy neighbors go bother someone else. (If you have serious secrets on your network, don't depend on Wi-Fi passwords. A bad guy using a laptop and one of the widely available Wi-Fi password-cracker programs can gather enough data from your network to break any password in less than a week. If you need better cryptographic protection, it's available, but it isn't exactly a do-it-yourself project to set up.)

Those creative Wi-Fi engineers created several flavors of passwords, too. Most new Wi-Fi equipment uses the secure password scheme Wireless Privacy Access (WPA). If all your Wi-Fi equipment can handle it, use WPA. WPA passwords can be almost any length, so you can pick something you can remember. (Don't use your last name or your address, which is likely to be the *only* information that a passerby might know about your house.) Some Wi-Fi equipment arrives configured with a network name and a random password, which you might as well use. It usually includes a card with the network name and password printed on it to help you set up your computer.

Older Wi-Fi equipment can't do WPA, and you may be stuck using the system named *WEP,* a term that allegedly means Wired Equivalent Privacy (which it's not). WEP passwords come in two sizes: 64 and 128 bits. Use 128 unless you have old equipment that can do only 64, in which case, 64 will do. (Your entire network has to use the same size.) The password can be represented as either a text string or a hexadecimal (base-16, also called *hex*) number — we leave it to you to choose which would be easier for you to type and remember. If you use 64-bit WEP, your password (in text format) must be exactly 7 characters long. For 128-bit WEP, you need a 13-character password. If you want to use a shorter password, pad it out with digits or punctuation.

The easiest way to set the password is to set it up at the same time you set up your network, as described in the next section.

Making the Wi-Fi connection

To create a Wi-Fi system, follow these steps:

1. **Get your router set up, and then set up your computers to connect to it.**

   See the section "Setting up a router," earlier in this chapter. Even if you plan to use an all-Wi-Fi network, to do the setup process, plug in one computer with a cable and use it to set up the Wi-Fi.

2. **Use your web browser to display the router's control page (usually at 192.168.0.1) so that you can configure the router.**

3. **Find the page where you can configure the router's Wi-Fi settings.**

   What you click depends on your router. On our D-Link router, we clicked Setup and then Wireless Settings to open the page shown in Figure 5-3. Look for a page with settings about wireless, a network name, and wireless security.

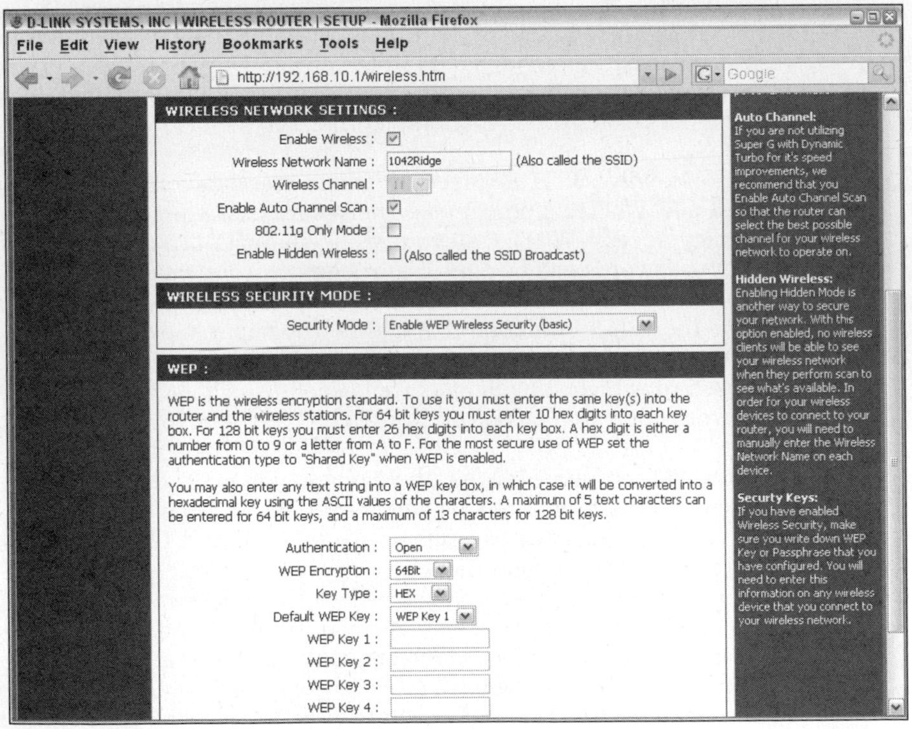

Figure 5-3:
Configuring your router to do Wi-Fi with a password.

4. **Give your network a name.**

   Every Wi-Fi network has a name. With typical machine imagination, your router suggests a name similar to linksys (a router manufacturer) or dlink (another manufacturer) or default. We suggest a name similar to FredsHouse so that any neighbors who happen on it know that it's you.

5. **Turn on Wi-Fi passwords and set one, as described in the preceding section.**

   Your router probably has lots of other options — such as MAC cloning (less pomological than it sounds, and nothing to do with Macintosh computers), all of which you can ignore.

6. **When your router is up and running and your computer can see the Internet (that is, you can display web pages), you're done configuring the router for your Wi-Fi network.**

Now, at last, you can cut the cord and go wireless. You need to tell every computer which Wi-Fi network to use and what the password is. The setup is quick.

For computers running Windows 8.1, 7, or Vista, try this:

1. **In Windows 8.1, look for the Network Connection icon near the right end of the Taskbar; click to make the Networks "charm" slide out from the right side of the screen. In Windows 7, click the Networking icon in the lower right corner of the screen, to the left of the digital clock. In Windows Vista, choose Start⇨Connect To.**

   You see a window with a list of available networks, one of which is yours. If you have neighbors with Wi-Fi networks, it may show them, too, but don't use your neighbors' networks unless they give you permission.

2. **Double-click your network.**

   In a moment, you see a dialog box that asks for the security key or pass phrase.

3. **Enter the network password, exactly as you did on the router, and click Connect.**

   Windows retrieves network settings from the router, and in a few seconds you're online. If you have trouble typing the password, click the box to display the characters of the password (unless, we suppose, someone you don't trust is looking over your shoulder.)

4. **Answer one more question.**

   If you see a question like "Do you want to find PCs, devices, and content on this network and automatically connect to devices like printers and TVs?", follow Windows' recommendation and click Yes if you are on your own home network or No if you are on a public network that includes devices you don't trust.

Mac users can click the Wi-Fi icon at the top of the screen toward the right; it looks like concentric curves. The message "Wi-Fi: Looking for Networks" appears and the networks your computer finds appear on a list. Click one to connect. If it requires a password, your Mac will ask for it.

For more on wireless networking, check out *Wireless Home Networking For Dummies.*

Shortcut setup with WPS

Most tablets and some smartphones can use Wi-Fi Protected Setup (WPS) to connect to a WPA router without using a password. Look at the back of the router to see if it has a button marked with two curved arrows that sort of make a circle. If so, it can use WPS. To connect your tablet or phone, open the Wi-Fi menu on the device and look for the same two-arrow symbol. Click the symbol on the tablet, press the WPS button on the router, and in a few seconds, the two devices should find each other and connect, no password needed.

In some cases, a WPS device will want you to enter an eight-digit security code into the other WPS device. We find that's more trouble than it's worth, so if it tells you to do that, configure the network the usual way, by entering the router's network password on the device.

Home and Office Setup

Lots of people have laptops or tablets they carry back and forth between home and the office. Many variables are involved in doing this successfully, depending on not only your particular device but also the networks you use at home and at the office. In general, however, this is how the various setups should work:

- ✔ **If both home and the office have wired networks,** your computer should work when it's plugged into either network. If your computer doesn't connect at work, talk to your network administrator.

- ✔ **If your office has local shared files and printers and your house doesn't,** or vice versa, Windows complains and sulks if it can't find them. As long as you don't try to print to a printer that's at the other place, though, you can go online just fine.

- ✔ **If both the home and office networks are wireless, or one is wireless and the other is wired,** set up each one as described earlier in this chapter and your computer should automatically recognize whichever is available — that is, the network where you are.

On the road with laptop and tethering or Mifi

One of the better new gadgets for road warriors is the portable Wi-Fi hotspot, often known as MiFi after the name of one of the most popular models. You pull a little credit card sized box out of your briefcase, purse, or pocket, push a button to turn it on, and it's a Wi-Fi hotspot with a range of about 20 feet, ready for you to use with your laptop or smartphone, with the connection provided by a mobile carrier. If you find yourself paying $6 here and $10 there for Wi-Fi at hotels, coffee shops, and airports, a MiFi for which you pay $20 to $50 per month is a good alternative. Since it is a real Wi-Fi hotspot that can handle several computers, you can also make new friends by letting those envious bystanders share your connection.

All major mobile carriers offer some version of mobile hotspot, with the same baffling range of prices and plans found with cell phones, sold in the same places that sell phones. Some require a monthly plan, some are pay-as-you-go. John likes the Virgin Mobile MiFi that costs about $150, which you can enable for a month at a time when you need it, and not when you don't. Plans run $20/month for enough data to check your mail, or $50/month for no limit. Margy rented a MiFi from a group called Telecom Square for $14 a day in the U.S. and a little more than that for use in Brazil.

Some smartphones, particularly iPhones, can act as *personal hotspots* just like a Mifi device, known as *tethering* when a phone does it. Check your phone's instructions for details, and remember that all the data that runs through the hotspot also runs through your phone's mobile connection, so you probably only want to tether if your plan includes a lot of data.

Chapter 6

Welcome to the Wild, Wonderful, Wacky Web

In This Chapter

▶ Understanding web pages and URLs

▶ Pointing, clicking, browsing, and other basic skills

▶ Opening lots of web pages at the same time

▶ Discovering the web from your phone

▶ Discovering Internet Explorer and Firefox

▶ Installing a browser other than Internet Explorer

*P*eople now talk about the *web* more than they talk about the *Internet*. The World Wide Web and the Internet aren't the same thing — the World Wide Web (which we call *the web* because we're lazy typists) lives "on top of" the Internet. The Internet's network is at the core of the web, and the web is an attractive parasite that requires the Net for survival. However, so much of what happens online is on the web that you aren't really online until you know how to browse the web.

This chapter explains what the web is and where it came from. Then it describes how to install and use some popular web browsers and how to use web browsers to display web pages. If you're already comfortable using the web, skip to Chapter 7.

What Is the World Wide Web?

So what is the web, already? The *World Wide Web* is a bunch of "pages" of information connected to each other around the globe via the Internet. Each page can be a combination of text, pictures, audio clips, video clips, animations, fill-in-the-blank forms, and other stuff. (People add new types of other stuff every day.)

Linking web pages

What makes web pages interesting (aside from the fact that there seems to be a web page about every topic you can possibly think of) is that they contain *links* that point to other web pages. When you click a link, your browser fetches the page the link connects to. (Your *browser* is the program that shows you the web — read more about it in a couple of pages.) Links make connections that let you go directly to related information. These invisible connections between pages resemble the threads of a spider web — as you click from web page to web page, you can envision the "web" created by the links.

Figure 6-1 shows a web page. Underlined phrases are links to other web pages, but a lot of non-underlined text is, too — move the mouse pointer around a page and see wherever it turns into a little hand. Anywhere a hand appears is a link, even if it isn't underlined. Pictures can be links, too.

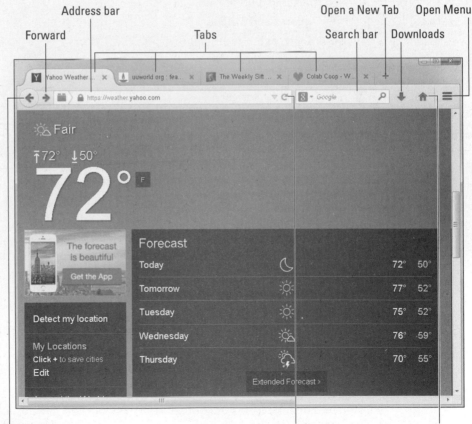

Figure 6-1:
This web page is displayed in the Firefox browser.

Forward   Address bar   Tabs   Open a New Tab   Open Menu   Search bar   Downloads

Back   Reload   Start Page

Where did the web come from?

The World Wide Web was invented in 1989 at the European Particle Physics Lab (CERN) in Geneva, Switzerland, an unlikely spot for a revolution in computing. The inventor is a British researcher named Sir Tim Berners-Lee, who is now the director of the World Wide Web Consortium (W3C) in Cambridge, Massachusetts, the organization that sets standards and loosely oversees the development of the web. Tim is terrifically smart and hard working and charming. (Margy met him when he played the part of an amoeba in a church pageant.)

Tim invented *HTTP* (HyperText Transport Protocol), the way web browsers communicate with web servers; *HTML* (HyperText Markup Language), the language in which web pages are written; and *URLs* (Uniform Resource Locators), the addresses used for web pages and most other information on the Net. He envisioned the web as a way for everyone to publish and read information on the Net. Early web browsers had editors that let you create web pages almost as easily as you could read them.

For more information about the development of the web and the work of the World Wide Web Consortium, visit its website at www.w3.org. You can also read Tim's book, *Weaving the Web* (HarperOne, 1999). He was knighted in 2004 and became Sir Tim. You may have seen him on TV about an hour into the opening ceremony for the London Olympics in 2012.

What's remarkable about the web is that it connects pieces of information from all around the *planet,* on different computers and in different databases (a feat you would be hard pressed to match with a card catalog in a brick-and-mortar library). Pages can be linked to other pages anywhere in the world so that when you're on the web, you can end up looking at pages from Singapore to Calgary, or from Sydney to Buenos Aires, all faster than you can say "Bob's your uncle," usually. You're only seconds away from almost any site, anywhere in the world.

Finding the page you want

An important characteristic of the web is that you can search it — over a trillion pages. For example, in fewer than ten seconds, you can find a list of web pages that contain the phrase *domestic poultry* or your own name or the name of a book you want to find out about. You can follow links to see each page on the list to find the information you want. See Chapter 13 to see how to use a search engine to search the web.

Where's that page?

Before you jump onto the web (boing-g-g — that metaphor needs work), you need to know one more basic concept: Every web page has a *web address* so that browsers, and you, can find it. Great figures in the world of software engineering (one guy, actually, named Sir Tim Berners-Lee) named this address the *Uniform Resource Locator,* or *URL.* Every web page has a URL, a series of characters that begins with `http://`. (How do you say *URL?* Everyone we know pronounces each letter, "U-R-L" — no one says "earl.") Many URLs include the letters *www,* but not all do. Now you know enough to go browsing. For more entirely optional details about URLs, see the later sidebar "Duke of URL."

Browsing to Points Unknown

It's time to check out the web for yourself, using a *browser,* the program that finds web pages and displays them on your screen. Fortunately, if you have any recent version of Windows, any recent Mac, any netbook, almost any other computer with Internet access, or a smartphone or tablet, you probably already have a browser.

Here are the most popular browsers:

✔ **Firefox** (shown in Figure 6-1) is the browser from the open source Mozilla project at `www.mozilla.org`. You can download Firefox for free for Windows, Macs, and Linux computers. Firefox is used by about 24 percent of web users.

✔ **Chrome,** shown in Figure 6-2, is from Google, the company responsible for the `www.google.com` search site and lots and lots of free, web-based services. About 60 percent of people use Chrome, which you can download for free for Windows, Macs, and Linux at `www.google.com/chrome`. It also comes on every Android phone and tablet. Google has a plan for Chrome to become its own operating system, competing with Windows, currently available on laptop computers called Chromebooks.

✔ **Internet Explorer (IE)**, shown in Figure 6-3, is the browser that Microsoft has built into every recent version of Windows. Fewer than 10 percent of people (and dropping) still use IE. It is available as a free download for many earlier versions of Windows (at `www.microsoft.com/ie`) but not for the Mac. IE also runs on Windows Mobile phones and tablets. See the nearby sidebar "Our advice: Switch from Internet Explorer to Firefox, Safari, or Chrome."

✔ **Safari,** shown in Figure 6-4, is the Apple browser for the Mac, iPad, iPhone, and iPod touch. Windows has a version, too, although we've never heard of anyone other than us using it. You can download the latest versions from www.apple.com/safari.

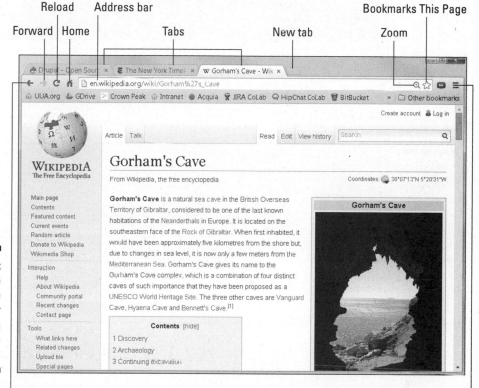

Reload

Address bar

Bookmarks This Page

Forward Home

Tabs

New tab

Zoom

Figure 6-2:
The Google Chrome browser displays another web page.

Back

Customize and Control

We describe Chrome and Firefox in detail in this book, and we mention Internet Explorer and Safari here and there. All browsers are similar, enabling you to view web pages, print them, and save the addresses of your favorite pages so that you can return to them later. If you want to try a different browser, see the section "Getting and Installing a Browser," later in this chapter.

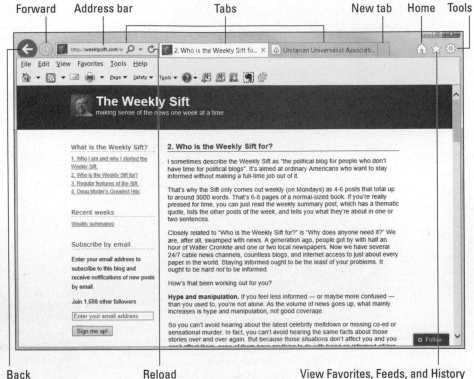

Forward   Address bar   Tabs   New tab   Home   Tools

Figure 6-3:
Your typical
web page,
viewed in
Internet
Explorer 11.

Back   Reload   View Favorites, Feeds, and History

Our advice: Switch from Internet Explorer to Firefox, Safari, or Chrome

Internet Explorer, Firefox, Safari, and Google Chrome are all free and downloadable from the Internet, but beyond that, they have some important differences.

The advantages of Firefox, Safari, and Chrome:

✔ They run faster. They're smaller and quicker.

✔ They don't use ActiveX controls, a feature of IE that spyware uses to infect your computer.

✔ If you use a Mac, iPhone, iPad, or iPod touch, you already have Safari.

✔ If you use an Android tablet or phone, you already have Chrome.

The advantages of Internet Explorer:

✔ Some websites (mainly sites run by Microsoft itself) require Internet Explorer because they use ActiveX controls.

✔ A few browser add-ins work only with IE.

✔ If you use Windows, you already have IE because it comes bundled with Windows.

Any browser can display and print web pages — don't get us wrong. However, we think that the security issue — avoiding spyware — trumps all other considerations hands down, and we recommend that Windows users install Firefox or Chrome and use it except for the few websites that require Internet Explorer. You can have more than one browser installed at the same time — you can even have two or three running at the same time — so switching to Firefox or Chrome doesn't mean that you can never use Internet Explorer again. Mac users can stick with Safari.

See the later section "Getting and Installing a Browser" for downloading instructions.

Figure 6-4:
Safari is Apple's web browser.

Web Surfing with Your Browser

When you start your web browser — Firefox, Chrome, Internet Explorer, Safari, or whatever — you see a window that displays one web page, with menus and icons along the top. Figure 6-1 (shown earlier in this chapter) illustrates Firefox, Figure 6-2 shows Google Chrome, Figure 6-3 shows Internet Explorer, and Figure 6-4 shows Apple's Safari. Other browsers look similar, but with different menus and icons along the top.

The main section of the browser window is taken up by the web page you're looking at. After all, that's what the browser is *for* — displaying a web page. Which page your browser displays at startup — your *start page* — depends on how it's set up. Many ISPs arrange for your browser to display their home pages; otherwise, until you choose a home page of your own, IE tends to display a Microsoft page, Firefox and Chrome usually show a Google search page, and Safari shows a page from the Apple website. Chapter 7 explains how to set the start page to a web page you want to see.

The buttons, bars, and menus around the edge help you find your way around the web and do things such as print and save pages. Here are some of the most important buttons and menus at the top of your browser window:

- **Back button:** Click to display the last page you looked at, as described in the later section "Backward, ho!"After you click Back, you can click Forward to return to the page you were looking at.

- **Reload button:** Click to reload the page you're looking at now from the web. Maybe something changed since you loaded it, or maybe it didn't load correctly the first time. F5 is a keyboard shortcut.

- **Home button:** Click to display your start page (or *home page*), as described in Chapter 7.

- **Address bar:** Displays the web address (URL) of the current page. You can enter the URL of a page to display, as described in the later section "Going places."

- **Search bar:** Firefox has a separate *Search bar,* to the right of the Address bar, where you can type search terms. Other browsers combine the Address and Search bars. See Chapter 13 for details.

The rest of this chapter explains how to use these and other features of your browser.

Getting around

You need two simple skills (if we can describe something as basic as making a single mouse click as a skill) to get going on the web. One is to move from page to page on the web, and the other is to jump directly to a page when you know its URL (web address). Okay, we know that you aren't actually *moving* — your web browser displays one page after another — but browsing feels as though you're cruising (or surfing, depending on which metaphor you prefer) around the web.

Moving from page to page is easy: Click any link that looks interesting. That's it. Underlined blue text and blue-bordered pictures are links, and sometimes other things are, too. Anything that looks like a button is probably a link. You can tell when you're pointing to a link because the mouse pointer changes to a little hand. Clicking outside a link selects the text you click, as in most other programs. Sometimes, clicking a link moves you to a different place on the same page rather than to a new page.

Backward, ho!

Web browsers remember the last few hundred pages you visited, so if you click a link and decide that you're not so crazy about the new page, you can easily go back to the preceding one. To go back, click the Back button on the toolbar. Its icon is an arrow or triangle pointing to the left, and it's the leftmost button on the toolbar, as shown in Figures 6-1, 6-2, 6-3, and 6-4. You can also press Alt+← or Backspace to return to the previous page.

Sometimes, clicking a link opens the new page in a new browser window or tab — your browser can display more than one web page at the same time, each in its own window or in tabs in one window. If a link opens a new window or tab, the Back button does nothing in that window, but you can still switch back to the old window by clicking it.

Going places

Someone tells you about a cool website and you want to take a look. Here's what you do:

1. **Click in the Address bar, near the top of the browser window.**

   Figures 6-1, 6-2, 6-3, and 6-4 show where the Address bar is.

TECHNICAL STUFF

Duke of URL

The World Wide Web will eventually link together all information in the known universe, starting with all the stuff on the Internet. (This statement may be a slight exaggeration, but not by much.) One key to global domination is to give everything a name so that no matter what a web page link refers to, a web browser can find it and know what to do with it.

Look at this typical URL:

```
http://airinfo.travel/index.
    phtml
```

The first item in a URL, the letters that appear before the colon, is the *scheme,* which describes the way a browser can get to the resource. Although ten schemes are defined, the most common by far is HTTP, which stands for HyperText Transfer Protocol, the web's native transfer technique. HTTP is the language that your browser uses to request a web page from the web server on which it's stored; it's also the language that the web server uses to send you back the page you want to see. (A conversation in HTTP can be translated into English as something like this: "I'd like a web page, please." "Here it is. Enjoy!")

Although the details of the rest of the URL depend on the scheme, most schemes look similar. Following the colon are two slashes (always forward slashes, never backslashes) and the name of the host computer on which the resource lives; in this case, `airinfo. travel` (one of the many names of John's Internet server). Then comes another slash and a *path,* which gives the name of the resource on that host; in this case, a file named `index. phtml`.

URLs allow a few other optional parts. They can include a *port number,* which specifies, roughly speaking, which of several programs running on that host should handle the request. The port number goes after a colon following the host name, like this:

```
http://airinfo.travel:80/
    index.phtml
```

The standard `http` port number is 80, so if that's the port you want (it usually is), you can leave it out. Finally, a URL can have a *query part* at the end, following a question mark, like this:

```
http://airinfo.travel:80/
    index.phtml?discounts
```

When a URL has a query part, it tells the host computer more specifically what you want the page to display. (You rarely type query parts yourself — they're often constructed for you from fill-in fields on web pages.)

Many URLs start `https:` rather than `http:`. The "s" stands for Secure, the connection between you and the server computer is kept private by high quality cryptography, and the server's identity was verified. You should see a little lock next to the URL if the verification worked.

Another useful URL scheme is `mailto`. A `mailto` URL looks like this:

```
mailto:internet14@gurus.org
```

That is, a `mailto` link is an email address. Clicking a `mailto` URL runs your email program and creates a new message addressed to the address in the link.

2. Type the URL in the box.

The URL is similar to `http://net.gurus.org` — you can just type `net.gurus.org` and your browser supplies the `http://` part. Be sure to delete the URL that appeared before you started typing.

3. Press Enter.

Here are a few shortcuts:

- ✔ If the entire address in the Address bar is highlighted, when you type, the new URL replaces what was there before. If not, click in the Address bar until the entire old address is highlighted.

- ✔ You can leave the `http://` off URLs when you type them in the Address bar. Your browser can guess that part! Many web addresses include a name that ends with `.com`, but not all do. See the later sidebar "Why .com?" for more information.

- ✔ When you start typing a URL, your browser helpfully starts guessing the address you might be typing, suggesting addresses you've already typed that start with the same characters. The browser displays its suggestions in a list just below the Address bar. If you see the address you want on the list, click it — there's no point in typing the rest of the URL if you don't have to!

If you receive URLs in email, instant messages, or documents, you can usually click on them — many programs pass along the address to your browser. Or, use the standard cut-and-paste techniques and avoid retyping:

1. Highlight the URL in whichever program it appears.

That is, use your mouse to select the URL so that the whole URL is highlighted.

2. Press Ctrl+C (Command+C on the Mac) to copy the info to the Clipboard.

3. Click in the Address bar to highlight whatever is in it. (Click again until the entire URL is selected, so the whole thing gets replaced.)

4. Press Ctrl+V (Command+V on the Mac) to paste the URL into the box, and then press Enter.

Bad guys can easily create email messages where the URL you see in the text of a message isn't the URL you visit; the bad guys can hide the actual URL. Keep this warning in mind if you receive mail that purports to be from your bank — if you click the link and enter your account number and password in the web page that appears, you may be typing it into a website run by crooks rather than by your bank. See Chapter 2.

Why .com?

When you want to put information on the Internet with your own name on it, you register a *domain name* such as yahoo.com or wikipedia.org. (See Chapter 17 if you're thinking of making your own website with your own domain name.) A domain name for an ISP in the United States usually ends with a dot and a two- or three-letter code (which is the *top-level domain,* or TLD) that gives you a clue to what kind of outfit owns the domain name. The following list briefly explains which type of organization owns which domain for each TLD code:

- ✔ **Commercial organizations** typically own domain names ending in .com, such as google.com (the most popular web search site), aa.com (AMR Corporation, better known as American Airlines), and taugh.com (John's hard-to-pronounce Taughannock Networks). Because "dot-com" has become a synonym for the Internet itself, lots of other organizations and even individuals have .com domains.

- ✔ **U.S. colleges and universities** typically own domain names ending in .edu, such as yale.edu.

- ✔ **Networking organizations** typically end with .net. These include ISPs, such as comcast.net, and companies that provide network services.

- ✔ **Government organizations** in the United States typically own domain names ending in .gov. For example, the National Do Not Call Registry, run by the Federal Trade Commission, is at donotcall.gov.

- ✔ **U.S. military organizations** use domain names ending in .mil.

- ✔ **Nonprofits** and **special interest groups** typically own domain names ending in .org. For example, the Unitarian Universalist Association (where Margy works) is at uua.org.

- ✔ **Organizations in specific countries** frequently own domain names ending in two-letter country codes, such as .fr for France or .zw for Zimbabwe. The full list of country TLD codes is at www.iana.org/domains/root/db. Small businesses, local governments, and K-12 schools in the United States may end with the two-letter state abbreviation followed by .us (such as John's church website at unitarian.ithaca.ny.us.

A good place to start browsing

You find out more about how to find things on the web in Chapter 13, but for now, here's a good way to get started: Go to the Yahoo! News page. To get to Yahoo! News, type this URL in your browser's Address bar and then press Enter:

```
news.yahoo.com
```

Who makes up these TLDs?

An international group (the Internet Corporation for Assigned Names and Numbers, or ICANN, at `icann.org`) is in charge of TLDs (top-level domains). Two-letter TLDs are for entire countries, such as `.us` for the United States, `.ca` for Canada, `.me` for (wait for it!) Montenegro, and `.zw` for Zimbabwe. The newest country domain is `.ss`, for South Sudan.

In 1997, ICANN proposed adding some extra, generic domains, such as `.firm`, `.arts`, and `.web`. After a lengthy detour through a maze of international intellectual-property politics, the first new domains (`.biz` and `.info`) appeared in 2001. The result is confusion that practically guarantees that, more often than not, `whatever.biz` and `whatever.info` are owned by the same group that owns `whatever.com`, and when they're owned by someone else, they're usually sleazy knockoffs. ICANN has since added domain extensions including these:

- `.name`: Personal vanity
- `.coop`: Co-ops
- `.museum`: Museum

- `.aero`: Air travel
- `.jobs`: Job offers
- `.travel`: Travel in general
- `.mobi`: For cellphones and other mobile devices

None is widely used.

ICANN threw open the domain floodgates to anyone who filled out the application form and sends it in with a check for a modest $185,000 application fee. They got over 1900 applications, about 2/3 of which are likely to be accepted, and which all should be started up by the end of 2015. Many are private vanity domains for companies, like `.bmw` and `.suzuki`, two car companies, or intended for people in particular places like `.berlin` or `.cymru` (Wales in Welsh). Some are for communities of interest like `.hockey` and `.dentist`, and some are just strange, like `.xyz` and `.wtf` (yes, really). We doubt that any will be particularly important, but don't be surprised if you start seeing them in advertisements.

The Yahoo! website includes lots of different features, but its news site should look familiar — it's similar to a newspaper on steroids. Just nose around, clicking links that look interesting and clicking the Back button on the toolbar when you make a wrong turn. We guarantee that you'll find something interesting.

For information related to the very book you're holding, go to `net.gurus.org`. If we have any late-breaking news about the Internet or updates and corrections to this book, you can find them there. If you find mistakes in this book or have other comments, by the way, please send an email to us at `internet14@gurus.org`.

What not to click

The web has some bad neighborhoods, and it isn't always safe to click whatever you see. For example, clicking a link on a web page can download and install a program on your computer, and that program might not be one you want to be running. So, exercise judgment when clicking.

Here are some links *not* to click:

✔ Don't click ads claiming that you just won the lottery or a free laptop or anything else too good to be true.

✔ Don't click messages on web pages claiming that your computer is at risk of dire consequence if you don't click there. Yeah, right.

✔ Don't click OK in a dialog box that asks about downloading or installing a program, unless you're deliberately downloading and installing a program. (See Chapter 7.)

✔ Don't click any link that makes you suspicious. Your instincts are probably correct!

If one of these messages appears in a browser window, the safest thing to do is to close the window by clicking the X box in the upper-right corner (or on a Mac, the red Close button in the upper-left corner).

This page looks funny or out of date

Sometimes, a web page becomes garbled on the way in or you interrupt it (by clicking the Stop button on the toolbar or by pressing the Esc key). You can tell your browser to retrieve the information on the page again. Click the Reload button (shown in Figures 6-1, 6-2, 6-3, and 6-4) or press Ctrl+R (Windows) or Command+R (Mac).

Some people hardly ever close their browsers, which probably isn't a good idea for their long-term mental stability. (Naturally, we aren't talking about anyone *we* know! Definitely not.) If you're this type of person, however, remember that your browser *caches* pages — it stores the pages temporarily on your hard drive for quick retrieval. If you want to make sure that you're seeing an up-to-date version of a page, reload it.

Get me outta here

Sooner or later, even the most dedicated web surfer has to stop to eat or attend to other personal needs. You leave your browser in the same way you leave any other program: Click the Close (X) button in the upper-right corner of the window (or on a Mac, the red Close button in the upper-left corner) or press Alt+F4 (Windows) or Command+W (Mac). Or, just leave the program running and walk away from your computer. If you have multiple tabs open (described in "Tab dancing," later in this chapter), the program asks whether you want to close them all.

Viewing Lots of Web Pages at the Same Time

When we're pointing and clicking from one place to another, we like to open a bunch of browser windows so that we can see where we've been and go back to a previous page by just switching to another window. You can also arrange windows side by side, which is a good way to, say, compare prices for *The Internet For Dummies* at various online bookstores. (The difference may be small, but when you're buying 100 copies for everyone on your Christmas list, those pennies can add up. Oh, you weren't planning to do that? Drat.) Your browser can also display lots of web pages in one window, by using tabs (as explained in the section "Tab dancing," a little later in this chapter).

Wild window mania

To display a page in a new browser window, click a link with the right mouse button and choose Open in New Window (or Open Link in New Window) from the menu that pops up. To close a window, click the Close (X) button in the upper-right corner of the window frame or press Alt+F4, the standard close-window shortcut. (On a Mac, click the red button in the upper-left corner of the window or press Command+W.)

You can also create a new window without following a link: Press Ctrl+N. (Mac users, press Command+N.)

Tab dancing

We've all heard about how multitasking is a bad idea, but sometimes it's very useful to have several web pages open at the same time. Web browsers have *tabs,* which are multiple pages you can switch among in a window. Figures 6-1, 6-2, 6-3, and 6-4 show browsers with several tabs across the top. The name of the tab is shown on each tab, like old-fashioned manila folder tabs. One tab corresponds to the page you see; that tab is a brighter color.

Just click a tab to show the page. To make a new, empty tab, click the New Tab (the tiny, blank tab to the right of the other tabs), press Ctrl+T (Windows) or Command+T (Mac), or right-click an existing tab and choose New Tab from the menu that appears. You can also open a new tab by right-clicking a link and choosing Open in New Tab (or Open Link in New Tab) from the menu that pops up. Click the X on the tab to get rid of it, or right-click the tab and choose Close Tab. (You may have to hover the mouse on the tab to see its X.)

IE normally displays your tabs in the same area as the Address bar, which can make the Address bar rather small. If you'd rather see your tabs below the Address bar, right-click any tab and choose Show Tabs on a Separate Row from the menu that appears. Ah, that's better!

For most purposes, we find tabs more convenient than windows, but multiple windows are useful if you want to compare two web pages side by side. You can use both tabs and windows; each window can have multiple tabs. In most browsers, you can drag a tab from one browser window to another, or drag a tab out to the desktop to make a new window. And like all windows, you can drag their edges to move or resize them.

Short-attention-span tips

If you have a slow Internet connection, use at least two browser tabs or windows at the same time. While you're waiting for the next page to open in one tab or window, you can read the page that opened a while ago in the other tab or window.

While your browser is downloading a big file, it may display a small window in the corner of your screen or an icon at the bottom of the browser window. You can click back to the main browser window and continue surfing while the download continues.

Warning: Doing two or three things at a time in your browser when you have a slow Net connection is not unlike squeezing blood from a turnip — only so much blood can be squeezed. In this case, the blood is the amount of data your computer can pump through its network connection. A single download task can keep your connection close to 100 percent busy, and anything else you do shares the connection with the download process. When you do two things at a time, therefore, each one happens more slowly than it would by itself.

Browsing from Your Smartphone or Tablet

Internet-connected phones and tablets — such as the iPhone and iPad and Android and Windows Mobile phones and tablets — can browse the web, too. Some use your cell connection to load pages and others use Wi-Fi. Of course, on a phone you can see only teeny, tiny web pages on their teeny, tiny screens, but phone-based browsing can still be incredibly useful, especially when you're looking for a good restaurant recommendation. The iPad and other Wi-Fi-connected tablets have browsers, too, and their screens are large enough for a tolerable browsing experience.

The iPhone and iPad come with Safari, Android phones come with Google Chrome, and Windows Mobile phones come with IE. All these pint-size browsers have Back buttons and Address bars and most of the same basic features as their larger siblings.

Some web pages look great on smartphones, when the page designers use a system called *responsive design* to automatically reformat pages to fit the small screens, dispensing with extraneous columns and graphics. Other pages are practically unreadable. As phone-based browsers become more popular, more websites have sites customized for mobile devices. If you find a site that's unusable, try adding m. to the domain name (in place of the www.) For example, m.netflix.com is the spare, usable version of the Netflix site designed for phones. Also try "unpinching" (using two fingers to "stretch out" the page) to magnify it.

Getting and Installing a Browser

Chances are, a browser is already installed on your computer. If you use Internet Explorer, we think you're better off installing either Firefox or Chrome, for speed and safety reasons. Fortunately, browser programs aren't difficult to find and install, and Firefox, Chrome, and Safari are all free.

Even if you already have a browser, new versions come out every 20 minutes or so. Your browser is probably set to update itself automatically by checking in periodically with its home website. If your browser suggests that it needs to be updated, go ahead and follow its instructions to do so, because occasionally the new versions fix bugs or solve security issues.

Hey, how about us Mac users?

Macs have always been famous for their slick, easy-to-use software, and the Internet software is no exception. Macs come with a nice web browser named Safari (refer to Figure 6-4). You use the Command key rather than Ctrl for the keyboard shortcuts, and nearly all the rest of the keys work the way they do in the other browsers we describe.

Or, you can do what we do and use Firefox or Chrome, which work quite nicely on a Mac, just as they do on Windows, with Command rather than Ctrl. You can use Safari to visit www. mozilla.com or www.google.com/ chrome to download and install Firefox or Chrome and then use it instead of or alongside Safari.

Getting the program

To get Firefox (for Windows or Mac or any of the other dozen computers it runs on), visit www.mozilla.com. For Chrome, go to www.google.com/ chrome. To get or upgrade Internet Explorer, go to www.microsoft.com/ ie. Safari is available at www.apple.com/safari. Use your current browser to go to the page and then follow the instructions for finding and downloading the program. (Take a look at Chapter 7 for advice about downloading files.) If you are using a smartphone or tablet, go to your app store (the App Store on Apple devices and the Play Store on Androids).

Running a new browser for the first time

To run your new browser, click the browser's attractive new icon. If you use Windows, the default browser also appears at the top of the left column of the Start menu, too.

Your new browser will probably ask whether you want to import your settings — including your bookmarks and favorites — from the browser program you've been using. If you've already been using the web for a while and have built up a list of your favorite websites (as described in Chapter 7), take advantage of this opportunity to copy your list into the new browser so that you don't have to search for your favorite sites all over again.

It will also ask whether to make it the "default" browser, that is, the one used when another program opens a web page. Browsers are very jealous, so if you don't say yes, it'll keep asking you each time you run it. Or if you do say yes, the next time you run any *other* browser, that browser, feeling jilted, will offer to make itself your default. Our advice is that once you find a browser you like, make it your default and stick with it.

Apple's iOS devices don't let you change the default browser from Safari. If you use an Android device, you can change the default; open Settings, choose More, choose Application Manager, and scroll right to choose All. Then choose the current default browser and choose Clear Defaults. The next time you click a link in an email or other message, Android will ask what program to use; choose your favorite browser.

Chapter 7

Taking Your Browser for a Spin

*I*f you've read Chapter 6, you're all set to browse the web. But to be an efficient, downright clever web surfer, you need to know about other browser features, such as printing web pages, displaying more than one web page at the same time, and storing the addresses of web pages you like to visit often. You also need to know how to handle spyware, an Internet menace we describe in Chapter 2. This chapter is your guide to these extra features and how you can make the most of them right away.

Saving Stuff from the Web

Frequently, you see something on a web page that's worth saving for later. Sometimes it's interesting information, a picture, or another type of file. There's not much point to saving an entire page: It's usually made up of several files — one for the text, one for each picture, and sometimes other files — so your browser can't just save the page in a file. However, you can save images and text from a page.

If you want to remember a page and come back to it, bookmark it in your browser, as explained later in this chapter.

Saving text from a page

You can copy and paste text from a web page into a word processing document or another type of file. Select the text with your mouse (click and drag the mouse over the text) and press Ctrl+C (Command+C on the Mac) to save the text on your computer's Clipboard. Then switch to the word processing or other type of program, position the cursor where you want the text to appear, and press Ctrl+V (Command+V on the Mac) to paste it. You'll probably need to do some reformatting once the text is in your document.

Saving an image

To save an image you see on a web page, follow these steps:

1. **Right-click the image.**

2. **Choose Save Image As (in Firefox, Chrome, or Safari) or Save Picture As (in Internet Explorer) from the menu that appears.**

3. **In the Save Image or Save Picture dialog box, move to the folder or directory in which you want to save the graphics file, type a filename in the File Name text box, and click the Save button.**

A note about copyright: Almost all web pages, along with almost everything else on the Internet, are copyrighted by their authors. (A notable exception is U.S. federal government websites, which are all free of copyright.) If you save a web page or a picture from a web page, you don't have permission to use it any way you want. Before you reuse the text or pictures, send an email message to the owner of the site. If an address doesn't appear on the page, write for permission to webmaster@domain.com, replacing *domain.com* with the domain name part of the page's web address.

Printing pages

To print a page, press Ctrl+P (Windows) or Command+P (Mac). Depending on your browser, you can also click something:

- ✔ **Firefox:** Click the Menu button in the upper-right corner of the window and choose Print from the menu that appears.

- ✔ **Chrome:** Click the Menu button (the three lines at the right end of the Address bar) and choose Print.

✔ **IE:** Click the Tools button (the little gear icon to the right of the Address bar and tabs) and choose Print.

✔ **Safari:** If you print a lot, you can use View⇨Customize Toolbar to add the Print button.

The browser has to reformat the page to print, which can take a minute, so remember that patience is a virtue. Fortunately, each browser displays a progress window to let you know how it's doing. You'll see your computer's usual Print dialog box, where you can choose your printer.

Chrome, Firefox, and Safari can print a page to a PDF file, which you can save and open later (as with any other PDF) with the Adobe Acrobat reader. It can be a handy way to save the whole page, images and all.

A Few of Your Favorite Things

You'll find some web pages that you want to visit repeatedly. (Both of us have visited the Google website thousands of times by now.) The makers of fine browsers have, fortunately, provided a handy way for you to remember those URLs so that you don't have to write them on the wall and type them again later.

The idea is simple: Your browser lets you add a web address to a list on your computer. Later, when you want to go back, you just go to your list and pick the page you want. Firefox, Chrome, and Safari call these saved web addresses *bookmarks;* Internet Explorer calls them *favorites.*

Bookmarking with Firefox

When you're looking at a page you want to bookmark, click the Bookmark This Page icon (a little star) at the right end of the Address bar. The star turns gold — the page is bookmarked.

To see your bookmarks, click the Show Your Bookmarks button that appears next to the Bookmark This Page icon. A menu of your items appears, including your bookmarks, as shown in Figure 7-1.

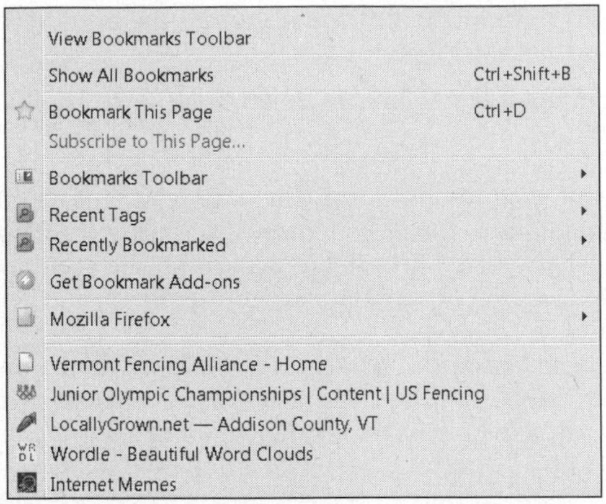

	View Bookmarks Toolbar	
	Show All Bookmarks	Ctrl+Shift+B
☆	Bookmark This Page	Ctrl+D
	Subscribe to This Page...	
▥	Bookmarks Toolbar	▸
▤	Recent Tags	▸
▤	Recently Bookmarked	▸
◎	Get Bookmark Add-ons	
▭	Mozilla Firefox	▸
▢	Vermont Fencing Alliance - Home	
▧	Junior Olympic Championships | Content | US Fencing	
▢	LocallyGrown.net — Addison County, VT	
▨	Wordle - Beautiful Word Clouds	
▨	Internet Memes	

Figure 7-1:
Your list
of Firefox
bookmarks
can quickly
get out of
control.

To go to one of the pages on your bookmark list, just choose its entry from the menu.

If you're like most users, your bookmark menu grows and grows and crawls down your screen and eventually ends up flopping down on the floor, which is both unattractive and unsanitary. Fortunately, you can smoosh (technical term) your menu into a more tractable form. Click the Show Bookmarks button and choose Show All Bookmarks (or press Ctrl+Shift+B in Windows or Command+Shift+B on a Mac) to display the Library window, which shows various kinds of items you can save.

When you create a bookmark, it appears in the Unsorted Bookmarks folder. You can click it and double-click any bookmark to see that bookmarked page. (You can leave this window open while you move around the web, or close it by clicking the X in its upper-right corner.) You can also organize your bookmarks into folders and rename your bookmarks with meaningful names — web page titles can be long and uninformative.

If you want to organize your growing list of bookmarks into folders, right-click the Bookmarks Menu folder, choose New Folder, give your folder a name, and click Add. Now you can put bookmarks into this folder, which appears as a submenu on the Bookmarks menu. Drag an item to a folder to put it in that folder's submenu, and click a folder to display or hide that submenu. Because any changes you make in the Bookmarks sidebar are reflected immediately on the Bookmarks menu, you can easily fiddle with the bookmarks until you have them arranged as you like. Firefox starts out your bookmarks with pages that the Firefox developers want you to look at, but feel free to delete those pages if your tastes are different from theirs.

Another way to create a bookmark, and put it where you want it on the Bookmarks menu, is to find the little icon at the left end of the Address bar. (The icon changes depending on the page.) Drag the icon over to the Bookmarks button, which responds by displaying your list of bookmarks. Keep dragging the icon down the list to where you want the bookmark to appear.

Creating one-click bookmarks in Firefox

Okay, you've got the Bookmarks menu, which is what you see when you click the Bookmarks button. You've got the Library window, described in the preceding section. Wait — there's more! The Bookmarks toolbar is a row of buttons that appears just below the Address bar. (If it doesn't appear, right-click just above the Address bar and choose Bookmarks Toolbar from the menu that appears.) This row of buttons gives you one-button access to a bunch of Firefox developers' favorite websites. Wouldn't it be nice if your favorite websites appeared there instead?

No problem! When you organize your bookmarks in the Library window, drag your favorite sites into the Bookmarks Toolbar folder — any sites in this folder automagically appear on the Bookmarks toolbar. Feel free to delete the bookmarks that come with Firefox — the only one we like is the Latest Headlines bookmark, which displays a menu of breaking news stories on the BBC website.

Storing favorites in Internet Explorer

Internet Explorer uses a URL-saving system similar to the one in Firefox, although it calls the saved URLs *favorites* rather than bookmarks: You can add the current page to your Favorites folder and then look at and organize your Favorites folder. If you use Windows, this Favorites folder is shared with other programs on your computer. Other programs also can add things to your Favorites folder, so it's a jumble of web pages, files, and other elements. (To avoid insanity, most people use favorites only for web pages.)

Internet Explorer 9 and later have the Favorites icon — a star — just above the upper-right corner of the web page. To add the current page to your favorites, click the Favorites icon (or press Alt+C) and choose Add to Favorites from the menu that appears. (Or, press Ctrl+D.) The Add a Favorite dialog box, shown in Figure 7-2, displays the page name (which you can edit) and the folder in which the favorite will be saved. Click the Create In box to choose a folder, or click the New Folder button to create a new folder in which to contain the page's address. Click Add when you're ready to save the favorite.

Figure 7-2:
Adding a
web page
to your
Internet
Explorer
favorites.

To return to one of your favorite pages, click the Favorites icon to see a menu of your favorites, shown in Figure 7-3. Click an item to view that page. Your Favorites menu can contain folders, too, so that you can organize pages into groups; click a folder to open it and see what's inside.

Figure 7-3:
The Internet
Explorer
Favorites
menu.

Creating one-click bookmarks in Internet Explorer

For quicker access to your top favorite pages, Internet Explorer has a Favorites bar that you can display just below the row of tabs. (If you don't see it, right-click above the Address bar and choose Favorites Bar from the menu that appears.) Click an icon on the Favorites bar to display that page. This feature is seriously handy for websites you visit often.

If you want to reorganize your Favorites menu, click the Favorites icon, click the down arrow to the right of the Add to Favorites button, and choose Organize Favorites. In the Organize Favorites window you can move favorites around, edit them, or delete them. To see what's in a folder, click it. When you're done organizing your favorite items, click Close.

In the Organize Favorites window, the Favorites Bar folder contains whatever you've added to your Favorites bar for instant access. Drag your favorite sites and folders into this folder — any sites in this folder automagically appear on the Favorites bar. Delete any sites in the Favorites bar folder that aren't your favorites. You can also delete icons right from the Favorites bar; right-click one and choose Delete from the menu that appears.

Adding web pages to your Windows taskbar

IE enables you to add an icon for a web page to the Windows taskbar (the icons that run along the bottom edge of your screen, with one for every running program and open document). To create an icon, click and drag a tab in Internet Explorer to the Windows taskbar.

Bookmarking (including one-click) with Chrome

 Google Chrome has a clean, spare look with no menus and only a few icons to clutter its window. But the features we love are there, including bookmarks. To add the current page to your list of bookmarks, click the Bookmark This Page star icon at the right end of the Address bar. A Bookmark Added box pops up so that you can edit the name for the bookmark and choose which bookmark folder to put the web page in. (Click Remove if you clicked this icon accidentally!) After a page is in your bookmarks, the star icon turns gold.

 To edit your bookmarks, click the Menu icon, the three lines to the right of the Address bar, and choose Bookmarks⇨Bookmark Manager from the menu that appears. The Bookmark Manager, shown in Figure 7-4, opens in a new tab. Click Organize to add folders into which you can drag your bookmarks.

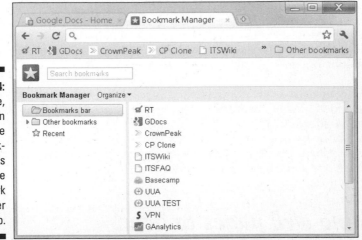

Figure 7-4:
In Chrome, you can organize your bookmarks on the Bookmark Manager tab.

When you drag a bookmark into the Bookmarks Bar folder, it appears (where else?) on the Bookmarks bar, between the Address bar and the top edge of the web page in the Chrome window. (If you don't see bookmarks below the Address bar, click the Customize and Control icon, choose Tools, and choose Always Show Bookmarks Bar so that it has a check mark next to it.)

One click and drag bookmarking with Safari

Safari comes from Apple, and Apple always does things a little differently. Unlike the other three browsers, new versions of Safari have an icon you click to show you your bookmarks, where you can then add your new bookmark. Ctrl+Command+1 also shows or hides the Bookmarks sidebar (see Figure 7-5).

The bookmarks pane has three tabs:

✔ The actual bookmarks, indicated by a little book, including the Favorites.

✔ The Reading List, indicated by a little pair of glasses, is a list of pages you intend to read real soon now.

✔ Social bookmarks, indicated by an @ sign, which are supposed to connect with your social media accounts.

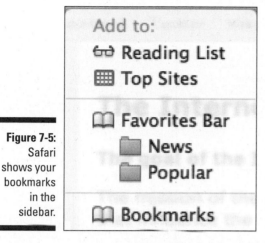

Figure 7-5:
Safari
shows your
bookmarks
in the
sidebar.

The Favorites section in the bookmarks are what appear on the Favorites bar, and are the buttons you see when you create a new tab, so that's usually the best place to make a new bookmark.

To make a bookmark, click in the address bar and drag the address into the place in the bookmark pane where you want your bookmark to be. (Bet you thought it'd be more complicated.) You can also drag bookmarks up and down in the bookmarks bar to reorganize them.

Once your bookmarks are perfect, click the bookmark icon at the top of the window again to make the bookmark pane disappear.

Your page history is in the History menu at the top of the screen. Select History, then the page you want to go back to, or History⇨Show History to see your history as a page of clickable links.

Filling In Forms

The web isn't just for reading — it's for buying stuff, signing up for stuff, and expressing your opinion about stuff. To put your two cents into a web page, you usually fill out a form that has boxes to type in, check boxes to select, and maybe other clickable stuff. Then you click a Submit button (or a button with another name) to send in the information you entered. Figure 7-6 shows a typical form.

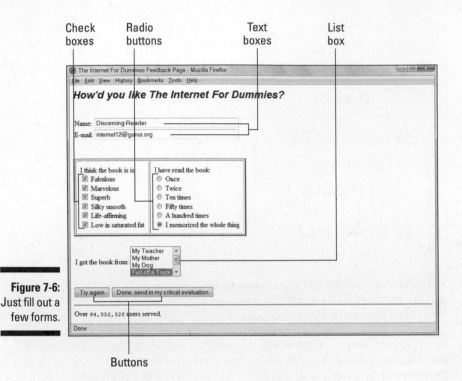

Figure 7-6:
Just fill out a
few forms.

Text boxes in a form are white, fill-in boxes in which you type information, in this case, your name and email address. *Check boxes* are little square boxes in which you check whichever ones apply (all of them, we hope, on our sample form). *Radio buttons,* the little round buttons, are similar to check boxes except that you can choose only one of them from each set. In Figure 7-6, you also see a *list box,* in which you can choose one possibility in the box. In most cases, you see more entries than can fit in the box, so you scroll them up and down. You can usually choose only one entry, although some list boxes let you choose more.

Forms also include buttons that determine what happens to the information you enter on the form. Most forms have two of these buttons: one that clears the form fields to their initial state and sends nothing, and one, usually known as the *Submit* button, that sends the filled-out form back to the web server for processing.

Some pages have *Search bars,* which are one-line forms that let you type some text for which to search. Depending on the browser, a Submit button may be displayed to the right of the text area, or you may simply press Enter to send the search words to the server. For example, the Google search page at www.google.com has a box in which you type a word or phrase; when you press Enter or click the Google Search button, the search begins. (See Chapter 13 to find out what happens!)

Your browser can keep a secret

When you fill out a form on a web page, you may need to provide information that you prefer to keep private — your credit card number, for example. Not to worry! Browsers can *encrypt* the information you send to and receive from a *secure web server.* You can tell when a page was received encrypted from the web server by the little padlock icon at one end of the Address bar or in the lower-right corner of the browser window. If the padlock doesn't appear, the page wasn't encrypted.

Typed-in data in forms on secure pages are almost always sent encrypted, making it impossible for anyone to snoop on your secrets as they traverse the Net. Encrypted pages are

nice, but in practice, it's unlikely that anyone is snooping on your web session anyway, encrypted or otherwise. The real security problems are elsewhere (refer to Chapter 2).

Some browsers have the habit of popping up little boxes to warn you about the dangers of what you're about to do. They display a box when you're about to switch from encrypted to non-encrypted (or back again) transmissions. Most of these warning boxes include a check box you can select to tell the program not to bother you with this type of warning again. After you read the warning, select the check box so that your browser stops nagging you.

Your browser can remember the entries, such as your name and address, that you frequently type into web page forms. As you type, your browser may try to spot entries you made earlier and suggest the rest of the entry so that you don't have to type it. If a suggestion pops up from your browser as you're filling in a form, you can click the suggestion to accept it. If you don't like the suggestion, just keep typing.

Knowing Where to Start

When you run your browser, it displays your *start page.* Unfortunately, the people who make browsers usually don't pick pages that we particularly like. Why not tell your browser to start where *you* want to start? You may want to start at the Yahoo! page (www.yahoo.com), which we describe in Chapter 6; or Google (www.google.com); or Wikipedia (en.wikipedia.org for the English language encyclopedia); or the home page of your local newspaper. You can even start with more than one page by setting multiple start pages, and your browser can open each one in a separate tab.

You can also specify a separate *home page,* which is the page you see if you click the Home icon in your browser. Where's the Home icon? Firefox, Chrome, and Internet Explorer display the Home icon automatically, and we tell you how to display one in Safari in the following sections.

The following sections show you how to set both your start page and your home page. Most people set them to the same page (or pages) anyway.

Specifying where Firefox starts

Display the page that you want to use as your start page and home page, and then follow these steps:

1. **Click the Firefox button in the upper-left corner, and choose Options or Preferences.**

   You see the Options dialog box, shown in Figure 7-7.

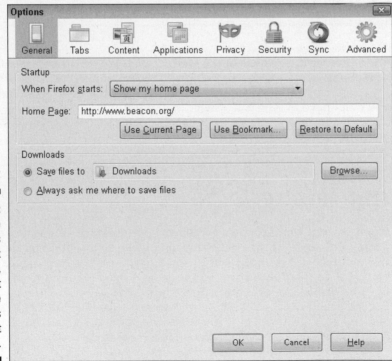

Figure 7-7:
In the Options dialog box in Firefox, you can set your favorite website as your start page.

2. **Click the General icon, if it isn't already selected.**

   This icon may already be selected, and its settings appear in the rest of the Options dialog box. The settings you're concerned with are in the Startup section.

3. **Set the When Firefox Starts option.**

   You can choose Show My Home Page (you set your home page in the next step), Show a Blank Page (make Firefox start faster), or Show My Windows and Tabs from Last Time.

4. **Set your home page(s) to the current page(s) by clicking (you guessed it!) the Use Current Pages button.**

5. **Click OK.**

You can set Firefox or Chrome to display a bunch of pages when it starts up, each on its own, separate tab. For example, you might want to have Firefox open a weather-reporting page, such as Weather Underground (www. wunderground.com), the *New York Times* (www.nytimes.com), or even a silly page (such as cuteoverload.com) every time you start Firefox. First display the web pages you want to start with. Then follow the preceding instructions to make the entire set of tabs open when you start your browser.

Configuring Internet Explorer start and home pages

Display the page that you want to use as your start page and home page, and then follow these steps:

1. **Click the Tools icon above the upper-right corner of the web page and choose Internet Options from the menu that appears.**

   You see the Internet Options dialog box.

2. **Click the General tab, along the top of the dialog box.**

   It's probably already selected, but we say this in case you've been looking around at what's on the other tabs.

3. **In the Home Page section, click the Use Current button.**

   The URL of the current page appears in the Address text box. To start with no page, click the Use Blank button.

4. **Click OK.**

Telling Chrome what to display at start-up

Display the page or pages that you want to use as your home page, and then follow these steps:

1. **Click the Menu three-line icon above the upper-right corner of the web page and choose Settings from the menu that appears.**

   You see the Settings page in a new tab. (It isn't a web page, but it looks like one.)

2. **In the On Startup section, choose Open the New Tab Page, Continue where you left off, or Open a specific page or set of pages.**

   If you choose the last option, you can click Set Pages to set the current page as your start page (or one of several start pages, using tabs).

3. **Set your home page to the current page by clicking Set Pages (in the On Startup section), then click Use current pages.**

   If you had more than one page open, it adds all of them. If you don't want one, mouse over it, which makes an X appear to the right of the URL, then click the X to get rid of that page.

4. **In the Appearance section, select Show Home button, if it's not already checked.**

5. **Click Close.**

You might consider setting your home page so that it's the New Tab page (as Chrome refers to it), shown in Figure 7-8. This page is pretty cool, actually — Chrome displays a bunch of tiny pages, like thumbnail pictures of the pages, each with a title, showing the pages you've visited most often. It also shows bookmarks you've recently used and pages you've recently closed. Very useful! It's the home page we use.

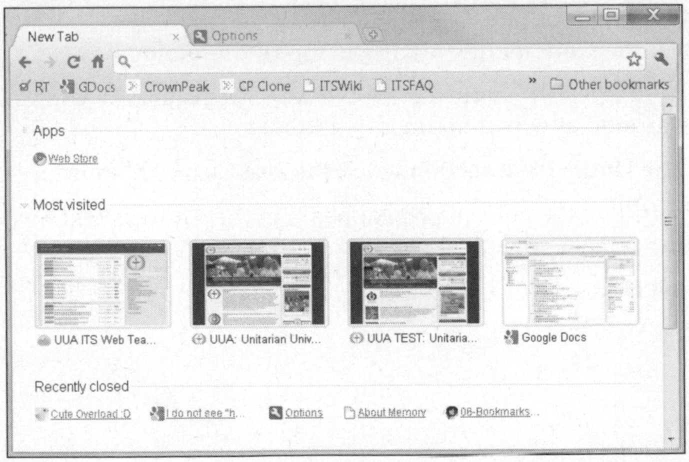

Figure 7-8:
The New Tab page in Chrome tells you what you visit most often and what you've seen recently.

Setting Safari's home page

Display the page that you want to use as your start page and home page, and then follow these steps:

1. **Click the Settings icon above the upper-right corner of the web page and choose Preferences. Or choose Safari⇨Preferences.**

   You see the General dialog box. If you don't, click the General Tab.

2. **Set the New Windows Open With option to Home Page.**

   On a Mac, enter the URL of your home page into the Homepage box, or if you have that page open, click Set to Current Page.

3. **Click the Close button in the upper-right corner of the window.**

You can tell Safari to display the Home icon by clicking the Settings icon above the upper-right corner of the web page, choosing Customize Toolbar, and dragging the Home icon to your Safari toolbar. (For example, you can drag it to between the Address bar and the Tools icon.)

 Safari has a cool Top Picks page, which shows the web pages you view most frequently. You can tell Safari to display it whenever you open a new tab or window by setting the New Windows Open With setting or the New Tabs Open With option to Top Sites. It's similar to Chrome's New Tab page (refer to Figure 7-8).

Who Can Remember All Those Passwords?

We certainly can't remember all our passwords. Many websites ask you to enter a username and password. If you're buying an item from an online store such as Amazon (www.amazon.com), you create an account with a username and password that you enter every time you want to buy something. Amazon.com remembers your name, address, and credit card information as part of your account, so you don't need to enter it every time. If you want to read the *New York Times* online at www.nytimes.com, you create an account with a password, too. The account remembers what kinds of news you're interested in reading. After you use the web for a while, you pile up a heap of usernames and passwords.

See Chapter 2 for advice on choosing passwords and keeping track of them safely.

Browsers offer to remember your usernames and passwords for you. Using this feature can be dangerous if other people use your computer or if you use a computer in a public place, such as a library or an Internet café. But if you're the only person who uses your computer, you may want to let your browser do the work of remembering some, if not all, of your usernames and passwords.

When a web page asks for a username and password, your browser may pop up a little window that offers to remember the username and password you enter, or the question may appear just above the top edge of the web page. If you click Yes, the next time you arrive at the same page, your browser may fill in your username and password for you.

Depending on who else has access to your computer, you might let your browser remember only passwords to accounts that don't involve spending money or revealing personal information. For example, if we have an account at a Harry Potter fan site that enables us to participate in online discussions, the danger of having someone break into this account is a lot less daunting than the thought of someone hacking into an online bank account. Unless your computer is in a physically secure place, don't let your browser remember passwords that have any real power.

Storing passwords in Firefox

You can control whether and how your browser stores these passwords. In Firefox, follow these steps:

1. **Click the Menu icon, then select Options.**

    You see the Options dialog box, with a list of the categories of options across the top (refer to Figure 7-7 earlier in this chapter). On a Mac, choose Firefox⇨Preferences.

2. **Click the Security icon and look in the Passwords section.**

3. **Set the Remember Passwords for Sites check box.**

    Click the box to clear the check mark if you want to turn off this feature (or click the box again to turn it back on).

4. **If you want to see the list of usernames that Firefox has saved, click the Saved Passwords button.**

    You can review or delete usernames that Firefox is remembering for you. You can even see the passwords by clicking the Show Password button. (And so can anyone else with access to your computer!) Click Close when you're done.

5. **Select the Use a Master Password check box to set a master password that you need to type only once, at the beginning of every Firefox session.**

    This option reduces the number of passwords you need to remember while maintaining some security. Don't forget the master password.

6. **Click OK to close the Options dialog box.**

Storing passwords in Internet Explorer

In Internet Explorer, remembering usernames and passwords is the job of the AutoComplete feature, which you set up by following these simple steps:

1. **Click the Tools icon, choose Internet Options, and click the Content tab.**

    You see the Content tab in the Internet Options dialog box.

2. **In the AutoComplete section, click the Settings button.**

    You see the AutoComplete Settings dialog box.

3. **Select the check boxes to control which kinds of entries Internet Explorer stores.**

    IE doesn't show you a list of the passwords you saved, but you can turn the feature on and off by selecting the Ask Me Before Saving Passwords check box. The User Names and Passwords On Forms check box controls whether Internet Explorer fills in your stored passwords on forms.

4. **Click OK to close the AutoComplete Settings dialog box, and click OK again to close the Internet Options dialog box.**

Storing passwords in Chrome

The Chrome settings for remembering passwords are more like those in Firefox. Follow these steps:

1. **Click the Menu three-line icon and choose Settings from the menu that appears.**

    You see the Settings page on a new tab.

2. **Click Show advanced settings at the bottom, then scroll down to Passwords and Forms.**

3. **In the Passwords section, check or uncheck Offer to save your web passwords.**

   It's your choice, depending on whether you trust the other people who use your computer.

4. **If you want to review the passwords that Chrome has already saved, click Manage Passwords.**

   You see web addresses and the usernames, and you can remove any you don't want saved by clicking the X to its right. To display a password, click the dots that represent it and click Show. Click Close when you're done.

5. **Click Close.**

Storing passwords in Safari

Same old, same old — Safari works similarly to other browsers. Follow these steps:

1. **Click the Setting icon and choose Preferences or choose Safari⇨Preferences.**

2. **Click the AutoFill icon.**

   These settings control which personal information Safari stores and then supplies on web page forms.

3. **Click the User Names and Passwords check box if you want Safari to remember these items.**

4. **To see and edit the usernames and passwords that Safari has stored, click the Edit button to the right of the User Names and Passwords check box.**

5. **Click the Close button in the upper-right corner of the window.**

Cookies Are (Usually) Your Friends

To enhance your online experience, browser makers invented a type of special message, known as a *cookie,* that lets a website recognize you when you revisit that site. They thoughtfully store this info on your very own machine. See Chapter 2 for a full description of cookies and how they compare to more serious security threats. You can control which sites can store cookies on your computer.

Usually, the website that sets a cookie is the only one that reads the cookie. However, *third-party* cookies can be set by one website and read by another. Third-party cookies are used by servers that deliver advertisements and those annoying pop-up and pop-under ads. We recommend that you accept most cookies but block third-party cookies.

Burning cookies in Firefox

Choose Firefox⇨Options (on a Mac Firefox⇨Preferences), click the Privacy icon, and look in the History section. If Remember History is selected, Firefox stores cookies. If you want more control over which cookies it stores, change it to Use Custom Settings for History. This setting displays these cookie-related check boxes:

- **Accept Cookies from Sites:** We recommend that you leave this one selected.
- **Accept Third-Party Cookies:** We recommend you set this to "From visited".

You can specify which sites can and cannot store cookies by clicking the Exceptions button. You can enter the web addresses that you definitely trust with your cookies (such as the shopping sites you frequent) or that you don't trust (such as advertising sites).

You can take a look at the cookies on your computer, too. Click the Show Cookies button and scroll down the list of sites. If you see one that you don't recognize or that sounds suspicious, click it and click the Remove Cookie button.

Exploring cookies in Internet Explorer

 Click the Tools icon, choose Internet Options, and click the Privacy tab on the Internet Options dialog box that appears. Internet Explorer displays a slider that you can drag up and down to increase or decrease your level of privacy. By default, Internet Explorer sets your privacy level to Medium, allowing cookies except for third-party cookies. If you want to specify exactly how cookies are saved, click the Advanced button to see the Advanced Privacy Settings dialog box and then select the Override Automatic Cookie Handling check box. The options are

- ✔ **First-Party Cookies:** You can choose to accept or to block or to be prompted to choose, though this option grows tiresome quickly if you encounter a lot of cookies. Some sites can store three or more cookies *per page*. Choose Accept.

- ✔ **Third-Party Cookies:** Just say no to (that is, choose Block) third-party cookies.

- ✔ **Always Allow Session Cookies:** This check box lets through all *session* cookies, a type of cookie used to track a single instance of your visit to a website. These cookies are commonly used by shopping sites such as Amazon.com and are harmless. Select this option so that it contains a check mark.

Cookies and Chrome

 Click the Menu icon, and choose Settings from the menu. In the Privacy section, click the Content Settings button to display the Content Settings dialog box. In the Cookies section, select the setting labeled Allow Local Data to Be Set. (In our humble opinion, it's your best bet.) Check Block third-party cookies, if it's not already checked. Then click Done.

Safari with cookies

 In Safari, click the Settings icon and choose Preferences or choose Safari➪Preferences. Then click the Privacy icon in the window that appears. Set Block Cookies and Other Website Data to From Third Parties and Advertisers or to Allow From Current Website Only.

Where Have You Been?

Browsers keep a *history list* of the websites you've been to. No, your browser isn't spying on you; the history list remembers pages you went to earlier, even days ago, so that you can find them again.

Your browsing history

You can see your history list, and you can return to any page on it by clicking it. Here's how:

✔ **Firefox:** Click the Menu button, then History to display the Library window with the History list selected. You can also press Ctrl+H to display the list down the left side of your browser window, arranged by day. Close the History list by clicking the X in its upper-right corner.

✔ **Internet Explorer:** Click the Favorites icon, click the History tab on the menu that appears, and then click a day (for example, Today).

✔ **Chrome:** Click and hold the Back button (or right-click it) to see a list of the pages you've been to recently. Or, click and hold and then choose Show Full History from the bottom of the menu. You see a new tab with a list of web pages by day, with the time you viewed each page.

✔ **Safari:** Select History⇨Show History to see the History tab.

Oh, nowhere, really

Some of our readers have asked us how to clear out their browsing, presumably because they meant to type www.disney.com but their fingers slipped and it came out www.mega-xxx-babes.com instead. (It could happen to anyone.)

If you're using someone else's computer, and especially if you're using a public computer in a library or Internet café, you should delete your browsing history and any other information about your session that might be stored on the computer. Otherwise, the next person to sit down at the computer might find your browsing history rather interesting, especially if the browser has thoughtfully stored the usernames and password you entered.

Whether you, um, mistyped web addresses or you don't want to leave your personal information on someone else's computer, follow these procedures:

✔ **Firefox:** Click the Menu button, then History, and click the Clear Your Recent History link. Choose how far back to forget and click Clear Now.

✔ **Internet Explorer:** Click the Tools icon, choose Safety, and choose Delete Browsing History from the menu that appears. (Hmm, it's right at the top. There must be a lot of sloppy typists out there.) In the Delete Browsing History dialog box, decide which information to clear (by selecting check boxes), and click Delete.

✔ **Chrome:** Press Ctrl+H (or Function+Y on a Mac) to display the History tab, then click Clear Browsing Data, then select how far back to delete, and if you want what kind of history to delete, then the Clear Browsing data button. Or in the history page, click the checkboxes next to the individual page(s) you want to forget, then click Remove Selected Items.

✔ **Safari:** Press Option+Command+2 (on a Mac, because no one uses Safari on Windows) or choose History⇨Show History to see the History tab. The pages you visited are arranged by day; click a day to see the pages you viewed. To remove one page from the list, right-click it and choose Delete.

Some browsers let you browse in a kind of "stealth mode," which leaves no trace:

✔ **Firefox:** Choose File⇨New Private Window or click the Menu button and choose New Private Window.

✔ **IE:** Click the Tools icon, choose Safety, and choose InPrivate Browsing.

✔ **Chrome:** You can browse incognito. (Don't forget your trench coat and fedora.) Click the Menu button and choose New Incognito Window.

✔ **Safari:** Click the Settings icon, choose Private Browsing, and click OK. On a Mac, choose Safari⇨Private Browsing or File⇨New Private Window.

Blocking Pop-Up Windows

Pop-up windows, as described in Chapter 2, are browser windows that open without your asking for them, usually at the command of the website you're viewing. Some websites display so many pop-ups that your computer becomes unusable until you can close them all. If you've encountered these sites, you'll be glad to hear that your browser can block most (though not all) pop-up windows.

No pop-ups in Firefox

Click the Menu button and choose Options or Preferences, click the Content icon, and you see the Block Pop-up Windows check box. We leave it selected.

Blocking all pop-ups makes a few websites stop working. In particular, some shopping sites pop up small windows in which you have to type credit card verification information. Online help sometimes appears in pop-ups, too. Firefox thoughtfully includes an Exceptions button that lets you specify websites whose pop-ups are okay with you.

When a website tries to display a pop-up, you see at the top of the web page a message saying "Firefox prevented this site from opening a popup window." Click the Options button and choose from the menu that appears:

> ✔ **Allow Popups from *Sitename*** puts this site on your Allowed list.
>
> ✔ **Enable Popup Blocker Options** displays the Allowed Sites dialog box so that you can edit your list of sites.
>
> ✔ **Don't Show This Message When Popups Are Blocked** continues to block pop-ups, without asking each time it blocks one.

Click the red X at the right end of the message to make the message go away.

Blocking pop-ups in Internet Explorer

Microsoft finally added a pop-up blocker in response to the growing popularity of Firefox. Click the Tools icon, choose Internet Options to display the Internet Options dialog box, click the Privacy tab, and click the Turn On Pop-Up Blocker check box to turn this feature off or back on. (We leave the check box selected.) You can tell Internet Explorer to allow pop-ups from specific sites by clicking the Settings button and adding web addresses to a list.

The Internet Explorer pop-up blocker displays a "Pop-up blocked" message at the top of the web page whenever it blocks a pop-up window, and clicking the message displays a similar set of options.

Chrome and pop-ups

Chrome includes a pop-up blocker, too. When Chrome blocks a pop-up, you see a message in the lower-right corner of the browser window. You can either click the message and choose the first option (the exact address of the pop-up) to display it or choose Always Allow Popups to allow pop-ups from the site. To set up Chrome to block all pop-ups, follow these steps:

1. **Click the Menu icon and choose Options or Settings.**

2. **Click Show Advanced Settings.**

   You might have scroll to the bottom of the window.

3. **Click the Content Settings button in the Privacy section at the top of the page and scroll down to the Pop-ups section.**

4. **Select the Do Not Allow Any Site to Show Pop-ups check box. Click the Manage Exceptions button to allow specific websites to display pop-ups.**

Safari stops pop-ups

In Safari, click the Settings icon or choose Safari⇨Preferences, select the Security tab in the settings window, and choose Block Pop-Up Windows from the menu that appears to turn the pop-up blocker on or off.

When Browsers Go Bad

If your browser looks odd, try these tricks:

- **If the web page looks garbled,** click the Reload or Refresh icon (the circular arrow) to load the page again. Maybe it was damaged during its arduous trek across the Net.

- **If the whole top of the window is gone** — you have no window title bar or menu bar — you're in Full Screen mode. In Windows, press F11 to return to normal. On a Mac, hover your mouse at the top center of the screen until an icon appears in the upper right corner of the screen; click it to get your screen back to normal.

- **If the browser restarted and is telling you which fabulous new features it now has,** it probably just downloaded an updated version of the program and had to restart itself to complete the installation. Read the message appreciatively and then close the tab or window.

- **If your browser is just acting weird,** close all your browser windows, take a few deep breaths, and run your browser again. If the situation is ugly, try restarting the computer. (Save any unsaved work first.)

- **If your browser still looks strange,** especially if it's showing a lot of ads that you didn't ask for, your computer is probably infected with spyware. See Chapter 2 for a definition of spyware, and see the section in Chapter 4 about detecting spyware for advice on getting rid of it.

Getting Plugged In with Plug-Ins

Web pages with text and pictures are old hat. Now web pages must have pictures that sing and dance or calendars that let you create events or games such as chess that play against you. Every month, new types of information appear on the web, and browsers have to keep up. You can extend your browser's capabilities with *plug-ins* — add-on programs that glue themselves to the browser and add even more features. Internet Explorer can also extend itself by using *ActiveX* controls, which are another (less secure) type of add-on program.

What are you to do when your browser encounters new kinds of information on a web page? Get the plug-in program that handles that kind of information and glue it to the browser program. *Star Trek* fans can think of plug-ins as parasitic life forms that attach themselves to your browser and enhance its intelligence.

When you restart your browser, maybe because it updated itself, it may display messages about add-ons that are installed or that need to be updated. You can display a list of your plug-ins at any time:

- **Firefox:** Click the Menu button and choose Add-ons to see a page about all kinds of add-ons and extensions. Click the Plugins tab to see a list of which ones are installed. You can click the More link for more information and click the Disable button if you don't want to keep the plug-in.

- **IE:** Choose Tools⇨Internet Options, click the Programs tab, and click Manage Add-ons. To disable a plug-in, select it and click the Disable button at the bottom of the Manage Add-ons dialog box.

- **Chrome:** Type "about:plugins" in the address box and press Enter. If you don't like the look of a plug-in, click Disable to turn it off.

- **Safari:** Click the Settings icon or choose Safari⇨Preferences and then select Extensions.

Four essential plug-ins

Here are four useful plug-ins you may want to add to your browser:

- **Flash Player:** Plays both audio and video files in addition to other types of animations. Widely used on web pages, it's available at `www.adobe.com/products/flashplayer`. Using Flash, you can view videos on YouTube (see Chapter 14). Flash can also play *streaming* sound and video files while you download them. Our favorite site with streaming audio is the National Public Radio website (`www.npr.org`), where you can hear recent NPR radio stories. Another favorite is the BBC at `www.bbc.co.uk`, with news in 43 languages (really) and other BBC programs 24 hours a day. For a combination of political and technical reasons, Flash is not available on tablets or most smartphones, but many sites have apps to get you your streaming stuff anyway.

- **QuickTime:** Plays videos in a number of formats. Download it from `www.apple.com/quicktime/download`. (Mac users already have it.)

- **Java:** All sorts of extensions are written in Java, from browser based animations games to remote control consoles. Java isn't available on tablets or smartphones, either, for similar reasons to Flash.

- **Adobe Reader:** Displays PDF (Portable Document Format) files formatted exactly the way the author intended. Lots of useful PDF files are out there, including many U.S. tax forms (at `www.irs.gov`). You can find Acrobat at `http://get.adobe.com/reader`.

Down it comes!

Downloading means copying files from a computer Up There on the Internet "down" to the computer sitting on or under your desk. By far the easiest way to download any kind of file is by using your browser. Follow these steps:

1. **Find the file on the web.**

   Search the web for it, as described in Chapter 13.

2. **Follow the instructions on the web page to download the file.**

   This step usually just means clicking a Download button.

3. **If your browser displays a Save or Save As dialog box, choose where to put the file.**

   Put it on your desktop, where it's easy to find later. Or, put it in the folder where you want the file to end up (otherwise, your browser will probably store the file in a Downloads folder). Your browser may display a Downloads window where the file appears, or the downloaded file may appear as an icon at the bottom of your browser window.

4. **Open the file with its matching program, usually by double-clicking the filename or icon.**

If you downloaded a Word document, it opens in Word or WordPad (or maybe LibreOffice, a nice freeware office suite you can download from www.libreoffice.org).

5. **If it's a program file, it runs.**

   The file should open itself and walk you through a wizard-style set of windows to collect any needed setup info — and then install itself. A box may pop up to ask whether you are an administrator to complete the installation. If you're sure that you trust the source of the program, click OK. (If you aren't sure, you might consider at this point whether you can live without this potentially malicious program.) The setup program probably creates an icon for the program on your desktop. In Windows, it may also add the program to your Start menu.

Lots of the programs that this book recommends can be downloaded from the web, often for free. But watch out! Any program can contain viruses and spyware, so don't run an executable file unless you're sure that you know what's in it! Stick with the software libraries we recommend in this book because they scan their files for viruses and spyware. And make sure that you are running a virus scanner, as described in Chapter 4.

How to use plug-ins

After you download a plug-in from the web, run it (double-click its icon or filename) to install it. Depending on what the plug-in does, you follow different steps to try it out — usually, you find a file that the plug-in can play and watch (or listen) as the plug-in plays it.

After you install the plug-in, you don't have to do anything to run it. It fires up automatically whenever you view a web page containing information that requires the plug-in.

Plug-ins, particularly Flash and Adobe Reader, are subject to security problems, and they may not be automatically updated by Windows Update or Apple's Software Update. Drop by the Flash and Adobe Reader websites at `get.adobe.com/flashplayer` and `www.adobe.com/products/reader` from time to time to see whether they have new versions.

Part III
Hanging Out with Friends Online

In this part . . .

- ✔ Send and receive email
- ✔ Organize your email
- ✔ Explore social media
- ✔ Get to know Twitter
- ✔ Communicate by Internet phone, chat, and webcam

Chapter 8

It's in the Mail: Sending and Receiving Email

....

In This Chapter

▶ Dissecting the anatomy of an email address

▶ Setting up email on your smartphone

▶ Mastering the maze of mail servers 'n' stuff

▶ Choosing an email program

▶ Sending and receiving email

▶ Finding email addresses

▶ Safe email practices

....

*E*lectronic mail, or *email,* is without a doubt the most popular Internet service after the Web, even though it's one of the oldest and least glitzy. Although email doesn't have the flash and sparkle of the World Wide Web, more people use it. Every system on the Internet supports some sort of mail service, which means that no matter what kind of computer you're using, if it's on the Internet, you can send and receive mail. Even some systems that aren't technically on the Internet — think mobile phone — can do email.

Regardless of which type of mail you're using, the basic tasks of reading, sending, addressing, and filing mail work in much the same way, so skimming this chapter is worthwhile even if you're not using any of the mail programs we describe here. The next chapter describes more advanced email features, like forwarding, printing, and filing mail messages.

 Young whippersnappers may think that email is for old people, and that the cool way to send messages is by using text messages on their phones, instant messaging (covered in Chapter 12), or messages within Facebook or another social networking site. However, email is still *the* way that businesses communicate with each other and with customers, and that most people send messages over the Internet. Not everyone is on Facebook, WhatsApp, or whatever the new system is, but almost everyone who has ever used the Internet has an email address, and every email system automagically (a technical term) can connect to every other. Don't worry: Email is still cool! (And anyway, nearly all those sites send you mail when someone sends you a message, so you just need to check your mail, not all umpteen websites, to see what's new.)

What's My Address?

Your *email address* is the cyberspace equivalent of a postal address or a phone number. When you send an email message, you type the addresses of the recipients so that the computer knows where to send it. Each email address has a *mailbox* where mail to that address is stored.

Before you can do much mailing, you have to figure out your email address so that you can give it to people who want to get in touch with you. You also have to figure out some of their addresses so that you can write to them. (If you have no friends or plan to send only anonymous hate mail, you can skip this section.)

Email addresses have two parts, separated by the @ (*at*-sign). The part before the @ is the *username* or *mailbox,* which is, roughly speaking, your personal name. The part after that is the *domain.* Capitalization never matters in domains and rarely matters in usernames. To make it easy on your eyes, therefore, most domain and mailbox names in this book are shown in lowercase.

The domain part

The domain (the part after the @) indicates where your mailbox is stored. Mailboxes usually live in one of four places:

- ✔ **Your Internet service provider (ISP):** Your ISP usually gives you a mailbox using their domain. If you sign up for a DSL account at Verizon, the domain is `verizon.net`. If you use Comcast, it's `comcast.net`.

- ✔ **Your school, employer, or other organization:** If you attend Columbia University (Go, Lions!), your student mailbox is at the domain `columbia.edu`. If you work for Microsoft, it's at `microsoft.com`.

- ✔ **Your own domain, such as** `gurus.org`: (That's one of ours.) You can own your domain name, as described in Chapter 17. You need to arrange for your domain to live somewhere, which is probably where your mailboxes will be stored, too.

- ✔ **A web-based email service, or** *webmail:* About 20 years ago, two people simultaneously had the idea of creating a website where you can sign up for an email account and then log in to read and send messages. Your email mailbox lives on the website's mail servers. Many websites now provide free mailboxes, like Gmail (at `gmail.com`). See the later section "Getting Your Own Mailbox" to find out how to sign up for a webmail account. (Both of the original webmail systems are still around, one as Microsoft's Hotmail, which was recently rebranded as Outlook.com, the other as Yahoo's webmail.)

Even if your ISP or employer offers mailboxes, you may want to sign up for a webmail account. Some of us prefer to separate our work-related messages from our personal ones. Another advantage of webmail is that if you change ISPs or jobs, your email address doesn't change.

The username part

Your *username* is the name assigned to your particular mailbox. For example, you can write to the president of the United States at `president@white house.gov`. The president's username is `president`, and the domain that stores his mailbox is `whitehouse.gov` — reasonable enough.

If you're lucky, you get to choose your username; in other cases, you receive a standardized username. You may choose (or be assigned) your first name as your username — or your last name, your initials, your first initial and last name, or a completely made-up name. At the major webmail sites, the best 50 million or so usernames have already been taken, so you may need to get creative. Try adding numbers or other information to create a username that isn't already in use.

Many organizations assign usernames in a consistent format for all users, most often by using your first and last names with a dot (.) between them or your first initial followed by the first seven letters of your last name. In these schemes, your email address may resemble `elvis.presley@bluesuede.org` or `epresley@bluesuede.org`. (If your name isn't Elvis Presley, adjust this example suitably. On the other hand, if your name *is* Elvis Presley, please contact us immediately. We know some people who are looking for you.)

When you sign up with an ISP, the provider creates a mailbox for your username. Although some ISPs offer only one username per Internet account, many ISPs offer as many as five mailboxes with five different usernames for a single account so that every person in your family can have a separate mailbox.

Getting Your Own Mailbox

Don't share an email account with anyone else — you deserve your own. Many Internet services use your email address as your account identifier, send a message to your address to confirm your identity, and assume that anyone with access to your account is you.

A cool thing about webmail systems such as Google's Gmail and Microsoft's Outlook.com (a.k.a. Hotmail.com) is that you can read and send messages from any computer on the Net. Your mailbox is stored on the webmail server, and any computer with a browser can access it — you can check your mail from a friend's computer, at a cybercafé, or from the computer at the public library. Of course, no one should be able to read your messages, or send messages as you, without typing your password. One downside is that reading and sending messages tends to be slower with webmail than with an email program because you have to wait for a new web page to open every time you click a new message.

Some webmail accounts give you access to other services using the same username and password. If you sign up for Gmail, you can use the same account for Google Calendar, Google Drive (an online word processor, spreadsheet, presentation program, and storage) and other features. Your Outlook. com account includes access to storage and Microsoft's online versions of their Office programs.

Webmail addresses are free, so if you don't already have your own email address, get one by following these steps:

1. **Using your web browser, go to the webmail service's website.**

   Try Gmail at `www.gmail.com`, Outlook.com at `www.hotmail.com` or `www.outlook.com`, or another webmail service. See Chapter 6 for help starting your web browser. We could show you a picture of what these websites looked like when this book went to press, but they change every month or so, so it would just be confusing!

2. **Look for a link named Create an Account or Sign Up Now or similar wording and follow the instructions to create your account.**

   They don't ask anything too nosy; feel free to lie about your birthdate and gender. (Is it any of their business?) Microsoft lets you choose between `@outlook.com` and `@hotmail.com` for the second part of your email address.

   Be sure to click the links to read the *terms of service* (rules of the game) and *privacy policy* (what they plan to do with the information you give them).

3. **In Table 8-1, write down your email address and your password.**

   Your email address ends in `@outlook.com`, `@hotmail.com`, or `@gmail.com`, depending on which service you choose. Remember to create a hard-to-guess password for your email account, because if baddies can access your email account, they can probably reset the password on your other accounts.

You'll end up with a username and password that you can use for other services provided by these websites. You're ready!

Whaddaya mean you don't know your own address?

It happens frequently: You know the email address you requested for your new account, but you aren't absolutely positive that it was approved. Before you give out your address to everyone you know, test it out by sending a message to a friend or two. Tell them to reply to your message when they receive it and to let you know which address your message came from. Or, send yourself a message and use your email login name as the mailbox name. Then examine the return address on the message.

Better yet, send a message to *The Internet For Dummies* Mail Central, at `internet14@ gurus.org`, and a friendly robot will send back a message with your address. (While you're at it, tell us whether you like this book, because we authors read that mail and write back when time permits.)

Putting it all together

If you have to set up a mail program to read your email, you need to enter information about your email mailbox. Write in Table 8-1 your email address and other info that your ISP, employer, school, or other email provider gave you (and fold down the corner of this page so that you can find it again later). (Don't worry about the parts of the table you don't understand right away — we explain *servers* later in this chapter.)

Table 8-1	Information about Your Mailbox	
What You Supply	*Description*	*Example*
Your email address_____	Your username followed by @ and the domain name	`internet14@ gurus.org`
Your email password_____	The password for your email mailbox (usually the same as the password for your account)	`dum3myBook`
Webmail URL_____	The web address where you can check your mail	`https:// mail.google. com`

(continued)

Table 8-1 *(continued)*

What You Supply	Description	Example
Not Needed for Webmail:		
POP/IMAP server_____	Computer where your mail program picks up your mail	`pop.gurus.org`
POP/IMAP account_____	Log in to pick up your mail, often but not always your username	`Internet14` or `internet14@gurus.org`
SMTP server_____	Computer where your mail program sends outgoing mail	`smtp.gurus.org`

And I would read my mail how?

You can read your email in several ways:

- **Mail program:** You can use a *mail program* to read your email — a program that displays incoming messages and allows you to send messages. You can use any of a long list of mail programs, including Microsoft Outlook and Apple Mail. Android devices, iPads, and iPhones come with mail programs, too. We talk about the most popular mail programs later in this chapter.

- **Webmail:** The whole point of webmail is that you can read it on (drumroll, please) the web. Any web browser will do, as described in the next section.

If you use email at work, your organization may use a mail server called Microsoft Exchange. In addition to handling mail, Exchange also provides shared calendars, to-do lists, and other nifty features. If your company has bought Exchange, they've probably also bought licenses for Microsoft Outlook, so your organization usually insists that you use it. To learn Outlook, see *Outlook 2013 For Dummies* (John Wiley & Sons, Inc.). Exchange provides webmail, too. Check with your organization's information technology support group if you have trouble setting up your email.

The Web Is a Fine Place to Read Your Email

No matter which type of email account you have, even if you normally use a mail program such as Outlook or your smartphone or tablet to read your messages, your mail provider most likely has a webmail website where you can read and send mail. To find out whether your ISP provides webmail, go to its website and look around or write to its support email address. Most ISPs have a Mail or similar link on their home pages. You log in with the same account name and password that you may have jotted down in Table 8-1. For example, if you have an Internet account with Verizon, you can use its website to read and send messages at any computer on the Net; go to `webmail.verizon.com`.

If you use a computer on a wireless connection, particularly a connection without a password (see Chapter 5), people who are not your friends can snoop on your session. Fortunately, most webmail systems offer *https* sessions, which are encrypted so that snoops see only undecipherable noise. Start the web address with *https://*, as in `https://gmail.com`, and look for the Lock icon next to the address before logging in.

Reading webmail

You can read webmail — where else? — on the web, whether your mailbox is at a webmail site listed in the previous section or is hosted by your ISP.

To access your webmail mailbox, go to the website and log in:

1. **Go to the same website where you created your account.**

   If you created a webmail mailbox at Gmail (`www.gmail.com`) or Outlook.com (`www.hotmail.com` or `www.outlook.com`), log in at that website. If your mailbox is provided by your ISP, employer, or school or another organization, go to its website.

2. **Sign in with your new username and password.**

   You may see a web page that may have ads and news and all kinds of other information. If it doesn't include a listing of your email messages, look for an Inbox or Mail link to click.

   Your inbox looks something like Figure 8-1. You may not have any email yet, or you may have a welcome message from the webmail service. If so, you see the sender and subject line of the message.

3. **Click any message to read it.**

   Then you can click the Reply, Forward, or Delete button or link to deal with the message.

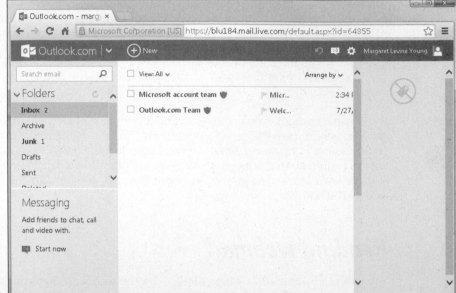

Figure 8-1:
Reading mail in Outlook.com (also known as Hotmail or Windows Live Mail).

More than webmail

If you sign up for Gmail, you get more than a web-based mailbox. You get a Google ID that enables you to use a whole bunch of online programs, including:

- ✔ Google Drive, where you can save files and access them from online anywhere

- ✔ Google Docs, a web-based word processor

- ✔ Google Sheets, an online spreadsheet program

- ✔ Google Calendar, an appointment calendar

Similarly, signing up for Outlook.com gets you a Microsoft account and a bunch of apps that include:

- ✔ One Drive, where you can save files and access them from online anywhere

- ✔ Word Online, a web-based word processor

- ✔ Excel Online, an online spreadsheet

- ✔ Calendar, an appointment calendar

It is just us, or do these two systems seem eerily similar? Both are described in Chapter 17, "Making a Splash Online."

Sending email with webmail

To send an email message using webmail, follow these steps:

1. **Sign in.**

   See Steps 1 and 2 in the previous section.

2. **Click the Compose button, New button, or any link that seems to be about writing and sending a message.**

   Your browser displays a form with boxes for To or Recipients (the address) and Subject and a large, unlabeled box for the text of the message, as shown in Figure 8-2.

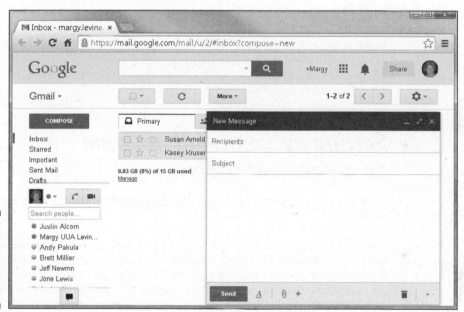

Figure 8-2: Sending mail from Google's Gmail.

3. **Type one or more addresses in the Recipients or To box.**

   If you want to send your message to more than one address, separate each address with a comma.

4. **If you see a Cc box, you can enter addresses there, too.**

   The Cc (*carbon copy*, for you historians) is for people to whom the message isn't directly addressed but who might want to be aware of your message. See the "Cc and Bcc" sidebar later in this chapter.

5. **Type a subject line in the Subject box.**

6. **Type your message in the big box.**

7. **Click the Send button.**

That's all it takes!

If you aren't at home, be sure to log out from the webmail site when you're done reading and sending mail, especially if you're using a friend's computer or a computer in a public place. Otherwise, someone else can come along and read or send messages using your account.

Doing Email on Your Smartphone or Tablet

Regular old cellphones can't send or receive email, but so-called *smartphones* can. (To find out what a smartphone is, see the section in Chapter 4 about getting an Android, iPhone, or Windows phone.) So can many tablets and e-readers, including iPads and Android tablets.

Setting up your mail program on a phone or tablet

Here are some tips for reading and sending mail depending on which device you have:

- ✔ **Androids:** Phones and tablets that run Android software come with one email program for Gmail and one for other accounts. For webmail other than Gmail, most providers have an app, or you can just use the device's web browser. For non-webmail mailboxes, Android configuration to add a mail account varies from one device to another. Open the Settings Menu, then if it has an Accounts section, scroll down to Add account, then the mail program (sometimes unhelpfully listed as IMAP), and add your account details. Or if there's an Accounts & Sync entry, pick that, then pick the Email program, then enter your account details. In Android 5.0 ("Lollipop") Google combined all the mail programs into the Gmail app, but it can still check mail accounts anywhere, not just at Gmail.

- ✔ **iPhones and iPads:** Choose Settings➪Mail Contacts Calendars➪Add Account. You see a list of popular mail providers, including AOL, Gmail, Microsoft Exchange (used by many corporations and other organizations), and Outlook.com. If your mail is somewhere else, choose Other➪Add Mail Account and enter your name, email address, email password, and a name for the account. Click Save. Choose IMAP or POP, fill in the names of your incoming (IMAP or POP) and outgoing (SMTP) mail servers from Table 8-1, and click Save.

✔ **Windows phones and tablets:** To set up a new account, display the App list, choose Settings⇨Email + Accounts⇨Add An Account, and follow the instructions on the screen. If you have an Outlook.com or Hotmail.com account, choose Windows Live as the type of account. If you use Gmail, choose Google.

If you are setting up a non-webmail account and you see an option similar to Leave Messages on Server, we recommend that you select it. If you have a choice between POP and IMAP as the account type, choose IMAP. (These two types of mail servers are described in the next section of this chapter.) Although checking email on a phone is cool, you *also* want to be able to check it on your computer!

Reading your email on a phone or tablet

Once you have told your phone or tablet about your mailbox, it's easy to read your email; in fact, checking your email 25 times a day can get to be a bad habit. The process is the same on almost all phones and tablets:

1. **Tap the Email or Mail icon.**

   On Windows devices, the icon has the name of your email account.

2. **Tap Inbox if it's not already selected, so you see arriving messages.**

   Unread messages are usually marked by a blue dot or appear in bold.

3. **Tap the message you want to read.**

When you have read your message, you can reply to it, forward it, or save it.

Sending email on a phone or tablet

From your Mail or Email program, follow these steps to send an email message:

1. **Click the New, Compose, or other button that suggests writing a message.**

   On iPhones and iPads, it's a little pencil-and-paper icon.

2. **Type one or more addresses in the To box.**

   If you want to send your message to more than one address, separate each address with a comma.

3. **If you see a Cc or Cc/Bcc box, you can enter addresses there, too.**

4. **Type a subject line in the Subject box.**

   Be specific and personal so recipients can distinguish your email from spam.

5. **Type your message in the big box.**

   iPhone and iPad users can touch the microphone icon and dictate your message. Try it one sentence at a time, and be prepared to correct what voice recognition gets wrong.

6. **Click the Send button.**

Figure 8-3 shows the email composition screen on an iPhone.

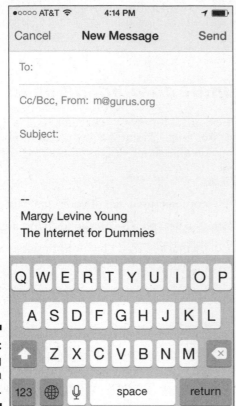

Figure 8-3:
Sending mail from an iPhone.

Reading Your Email in a Mail Program

Although reading your mail on the web is convenient, it's usually slower than using a *real* mail program. Mail programs have more features than many web-mail sites, too. Many mail programs are available. Many businesses and other organizations use Outlook, which comes with Microsoft Office. Macintosh computers come with Apple Mail.

IMAP: Mail anywhere and everywhere

When you use POP to pick up your mail, the messages are downloaded to your PC and stored there and are deleted from your mailbox on the mail server. If, like most people, you build up large files of saved messages, the saved messages are on your PC and accessible only from your mail program on that PC. Often, that's good enough, but if you read your mail in more than one place (say, at home and at work or at home and on your phone), it can be a pain if you're one place and the saved message with a crucial work-related item (a recipe for Killer Tequila Nachos, for example) is in the other. IMAP solves this problem by storing all your mail on the mail server so that you can access it from any mail program, and you have the same set of mailboxes no matter which computer you use. Many mail systems offer both IMAP and webmail, in which case you see the same mail in your mail program as you see in the webmail. IMAP can be tricky to set up in your mail programs; be sure to set your mail program to leave messages on the IMAP server, so that they are available to read on your other devices.

To use IMAP, you need a broadband connection at each place you read your mail, because IMAP is unusably slow on dialup. Because all your mail folders are on your ISP's computer, see how much mail you're allowed to store there because folders can get pretty big. One or 2 megabytes is tight, whereas 100 megabytes should be plenty unless you mail around a lot of video files. Most webmail providers now allow thousands of megabytes so space shouldn't be a problem.

If you want to use a mail program (we do!), you need to figure out which mail servers it uses for sending and receiving mail, choose a program (download it if you don't already have it), and set it up. This section walks you through the process.

Mail servers galore

If you use a mail program to read your email, you have to tell it about your mail servers:

- ✔ Your *incoming mail server* holds your mail until your mail program picks it up. The usual way to pick up mail is known as *POP* (Post Office Protocol, sometimes also written as *POP3* because it's version 3). All ISPs (Internet Service Providers) offer POP as one way to receive your mail. Most also offer IMAP, described in the sidebar "IMAP: Mail anywhere and everywhere."

- ✔ Your *outgoing mail server* (or *SMTP server*, for the badly misnamed Simple Mail Transfer Protocol) is where your mail program sends messages.

Write the names of your incoming (POP or IMAP) and outgoing (SMTP) mail servers in Table 8-1. If you don't know what to write, ask your ISP or whichever organization hosts your email mailbox. With luck, your mail program has the server names set automatically, but when the setup gets screwed up, you'll be glad that you know how to restore its settings.

Here are the servers that Gmail and Outlook.com use:

- ✓ Gmail's POP server: pop.gmail.com, port 995
- ✓ Gmail's SMTP server: smtp.gmail.com, port 587
- ✓ Outlook.com's POP server: pop3.live.com, port 995
- ✓ Outlook.com's SMTP server: smtp.live.com, port 587

Some popular mail programs

You can easily make a specific email program do what you want — after all, dealing with mail is what these programs are for. Popular email programs include:

- ✓ **Outlook:** Organizations use Outlook, which comes with most editions of Microsoft Office. (It's not the same as Outlook.com, the webmail service, or Outlook Express, the mail program that used to come with Windows.) It's helpful in organizations because it connects to Microsoft Exchange servers and provides email, shared calendars, and other features that are useful in offices. See *Outlook 2013 For Dummies,* by Bill Dyszel (John Wiley & Sons, Inc.).

- ✓ **Apple Mail:** Macs come with the creatively named Apple Mail. It's not bad, and has the advantage of already being there on your Mac. If your mail system uses Microsoft Exchange, it's one of the few alternatives to Outlook.

- ✓ **Mail app on your phone or tablet:** Yes, those Mail or Email apps on your favorite handheld device are also mail programs.

- ✓ **Thunderbird:** Our favorite, but not actually that popular with the rest of the world. Thunderbird comes from the same people who make Firefox, an excellent free web browser we describe in Chapter 7. It works with regular Internet accounts as well as with some webmail accounts. You can download Thunderbird from `www.mozillamessaging.com/thunderbird`.

Follow the instructions in the following sections to get your mail program up and running. Later sections describe how to send and receive mail with Outlook and Apple Mail (we described phone and tablet mail programs earlier in the chapter).

Setting up Outlook

Outlook comes with most editions of Microsoft Office or you can buy it separately. If you're using Outlook at your office, check with your information technology support folks to set up Outlook.

If you use Windows, to tell Outlook about your email account, follow these steps:

1. **Choose File⇨Info⇨Account Settings⇨Account Settings.**

   You see the Account Settings dialog box.

2. **On the E-mail tab click New.**

   You see the Add New Account dialog box.

3. **Choose E-mail Account and click Next.**

   You see yet another Add New Account dialog box.

4. **Fill in your name, your email address, and your email password. Click Next.**

   Outlook tries to guess based on your email address what your incoming and outgoing mail servers are. If it succeeds, skip to Step 6.

5. **If Outlook can't guess, it'll tell you so. Click Next to try again and if you are still out of luck, select the Manually Configure Server Settings checkbox and click Next again. Enter the server names from Table 8-1 and answer any other questions it might have.**

   Choose Internet E-mail for the service and POP3 for the Account Type. Refer to Table 8-1 for the information you collected about your account.

6. **Click Next and Finish.**

Outlook now retrieves any messages and displays them in your Inbox folder. If you have trouble setting up an account, contact your ISP, employer, or whoever hosts your mail account and ask them to talk you through it; there may be organization-specific settings.

On a Mac, choose Tools⇨Accounts to display the Accounts dialog box. Click the + button in the lower left corner and choose E-mail to add an account. First you enter your email address and password, and if Outlook doesn't recognize the mail server, it asks you to enter them from Table 8-1.

Setting up Apple Mail

Apple Mail comes on your Mac and may appear as just Mail or Mail.app. To set it up, follow these steps:

1. **Start Apple Mail by clicking the Applications icon on the Dock and clicking Mail or Mail.app.**

   Or click its icon on the dock – it looks like a postage stamp. The first time you run Mail, it asks for information about your mail account.

2. **Choose your mail server.**

   If you use Gmail, choose Google. If you don't see yours choose Add Other Mail Account.

3. **Type your information, copying the information from Table 8-1, clicking Continue or Create to move to the next step.**

   If you chose Add Other Mail Account, you need to enter your incoming and outgoing mail server names from Table 8-1. When you're done, you see your new account in the Mail window.

If you need to change your email account information later or set up Apple Mail to work with a different email account, choose Mail⇨Preferences and click the Accounts tab.

The Mail window looks like the one shown in Figure 8-4. A list of the messages in your Inbox is on the left and the text of the selected message is on the right. You can add a list of your mailboxes by choosing View⇨Show Mailbox List or pressing Command-Shift-M

Figure 8-4: Apple Mail displays your messages to the left and the selected message to the right.

Sending Mail Is Easy

Whether you use an email program or webmail, sending messages is easy enough that we show you a few examples rather than waste time explaining the theory. It works much the same way in all email programs.

Follow these steps to write an email message and send it off:

1. **Click the Write, New, or New Message icon or button.**

   A window (either the Compose or New Message window) opens. In webmail, your composition area appears in the web browser.

2. **Fill in the recipient's address (or recipients' addresses) in the To box.**

   You can send this message to more than one person at a time by entering more than one To address. This feature works a little differently in different programs. In Apple Mail, type a comma between the addresses. In Outlook, type a comma or semicolon between addresses.

   Remembering people's email addresses is annoying (or, for those of us at a Certain Age, just plain impossible). See the section in Chapter 9 about keeping track of your friends to find out how to add people to your address book and use it when sending messages.

3. **Add any Cc or Bcc addresses that you want the messages to go to.**

   See the later sidebar "CC and BCC" if you're wondering what we're talking about. In Outlook, enter addresses in the appropriate To or Cc box. In Apple Mail, use the Cc box.

4. **Type the subject in the Subject box.**

   Make it specific. If you want help, don't type Help! as the subject. Type **Need help getting my cat not to spit out his pills**.

   Press Tab to move to the message box.

5. **Type the message in the big box.**

   The cursor should be blinking in the *message area,* the large, empty box where you type the message.

6. **Click the Send icon or button to send the message.**

Spell-checking your message is a good idea; avoid the embarrassment of spotting your typos only after it's too late to fix them. You can ask your mail program to check the spelling in your message before you send it. Click the Spell icon to see which typos your program finds. In Outlook, press F7 or choose Tools⇨Spelling and Grammar; in Apple Mail, choose Edit⇨Spelling and Grammar⇨Check Spelling.

CC and BCC

The term *carbon copy* should be familiar to those of you who were born before 1965 and remember the ancient practice of putting sheets of carbon-coated paper between sheets of regular paper to make extra copies when using a typewriter. (Please don't ask us what a typewriter is.) In email, a *carbon copy* is simply a copy of the message you send. All recipients, on both the To and Cc lines, see who's receiving the message — unless a recipient's email address is typed in the BCC field instead. *Blind carbon copies* (BCCs) are copies sent to people without putting their names on the message so that the other recipients are none the wiser. You can figure out why you may want to send a copy to someone but not want everyone to know that you sent it.

If you want to send a message to a bunch of people without telling anyone who else got the message, send it to yourself, and put all the recipients in the BCC field. Actually, this is a good idea whenever you send a message to a lot of people, because it doesn't reveal all your correspondents' addresses to one another.

After your mail program sends a piece of email to the outgoing mail server, you can't cancel it! Check for misspellings or peculiar autocorrect errors.

Mail Coming Your Way

If you send email, and in most cases even if you don't, you most likely receive it also. The arrival of email is always exciting, even when you receive 200 messages a day. (It's exciting in a depressing kind of way, sometimes.)

A helpful feature of mail programs (not webmail) is that you can compose messages while you're offline. On the other hand, when you want to check your mailbox for your most current messages, you have to connect to the Internet. Webmail users have to be online to do anything. (That's not quite true: Gmail can do some work in your browser while offline.)

Reading your messages

To check your email in almost any email program, follow these steps:

1. **Start your email program, if it isn't already running.**

   If you use webmail, start your web browser and go to your webmail website.

2. **If your program doesn't retrieve mail automatically, click the Get Mail, Sync, or Send/Receive button on the toolbar to retrieve your mail.**

   If you have a full-time Internet connection, your mail program may retrieve your mail automatically, in which case you only have to start the program to fetch your mail. In addition, if you leave your mail program running, even hidden at the bottom of your screen as an icon, it may automatically check for new mail every once in a while. Mail programs can even pick up mail while you're reading or sending other messages.

   The program may play a tune or display a message when you receive messages. The mail appears in your inbox (usually in a window or folder named In or Inbox), showing one line per message. If you don't see it, double-click the In or Inbox mailbox in the list of mailboxes that usually appears on the left side of the window.

3. **To see a message, double-click the line or click the line and press Enter.**

   You see the text of the message, along with buttons for replying, forwarding, and deleting the message. Figure 8-5 shows an email message as it appears on the iPhone.

4. **To stop looking at a message, click the Close (X) button in the upper-right corner of the message window (the standard way to get rid of a window) or press Ctrl+W or Ctrl+F4.**

   On a Mac, click the red Done button in the upper-left corner.

Figure 8-5: The iPhone displays an email message.

One-click surfing

Most email programs display web addresses as links. That is, if the text of a message includes a web address (such as `http://net. gurus.org`), the address appears underlined and perhaps in blue. Just click the link to display the page in your browser.

When you send messages, you don't have to do anything special to display a web address as a link — the recipient's mail program should do it automatically.

Deleting messages the quick-and-easy way

You don't have to read every single message before you delete it; sometimes, you can guess from the sender's name or the Subject line that reading the message would be a waste of time. If you subscribe to email mailing lists or newsletters, certain topics may not interest you. And, of course, you may receive messages that are obvious spam.

Buttons on the email program's toolbar at the top of its window let you dispose of your mail. First, click once to highlight the message. Then (in most mail programs) click the Trash or Delete button on the toolbar to discard the message.

In webmail, on the web page that displays messages, is a Delete button of some sort. Some webmail systems have a check box next to every message in your inbox folder and a Delete button at the bottom of the list. To delete a bunch of messages, select their check boxes and then click Delete.

When you delete a message, most email programs don't throw it away immediately. Instead, they file the message in your Trash or Deleted Messages mailbox or mail folder or just mark it as deleted. From time to time (usually whenever you close the email program), the program empties your trash, truly deleting the messages. Until then, you can undelete it if you deleted it by mistake.

To Whom Do I Write?

As you probably have figured out, one teensy detail is keeping you from sending email to all your friends: You don't know their addresses. In this chapter, you find out lots of different ways to look for addresses. Start out with the easiest, most reliable way to find out people's email addresses:

Call them on the phone and ask them.

Pretty low-tech, huh? For some reason, this technique seems to be absolutely the last thing people want to do. (See the nearby sidebar "Top ten reasons *not* to call someone to find an email address.") Try it first. If you know or can find out the phone number, this method is much easier than any of the others.

Another approach is to go to a search engine, such as Google (`www.google.com`) or Bing (`www.bing.com`), and type the person's full name, enclosed in quotes. You see a list of pages that include the name — of course, many people may have the same name if your friend is named Allen Johnson or Bob Smith. Or, try Yahoo! People Search at `people.yahoo.com`, which enables you to search by name and state. Try searching for your own name and see what you find!

If you're in contact with someone by way of Facebook or another social networking site (described in Chapter 10), you can send them messages through that site to ask for an email address.

Top ten reasons *not* to call someone to find an email address

10. You want to surprise a long-lost friend.

9. You want to surprise a long-lost *ex*-friend who owes you a large amount of money and thinks that she has given you the slip.

8. Your friend doesn't speak English. (That happens — a majority of email users are outside the United States.)

7. You don't — or your friend doesn't — even speak. (That happens, too — networks offer a uniquely friendly place for most people with handicaps; nobody has to know or care whether someone has a disability.)

6. It's 3 A.M. and you need to send a message right now or else you'll never get to sleep.

5. You don't know the phone number, and, because of an unfortunate childhood experience, you have a deathly fear of calling directory assistance.

4. The pay phone takes only quarters; nobody around can break your $100 bill.

3. Your company has installed a new phone system, no one has figured out how to use it, and no matter what you dial, you always end up with Dial-a-Prayer.

2. You inadvertently spilled an entire can of soda into the phone and can't wait for it to dry out to make the call.

1. You called yesterday, didn't write down the answer, and forgot it. Oops.

Avoiding Viruses, Malware, and Other Mailborne Annoyances

A virus or another type of malware arrives on your computer as an attachment to an email message. (Refer to the section in Chapter 2 about viruses and malware arriving by email for a description of how viruses work.) In most mail programs, programs contained in attachments don't run until you click them — so *don't* open programs that come from people you don't know. Don't even open attachments from people you *do* know if you weren't expecting to receive them. Many successful viruses replicate themselves by sending copies of themselves to the first 50 people in an address book, so a message that appears to be from a friend is actually from a virus in the friend's computer.

It used to be that only an attachment that looked like a program (for example, a file with the filename extension .com or .exe) could contain a virus. Then the bad guys (aided by software written without security in mind) came up with ways to hide viruses in ZIP files (which Windows calls Compressed Folders), word processing documents, PDF files (print-ready formatted documents), and even pictures. Bad guys can also hide malware in web pages (more of a problem if you use Internet Explorer than other browsers), so if you receive an unexpected message with a link, think twice before clicking on it.

One-click surfing, but no phishing

Most email programs convert URLs (website addresses) in your email messages into links to the actual websites. You don't have to type these addresses into your browser. All you have to do is click the highlighted link in the email message and — poof — your browser opens and you're at the website. If your email program has this feature (all programs mentioned in this chapter do), URLs in email messages appear underlined and in blue — a nice feature.

Unfortunately, this feature is abused by phishers. *Phishing* is sending faked email that claims to be from your bank, store, delivery service, or another official organization to trick you into revealing personal information, and we describe it in Chapter 2. If you click one of these links and it opens a website that asks for a password or credit card number or the like, don't give it any information!

Most webmail and email programs have phish detection features. The features aren't perfect, but if either one says that a link looks phishy, you probably shouldn't click it.

Chapter 9

Putting Your Mail in Its Place

● ●

● ●

*A*fter you get used to using email, you start sending and receiving enough messages that you had better keep it organized. This chapter describes how to delete, reply to, forward, and file messages in webmail systems such as Gmail and Outlook.com, smartphones and tablets, Outlook (which comes with Microsoft Office), and Apple Mail (which comes with Mac OS X). Refer to Chapter 8 to find out how to get started using these programs.

After you read (or decide not to read) an email message, you can deal with it in a number of ways, much the same as with paper mail. Here are your usual choices:

✔ Throw it away (as described in Chapter 8).

✔ Mark it as spam so that your program and sometimes your mail provider can learn to identify spam before you even have to see it.

✔ Reply to it.

✔ Forward it to other people.

✔ File it.

You can do any or all of these things with any message. If you don't tell your mail program what to do with a message, it usually stays in your mailbox for later perusal.

A Few Words from the Etiquette Ladies

Sadly, the Great Ladies of Etiquette, such as Emily Post and Amy Vanderbilt, died before the invention of email. Here's what they may have suggested about what to say and, more important, what *not* to say in email.

Email is a funny hybrid, something between a phone call (or voice mail) and a letter. On one hand, it's quick and usually informal; on the other hand, because email is written rather than spoken, you don't see a person's facial expressions or hear her tone of voice.

A few words of advice:

- ✔ When you send a message, watch the tone of your language.

- ✔ Don't use all capital letters — it looks like you're SHOUTING.

- ✔ If someone sends you an incredibly obnoxious and offensive message, as likely as not it's a mistake or a joke gone awry. In particular, be on the lookout for failed sarcasm. Even if it wasn't, replying is rarely a good idea as we will see next.

Flame off!

Pointless and excessive outrage in email is so common that it has a name of its own: *flaming*. Don't flame. It makes you look like a jerk.

When you receive a message so offensive that you just *have* to reply, stick it back in your inbox for a while and wait until after lunch. Then . . . don't flame back. The sender probably didn't realize how the message would look. In about 30 years of using email, we can testify that we have never, ever, regretted *not* sending an angry message (although we *have* regretted sending a few — ouch).

When you're sending email, keep in mind that the person reading it will have no idea what you *intended* to say — just what you *did* say. Subtle sarcasm and irony are almost impossible to use in email and usually come across as annoying or dumb instead. (If you're an extremely superb writer, you can disregard this advice — but don't say that we didn't warn you.)

Another possibility to keep in the back of your mind is that it's technically easy to forge email return addresses. If you receive a totally off-the-wall message that seems out of character for the person who sent it, somebody else may have forged it as a prank. (No, we don't tell you how to forge email. How dumb do you think we are?)

Smile!

A *smiley* or an *emoticon* such as : -) means "This is a joke." (Try tilting your head to the left if you don't see why it's a smile.) In some communities, <g> or <grin> serves the same purpose. Here's a typical example:

```
People who don't believe that we are all part of a warm,
caring community who love and support each other are no
better than rabid dogs and should be hunted down and shot.
:-)
```

In our experience, any joke that needs a smiley probably wasn't worth making, but tastes differ. For more guidance about online etiquette, see our net.gurus.org/netiquette web page.

BTW, what does IMHO mean? RTFM!

Email users are often lazy typists, and abbreviations are common. Here are some of the most widely used:

Abbreviation	What It Means
AFAIK	As far as I know
BTW	By the way
DR	Didn't read — write something shorter next time
FWIW	For what it's worth
IANAL	I am not a lawyer, (but. . . .)
IMHO	In my humble opinion
LOL	Laugh out loud (*not* lots of love)
ROTFL	Rolling on the floor laughing (or ROFL)
RSN	Real soon now (that is, any time in the next century)
RTFM	Read the manual — you could have and should have looked it up yourself
TIA	Thanks in advance
TL;DR	Too long; didn't read — write something shorter next time
YMMV	Your mileage may vary

Spam: Kill, Kill, Kill!

Spam, unsolicited and unwanted bulk mail, is a scourge on the Internet. By most measures, upward of 90 percent of all mail is spam, which means that your mail provider has to filter out ten spam messages for every message it delivers. Spam filters work pretty well, but they aren't perfect. Here are some suggestions about how to make your mail's filtering closer to perfect.

Because nothing is perfect, be sure to check your spam folder from time to time to look for "ham" – good messages classified erroneously as spam.

Filtering spam in webmail

Webmail systems try to identify spam and move it to a Junk or Spam folder.

- ✔ **Gmail** separates your mail into Primary (mail that's actually for you), Social (notifications from sites like Facebook), and Promotions (ads, as shown in Figure 9-1). Take a look in these folders or tabs from time to time to look for any real messages that might accidentally have gotten marked as spam. It also has a spam folder for mail it thinks is plain spam.

- ✔ **Outlook.com** has a Junk folder in the list of folders down the left-hand side of the web page.

Figure 9-1: Gmail separates your incoming email into Primary, Social, and Promotions (ads).

If you see spam messages in your incoming mail, you can mark them as spam, which helps the webmail service identify this type of message in the future. From the list of messages, select the message and click the Spam, Report Spam, or Junk icon or link. If you find misfiled real mail in your junk folder, you can usually click a Not Junk or similar icon to "unreport" it.

Outlook.com has a Sweep option that can delete all the messages in your inbox that are from a specific email address and block all future messages from that address.

Filtering spam on a phone or tablet

The iPhone and iPad Mail app has an easy way to move a message to your Junk folder. Click the little flag icon and choose Move to Junk. Your mail server (Gmail, Outlook.com, etc.) may also do spam filtering before the messages even hit your inbox.

The Android apps for major mail systems such as Gmail and Outlook.com all have an option to mark a message as spam or junk, either as a button or a menu option. The regular email app lets you move mail to different folders. If your mail system provides a Spam or Junk folder, move the junk there.

Filtering spam in Outlook

Outlook has a Junk Email folder into which it puts anything it thinks is spam. You can look at what's in it just as you use any other folder, by clicking it in the folder list in the left pane of the Outlook window.

When you get a spam message, right-click the message and choose Junk⇨Block Sender. Future messages from that sender will automatically move into the Junk folder.

Be sure to check your Junk Email folder every few days, in case a good message gets misfiled there. If you see a nonspam ("ham") message in your Junk folder, right-click the message and choose Junk⇨Not Junk. Or choose Junk⇨Never Block Sender to "whitelist" the sender so that no future messages from that person are considered to be spam. You can whitelist an entire domain, too, by right-clicking a message from someone at the domain and choosing Junk⇨Never Block Sender's Domain. This command can be useful if you're doing business with an organization and you want to receive mail from anyone with an address at that organization's domain.

Filtering spam in Apple Mail

Apple Mail has a simple but usable spam filter. To use it, follow these steps:

1. **Choose Mail⇨Preferences. Click the Junk Mail icon at the top of the panel.**

   You should see the Junk Mail tab in the Mail Preferences dialog box.

2. **Check Enable Junk Mail Filtering, if it isn't already checked.**

   You have your choice of leaving junk mail in your inbox marked as junk or moving it to the Junk mailbox. We suggest using the Move It to the Junk Mailbox option.

3. **Select the message types to exempt from filtering.**

   Select the box to exempt senders in your address book. Deselect the other two boxes, Previous Recipients and Messages Addressed Using Your Full Name — leaving these two boxes selected has caused plenty of junk to come our way.

4. **Select Trust Junk Mail Headers Set by My Internet Service Providers.**

   Some providers mark junk but leave it in your inbox. This option tells Mail to use the markings to recognize junk.

5. **Close the Preferences box.**

Back to You, Sam: Replying to Mail

To reply to a message, look for the Reply link or a leftward-pointing curved arrow icon that means the same thing. Pressing Ctrl+R (Command+R on the Mac) works in most mail programs, too. Some programs show a list of options that include Reply (which replies to the sender of the message), Reply All (which replies to everyone who was included on the original message), and Forward (described in the next section). Reply and Reply All create a new email message from you, preaddressed to the sender(s) and with the Subject line filled in with the subject of the original message plus something like "Re:" at the beginning. The text of the original message is included, too.

Re: That thing

Why does the subject line of an email reply usually start with "Re:"? Prepare for some High Culture: It's from the Latin "in re," meaning "in the matter of" or "about that thing." Haven't you always wondered?

After you open the reply message, ask yourself two important questions:

- ✔ **To whom does the reply go?** Look carefully at the To line, which your mail program has filled out for you. Is that the person or group you thought you were addressing? If the reply is addressed to a mailing list, did you truly intend to send a message to the entire list, or is your reply of a more personal nature, intended only for the individual who sent the message? Did you mean to reply to a group? Are all the addresses that you think you're replying to included on the To list? If the To list isn't correct, click and edit it as necessary.

  Occasionally, you may receive a message that has been sent to a zillion people and their addresses appear in dozens of lines in the To section of the message. If you reply to a message such as this one, make sure that your reply isn't addressed to the entire huge list of recipients unless that's really what you want to do.

  Some mail programs have a separate Reply All command or button that addresses your reply to the people that the message was from *and* the people who received copies of the message (the "To" people and the "Cc" people). Outlook and Apple Mail have the Reply All button on their toolbars. Webmail systems may make you choose it from a dropdown menu.

- ✔ **Do you want to include the content of the message to which you're replying?** Most mail programs include the content of the message to which you're replying, usually formatted to show that it's a *quotation* or *quoted text*. Edit the quoted text to include only the relevant material, so as not to bore or confuse the recipient with unrelated stuff. If you don't provide some context to people who receive a great deal of email, your reply makes no sense, so including part of the original message can be helpful. If you're answering a question, include the question in the response. You don't have to include the entire text, but give your reader a break. She may have read 50 messages since she sent you mail and may not have a clue what you're talking about unless you remind her.

When you have the message headers straightened out, type your message above the quoted text from the original message and click Send.

Keeping Track of Your Friends

After you begin using email, you quickly find that you have enough regular correspondents that keeping track of their email addresses is a pain. Fortunately, every popular email program provides an *address book* or *contacts list* in which you can save your friends' addresses so that you can send mail to Mom, for example, and have it automatically addressed to chairman@ exec.hq.giantcorp.com. You can also create address lists so that you can send mail to family, for example, and it goes to Mom, Dad, your brother, both sisters, and your dog, all of whom have email addresses.

All address books let you do the same things:

✔ Save in your address book the address from a message you have just read.

✔ Use addresses you have saved for outgoing messages.

✔ Edit your address book, including deleting former friends and updating addresses.

Some address books also provide space for you to store other information about your friends and coworkers.

Who's who

Click the Address Book, People, or Contacts icon or link to see your address book. Most programs open a new window for your contacts list. In most address books, you double-click a contact's name to edit the person's information and click a New or Add link or icon to add a new friend.

Here's how to add people to your address book:

✔ **Gmail:** Gmail has a separate Contacts page that you see by clicking the Gmail link in the upper left corner of the page (below the Google logo) and choosing Contacts. As least that's the way it worked in 2014; Google may redesign the Gmail page any time. Click a person's name to enter information about them. When you are reading a message from someone in Gmail, you can hover your mouse on the person's name (don't click!) to see a little box pop up that includes a Contact Info link; click that to add the person to your contacts.

✔ **Outlook.com:** Click the little down-arrow next to the Outlook.com logo in the upper left corner of the page to see a page of bold icons for the other apps you can use with your Outlook.com account. (These instructions are approximate because webmail sites change their designs all the time.) Click People to set up your address book. The People website, shown in Figure 9-2, offers to sign you up for Skype, a phone and video messaging service that Microsoft owns, but you can click No Thanks. Click New at the top of the page to add a new contact. When you are reading a message in Outlook.com, an Add to Contact link appears to the right of their name, too.

✔ **iPhone and iPad:** These devices come with a separate Contacts app that stores information about people, including their email addresses. When you are addressing an email in the Mail app, start typing a name and if you have the person in your Contacts, their name pops up. A search box at the top of the page enables you to search for people by name or email address. When you are reading an email message, you can touch the person's name in the From line to see their name and email address and add it to your contacts.

✔ **Android:** The Android address book is your Google account contacts, the same as you use if you have a Gmail account. In most places where you can enter a name or address, the app looks at your contacts and suggests ones that match what you're typing. The People app lets you edit your contacts, but John, who has large fingers, finds it easier to edit them in Gmail on his laptop, where they will automagically be synced into his Android tablet and phone.

✔ **Outlook:** Click the Contacts button in the left pane of the Outlook window or click the Address Book on the Home tab of the toolbar. You see Outlook's Contacts list, showing people alphabetically by last name. Click the New button to display a dialog box with spaces for all the information you could possibly want to store about someone. Then click Save and Close.

✔ **Apple Mail:** Apple Mail uses the Contacts program that comes with Mac OS X. Open it by clicking the book icon in your dock (or in your Applications folder if it's not in the dock). Click the + icon at the bottom of the Contacts window and choose New Contact, enter as much info as you have about the person (at least name and email address), and then click Done. When you are reading a message in Apple Mail, you can right-click a person's name and choose Add to Contacts.

Figure 9-2:
Outlook.com comes with the People website, an online address book.

Apple Mail and the iOS Mail app have a VIP feature that allows you to identify people whose email messages you'd particularly like to know about. In Apple Mail, make someone a VIP by hovering your mouse to the left of someone's name and clicking the star icon that appears. On your iPhone or iPad, open a message from the person, tap their name to display information about them, and touch Add To VIP. Now messages from your VIPs appears in a special VIP folder.

Addressing messages the easy way

Composing a message is a good time to use your address book, because who can remember all those weird email addresses your friends pick? When you're writing a new message (or replying to or forwarding a message, as described later in this chapter), here's what to do in all these systems:

1. Click the Write, New, or New Message icon or button to create a new message.

2. Start typing the person's name or email address. If they are in your address book, the system will find it and display the name or address. If more than one entry matches, you may see a list you can choose from.

Or, open the address book or contacts list, click the person to whom you want to write, and look for an envelope icon or something else that suggest sending them a missive. Clicking or double-clicking the person's email address might do it, too. (Sorry to be vague, but these services redesign their web pages so often that even veteran users have to figure things out all over again from time to time.)

Hot Potatoes: Forwarding Mail

You can forward email to someone else. It's easy. It's cheap. Forwarding is one of the best things about email and at the same time one of the worst. It's good because you can easily pass along messages to people who need to know about them. It's bad because you (not *you* personally, but, um, people around you — that's it) can just as easily send out floods of messages to recipients who would just as soon not hear *another* press release from the local Ministry of Truth or another joke that's making the rounds. Think about whether you will enhance someone's quality of life by forwarding a message to him. If a message says "Forward this to everyone you know," do everyone you know a favor and delete it instead.

Forwarding a message involves wrapping the message in a new message of your own, sort of like putting sticky notes all over a copy of it and mailing the copy and notes to someone else.

Forwarding mail is almost as easy as replying to it: Select the message and click the Forward button or link, or the right-pointing arrow. The mail program composes a message that contains the text of the message you want to forward; all you have to do is address the message, add a few snappy comments, and send it.

The Reply icon points back, or left, and the Forward icon points forward, or right, in all mail systems we know of. If there's only a Reply icon, click it and you may get a list of options that include forwarding. On the iPhone or iPad, touching the left-pointing curved arrow icon at the bottom (iPhone) or top (iPad) of the email message displays a menu from which you can choose Forward.

The text of the original message appears at the top or bottom of the message, usually formatted as quoted text and preceded by a line that specifies whom the original message was from, and when. You then get to edit the message and add your own comments.

Cold Potatoes: Saving Mail

Saving email for later reference is similar to putting potatoes in the fridge for later. (Don't knock it if you haven't tried it — day-old boiled potatoes are yummy with enough butter or sour cream.) Lots of your email is worth saving, just as lots of your paper mail is worth saving. Lots of it *isn't,* of course, but that's what the Delete icon is for.

You can save email in a couple of different ways:

✔ Save it in a folder full of messages.

✔ Print it and put it in a file cabinet with paper mail. (Spare a tree; don't use this method.)

The easiest method usually is to stick messages in a folder. Webmail and mail programs usually come with folders named In (or Inbox), Outbox, Sent, and Trash, and perhaps others. But you can also make your own folders.

People use two general approaches in filing mail: by sender and by topic. Whether you use one or the other or both is mostly a matter of taste. For filing by topic, it's entirely up to you to come up with folder names. The most difficult part is coming up with memorable names. If you aren't careful, you end up with four folders with slightly different names, each with a quarter of the messages about a particular topic.

You can save all or part of a message by copying it into a text file or word processing document. Select the text of the message by using your mouse. Press Ctrl+C (Command+C on a Mac) or choose Edit➪Copy to copy the text to the Clipboard. Switch to your word processor (or whatever program in which you want to copy the text) and press Ctrl+V (Command+V on the Mac) or choose Edit➪Paste to make the message appear where the cursor is.

Filing messages in webmail systems

Webmail systems change every time the company decides to redesign the website, but here's how the Gmail and Outlook.com worked the last time we checked.

Your folders appear in the list of folders down the left side of your browser window (Figure 9-1 shows Gmail's list). Your folders include names such as Inbox, Sent, Draft, Spam (or Junk), Archive, and Trash (or Deleted). Click a folder name to see the messages in that folder. To save a message in a folder, drag the message from the list of messages into the folder.

To create a new folder in Outlook.com, right-click (Command-click or right-click on the Mac) the Folders title at the top of the list of folders, then choose Add a New Folder.

In Gmail, rather than put mail into folders, you label it. All mail with the same label acts sort of like a folder. Click the Labels icon (which looks like a little luggage tag) and choose from the list. If you're creating a new label, click the Labels icon and choose Create New.

Filing messages on a smartphone or tablet

On an iPhone or iPad, when you are looking at a message, a Folder icon appears at the bottom (iPhone) or top (iPad) of the screen. Click it to see a list of folders to which you can move the message. On Android mail, there is a file folder icon at the top or bottom of the screen which you tap to see the list of folders. If you want to create a folder, do it on your computer.

Filing messages in Outlook

Outlook starts with a bunch of folders, including Inbox, Deleted Items, Drafts (messages you haven't sent yet), Junk Email, and Sent Items. They appear indented under your mailbox name (the name you gave when you configured Outlook for your email account; for example, Mailbox – Margy Levine Young). You can create a new folder by right-clicking the mailbox name and choosing New Folder from the menu that appears. You can also make folders within folders: Right-click *any* folder to make a folder inside it.

To move a message from one folder to another, just drag it from its current location onto the name of the folder where you want to store it.

Filing messages in Apple Mail

What other people call folders, Apple calls mailboxes. To make a new one, choose Mailbox⇨New Mailbox. You might be able to choose the location of the mailbox (on your Mac, or with the rest of the mail in your mail account). Enter the name of the new mailbox and click OK.

To move a message, click on the message in the message list and drag it to the mailbox where you want it to go.

Sending Files by Email

Back in the old days, when dinosaurs roamed the Earth, email contained only text, with no formatting. Good old Courier font was good enough for us! But nowadays, email can be as all-singing, all-dancing as web pages, with formatting, pictures, and even video. Sooner or later, someone will send you a picture you just have to see, or you will want to send a video clip of Fluffy to your new best friend in Paris. To send stuff other than text through the mail, you can *attach* a file to your message or include a link to something on the web.

Attachment can be good

When you receive an email with pictures, your mail program usually displays the pictures right in the email. When you receive a file attachment, your mail program shows the name of the file, and you can click it to open it. This happens with pictures, too, if the image format is too exotic for your mail program to display.

Too big for email

What if you need to send a file that it too large for your mail system to accept? You have a number of options:

✔ Use a file transfer website like `dropbox.com` or `WeTransfer.com` to send the file. You can upload up to 2GB of files to the website and provide your email address and the address(es) to which you want to send the file. WeTransfer sends an email message to the addresses, with instructions for downloading the file from their website. They hold onto your files for two weeks and then delete them.

✔ For video files, upload them to YouTube, Vimeo, or another video-sharing site and then email the web address of your video to your friends. Chapter 14 describes video-sharing on the web.

✔ Upload the file to your Google Drive (if you use Gmail or have a Google ID) or OneDrive (if you use Outlook.com or Hotmail.com), then share it with your friends. Chapter 17 explains how.

You can save an attached picture or file for later use; most programs let you right-click the picture and choose Save Image As to put the picture in the folder of your choice. Then you can use it just like you use any other file.

These types of files are often sent as attachments:

✔ Pictures, in image files

✔ PDF files (printable, viewable formatted documents)

✔ Programs, in executable files (no longer recommended, since malware is also sent as executable attachments)

✔ Movies, in video files

✔ Sounds, in audio files

✔ Compressed files, such as .zip files

✔ Word processing documents

 Email viruses often show up as attachments. If you receive a message with an unexpected attachment, even from someone you know, **DO NOT OPEN IT** until you check with the sender to make sure she sent it deliberately. Viruses often suck all addresses from a victim's address book so that the virus can mail itself to the victim's friends. A few kinds of attachments can't carry viruses — notably, GIF and JPG images.

Many mail systems limit the size of email messages, including attachments, to something like 4MB. Your ISP or webmail service may also place a limit on the size of your mailbox (the place on its server where your messages are stored until you pick them up). You may run into a size limit if someone sends you a truly gigantic file, such as a video file.

When you receive a picture as an attachment, it's sometimes so large that all you see in your message window is one corner of a picture that would measure about 4 feet by 6 feet if viewed in its entirely. When this happens, right-click the picture and save it as a separate file, and then view it using another program.

If you receive an attachment on your smartphone, you may want to wait to open it until you're reading the message on your computer, where you're more likely to have the program required to open the attached file.

Forming attachments

Before you send someone a file, think about whether they will be able to open it. Almost everyone can open a photo or PDF file, but not everyone has Microsoft Word or other programs needed to open document files.

To attach a file to your message, just drag the file from the Windows Explorer or Finder window and drop it on the message. Or, click the Attach, Insert, or paper clip link and choose the file to attach.

On an iPhone or iPad, you send a file from the program that handles that file. For example, to send a picture, open the Photos app and display the photo you want to send. Touch the Send icon in the lower left corner of the screen. You have a number of choices for how to send the photo, as shown in Figure 9-3; choose Mail to create an email message with the photo attached. Then address and send the message as usual. It may ask what size photo you want to send (small, medium, or large). Choose based on how important picture quality is to you for this photo, and whether you are paying for data transfer from the device.

Figure 9-3:
On an
iPhone or
iPad you
can email a
photo from
the Photos
app.

Getting attached

If you receive a message with attached files, you see the filenames at the top or bottom of the message. A paper clip may indicate that a file came along for the ride. You can double-click or touch a filename to open it and then save it where you want it.

Chapter 10

Getting Social with Facebook and Google+

A social networking site lets you easily create an online profile about yourself and browse the online profiles of other people. You can add basic information about yourself, photographs, and announcements to your personal profile. You can also use social networking sites to communicate with friends, organize events, create groups, and meet new people.

Facebook Isn't the Only Social Network

Social networking sites have become hugely popular with all kinds of people. Facebook (facebook.com) was started for college students and expanded to teenagers in general. But Facebook has now attracted a large and diverse uscr base of more than 700 million people. And the percentage of older people using social networks has increased significantly. Facebook is used by everyone from grandmothers seeking to connect with their grandchildren to coworkers sharing conversations outside of work to politicians looking to update their supporters and gain new ones.

Before Facebook's ascendance, MySpace (myspace.com) was perhaps the leading social network. In addition to facilitating connections with friends and family members, MySpace carved out a niche as a site where rock bands and other musical groups can easily market to fans. MySpace is still active, but Facebook has left it in the dust.

Enter Google with Google+ in early 2011. It's nowhere near as popular as Facebook, but it's growing. Go to plus.google.com to try it. Ello (at www.ello.co, not .com), is a non-commercial upstart.

Though Facebook, Google+, and MySpace serve the purpose of connecting users to as many people as possible for all sorts of purposes, other social networks are intended for a specific audience and purpose.

For example, LinkedIn (linkedin.com) is designed for professional networking and can be particularly useful for job searches. After you connect with your business contacts on LinkedIn, you can post news about your work, write recommendations for colleagues, and see who your contacts know at other organizations. Many people use LinkedIn to make personal connections at places where they are applying for jobs, and to stay in touch with business contacts, since you never know. One feature lets you post and answer questions. The idea is to write useful answers so that people looking for employees or contractors will see your profile and decide to contact you by way of a mutual connection.

Since their creation, these sites have been a way for people to keep in touch with contacts and reach new people, for free. (In a few cases, including LinkedIn, sites provide basic service for free and more advanced services for pay.)

Facebook is the most popular social network in the world, so we describe it in detail here. How do you decide which social network to join? Ask your friends and colleagues which networks they belong to.

Because social networking is trendy, you can find a vast number of sites, most of which will never amount to anything. Some sites are popular in specific niches or in specific countries, but if you've never heard of a site, nobody else you'd be interested in has likely heard of it, either.

Before joining a site, think of people you'd expect to find there, and search for them. If you don't find at least a few of them, the site isn't likely to interest you. Some sleazier wannabe sites scoop all the addresses out of members' address books and send invitations "from" them. So if you receive an invitation you weren't expecting, first write back to the alleged sender to see whether they intended to invite you.

Different sites have different age restrictions for users, along with rules that apply to all users regardless of age. Facebook, like most networking sites, requires users to be 13 or older, although there are a lot of younger children who lie about their age.

It's entirely possible to join several social networks — and sometimes sensible to do so. We know many people who use LinkedIn for business contacts and Facebook for everyone else. Remember that the main reason to use a social network is to stay in touch with people, so there isn't much point in joining a network unless you already know people there.

Getting Started with Facebook

The best way to discover Facebook is to set up an account. Social networking sites want to have as many users as possible, so they make it easy to join.

Facebook in your browser

Start by opening your browser and visiting `facebook.com`. You see a form requesting basic information — including name and email address — that is required to set up an account on Facebook.

When you finish signing up for a Facebook account, Facebook sends you an email asking you to confirm your registration by clicking a link in the message. If you don't click the link, after several days you can no longer use your Facebook account.

Figure 10-1 shows a typical Facebook page (okay, it's the page of one of the authors of this book), also known as a *profile*. Your page can include photos, videos, announcements, and other elements to present the Real You (or, optionally, the Fake You).

Figure 10-1:
Social
networking
sites, like
Facebook,
display
information
about you
and make
links to your
friends.

If you are creating a Facebook presence for an organization instead of a person, you can create a Facebook *page*, which has *fans* instead of *friends*.

Facebook in your pocket

As our niece once said, "Facebook isn't what you do on your computer; it's what you do on your phone." Get the Facebook app shown in Figure 10-2 from the App Store or Play Store on your iOS or Android device. Log in with the same username and password that you used when you created your account.

When you open the Facebook app on your smartphone or tablet, the News Feed appears, with news of your friends. Icons along the bottom of the screen provide access to friend requests, messages, and notifications. The More icon in the lower right corner displays a menu of other options.

Figure 10-2:
Facebook is more fun on a smartphone or tablet, because you can post from anywhere.

Expanding Your Profile

After setting up your account, Facebook invites you to add information to your profile. You also have the opportunity to upload your photograph. Photographs are optional, but they help your friends recognize you on Facebook and help distinguish your profile from those of other people with the same name.

Connecting with your friends

The whole point of social networking sites is, believe it or not, social networking. Your Facebook profile isn't complete until it includes links to lots of friends and, preferably, people you actually know. (We don't try to explain the difference between a Facebook friend and an actual friend.)

Facebook offers multiple ways for you to find other people you know on the site.

After signing up, Facebook prompts you to allow Facebook to access your email address book. Facebook can then identify people you know who are also on Facebook and with whom you may want to become friends. This feature is entirely optional; if your address book is like ours, with a lot of addresses of people you barely know, this can be a way to annoy a lot of near strangers *very quickly.*

Based on the other information you add when setting up your profile, Facebook generates a list of other Facebook users whom you might know in real life and invites you to become their Facebook friend. In our experience, it does a creepily good job of finding possible friends.

You can also use the Search bar at the top of any Facebook page to search for a friend by name or email address. If one of the people listed looks right, click the name to see their profile. You'd be amazed how many people have the same name, but you can usually identify people by photo or location.

After you see your friend's profile listed, simply click the Add Friend button to the right of her name. Before sending your friend request, you can also add a personal message. Social norms do not require you to include a personal message when making a request to someone who knows you, but if your name has changed or the person might not recognize you for another reason, it can be helpful.

After you click the Send Request button, you just sit back and wait for your friend to (if they really are your friend) accept your request.

Some people have set their privacy settings so that no Add Friend button appears; instead, a Message button appears so you can tell them how you know them.

Groups of friends

Once you have more than a couple of dozen Facebook friends, you may want to organize then into groups. For example, you could have friends that live in your town, friends from high school or college, and work colleagues. There may be times when you want to share information with specific kinds of friends – or not share it with them.

When you are looking at a friend's profile page, the Friends button appears (to show that you are already friends). You can click it to add the person to your Close Friends or Acquaintances group, which Facebook makes for you, or to a group that you create. Choose Add to Another List to make a group and add this person to the group.

Do you want the whole world to see this?

To edit your privacy settings, click the Privacy Shortcuts icon in the upper right corner of every page (it looks like a little lock) and choose See More Settings. Note that this icon may have moved or changed since we wrote this; Facebook is constantly tweaking their pages. In the Facebook app on your smartphone or tablet, click the More menu (in the lower left-hand corner of the screen as of early 2015), scroll down to Settings, touch Settings, and touch Privacy.

In the Privacy Settings and Tools window, shown in Figure 10-3, you see options to select how wide a circle of people can see your friend list or send you messages or otherwise view your information and interact with you. Every action listed on this page can be adjusted.

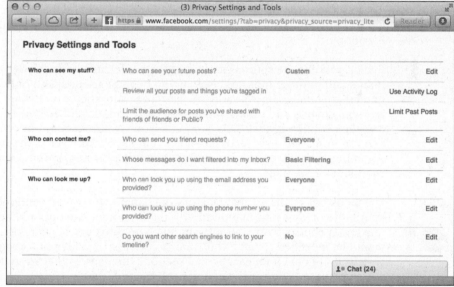

Figure 10-3: Specifying what people can see and who can connect with you.

A number of settings are available. You can

- Choose specific subsets of your friends, or specific individuals, who can see particular types of information
- Choose specific people to "hide" different types of information from
- Make some of your information visible only to you

For example, if you choose Public for the Who Can See Your Future Posts setting, your updates and certain information associated with your profile are visible to the general public. If you choose Friends, only people you've connected with directly on Facebook can see your information. You can also choose Only Me (then why post at all?), Friend Except Acquaintances, or any of the groups that you have created to organize people.

To change your choice for a privacy setting, click the Edit button to the right of setting. Options appear below the setting; make your changes and click Close to save them.

An ounce of prevention

If you take a little extra time to become familiar with the Facebook privacy settings, you can exercise a lot of control over how your profile posts, photos, and other information are seen (or not seen) by the world. But keep in mind that nothing is totally private on the Internet, particularly on Facebook.

Even if you choose settings so that only your friends can see your announcements and photographs, and even if you become friends with only your immediate family, there's sadly no guarantee that they won't share those announcements and photographs with their friends and coworkers. Neither are you guaranteed that their accounts won't be broken into or otherwise used by someone else. Also remember that Facebook itself is reading and watching *everything* you post so that it can display appropriate ads along the right side of the page.

Facebook has an unfortunate history of changing its privacy options to show ever more of your information to ever more people. The option that gives you maximum control over your information is to think before you post. If you would be mortified to have your snarky comment or silly photograph shared widely, don't post it on Facebook. Facebook themselves may even decide to use your material in ways you don't anticipate.

Don't Miss a Thing That Happens

Sharing appropriate information is what makes Facebook fun and worthwhile for millions of people. Every time you log in to your Facebook account, you see your News Feed page, with notices of what your friends are have posted, with the most recent posting at the top.

Some people log in to Facebook once a week to see whether new comments or messages are posted online. Others feel the need to update their accounts several times a day. (Perhaps these people check their voice mail every hour, too.) It's all up to you. Still others configure the Facebook app on their phone so that they get notified every time someone they know posts something.

You can receive updates from Facebook via email so that you don't need to log in to see whether anyone has sent you a message, written a comment on your profile, or otherwise interacted with you on Facebook. To change your email notification settings, click that little Privacy Settings icon again, choose See More Settings, and click the Notifications tab on the left side of the page. You can choose how to get notification (only on Facebook, via email, or by text message) and what you get notified about (updates, birthdays, and other events).

You can also get notifications on your smartphone or tablet. In the Facebook app, touch More in the lower left corner, scroll down and touch Settings, and touch Notifications. Touch Mobile Push to choose what pops up on your phone or tablet.

Updating your status

Posting status updates, photographs, and links are three especially popular ways of sharing news on Facebook. Your Facebook *status* is simply a written update from you that is displayed to your friends and on your profile. You can write a status message when you are looking at your profile page, which you go to by clicking your name in the upper left part of the Facebook page. You can also write one when you are looking at your News Feed page, which you get to by click the "F" Facebook icon in the upper left corner of the page. Either way, click in the What's On Your Mind box (underneath the Share options). The question disappears from the box and you're free to enter whatever text you want. In this box, you might write *Making chocolate chip cookies for a friend's birthday* or *Took a walk by the river today since the weather was so beautiful!*

If you are using the Facebook app on your smartphone or tablet, click the Status icon near the top of the screen to see the What's on Your Mind box.

After you click in the What's On Your Mind box, you can enter lots of things other than plain text:

✔ **A link to a web page:** Type or paste in the link to the web page you want to post, along with any comments you have about it. Don't just post a link; people want to know *why* you are posting it.

When Facebook identifies what you entered as a link, a summary of the web page you've linked to appears, usually with a little picture from the page.

✔ **A photograph or other image:** Click the little camera icon below the box where you are typing. Facebook displays a dialog box where you can choose a picture to upload. Or click the Add Photos/Video link above the box.

The Facebook app asks for permission to access the photos stored on your phone and enables you to share one or more. Another way to post a picture from your phone is to share it from your phone's photo album app.

After you write your update, paste in your link, or upload a photograph, the next step is to decide who you want to be able to share this information with. The default option is Public, which is probably not what you want. We usually set ours to Friends, so only our Facebook "friends" can see our posts.

The last step is to click Post. Your update appears on your profile and may show up in the News Feeds of your friends.

Keep in mind that just because you post an update that all your friends can see doesn't necessarily mean that all your friends will notice and read your update. Don't be surprised if you show up to a party and your friend doesn't know that you just got a new dog or walked in the park earlier that day. A Facebook user with lots of friends can't possibly keep up with everyone's updates (unless they have an extraordinary amount of free time). And Facebook has decided not to even display all your friend's updates so as to make room for their own ads, which they intersperse in your news feed. Well, Facebook is free, and someone has to pay for it. That someone turns out to be you, by sharing your personal information with advertisers and seeing their ads.

You can post on someone else's Facebook page, too. When you are looking at a friend's page, you can type into the Write Something page, or post photos or videos with the Photo/Video link.

Responding to and Arguing with Your Friends

After you have your hundreds of Facebook friends, you have lots of ways to keep up with them and to let them know what you're doing and thinking.

Keeping an eye on the News Feed

The News Feed is displayed when you log in to Facebook. If you scroll down the page, you can see posts from your friends and announcements about their activities on the site. You can also "like" those updates and comment on them. For example, if your friend posts that she has gotten a new job, you might click the Like link underneath her post, as a way of expressing congratulations. Or, you can click the Comment link and write a few sentences in response.

To see more of what's been going on in your friend's life, click her name to visit her profile. From her profile, you can read her past updates, view her photos, look at her friends, and (depending on people's privacy settings) look at her friends' pages.

You can also see on your friend's profile the Write Something box, similar to the What's On Your Mind box on your home page. If you type an update in this box, it appears on your friend's profile as a note from you to her; it's a kind of digital graffiti.

Sending messages

If you want to write a note to your friend that only she can see, send her a message. Start by visiting her profile and clicking the Message button in the upper-right corner. Facebook messages are more like texts or instant messages than like emails. You also have the option to add a photo to your message by clicking the camera icon at the bottom of the Message box.

To see your sent messages, and to read messages you have received, click the Messages link in the left-hand list of links on your News Feed page.

Hiding and unfriending

Every one of us has that friend who is fun to spend time with in real life but who continually posts random, uninteresting updates. After the fourth time in one afternoon that this person's update appears in your News Feed, you may be tempted to unfriend the poor soul, regardless of the consequences for your relationship. But there's a better way.

Click the little downward-pointing caret to the right of the person's latest post. You see several options, including the following:

- ✔ I Don't Want To See This hides this specific post and posts like it.

- ✔ Unfollow turns off all posts from this person while still remaining friends. Your friend will never know the difference. Hiding a friend doesn't limit her access to your information, but it prevents her information from popping up in your News Feed.

- ✔ Report Post sends a report to the Facebook people to complain about an inappropriate post. Facebook asks what the problem is.

But relationships end in real life, and sometimes when that happens, the online friendship also ceases. The easiest way to *unfriend* someone (so that she's no longer your Facebook friend) is to go to her profile, click the Friends button and choose Unfriend. Your former friend doesn't receive a notification. However, she may notice if she decides to check in on you sometime by visiting your profile (where she will see an Add As Friend button next to your name) or by looking for your name on her list of friends (where you will no longer be included).

Facebook galore

Facebook can take over life, but in moderation it can be a wonderful way to stay in touch with friends near a far. For more about how to use Facebook, get *Facebook For Dummies*, by Carolyn Abrams (John Wiley & Sons, Inc.)

Google Goes Social with Google+

Google+ is Google's answer to Facebook. It has many of the same features as Facebook (friends, messages, photo-sharing, and chat), but it makes it easier for you to control who can see what parts of your online material. Sign up at plus.google.com. If you use Gmail, you are already signed in. Google+ looks like Figure 10-4 — not unlike Facebook.

In Google+, you organize your friends into *circles*. When you post a comment, photo, or other information, you can choose which circles will be able to see it, as shown in Figure 10-5. This is useful when posting a message about how bored you are at work, if perhaps you don't want your work colleagues to know it.

Hangouts

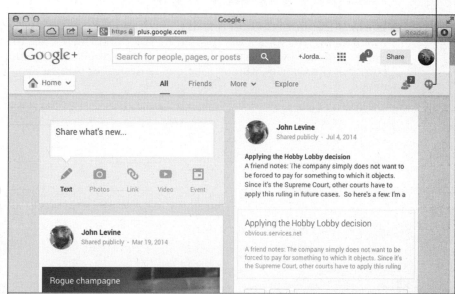

Figure 10-4:
Google+
displays a
news feed
not unlike
Facebook's.

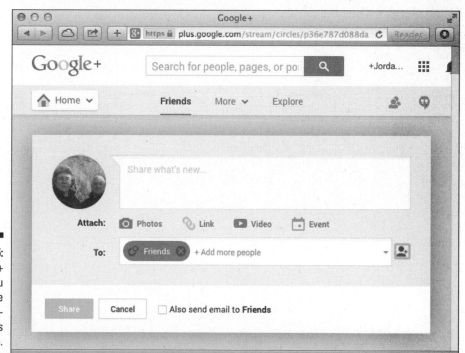

Figure 10-5:
Google+
enables you
to organize
your count-
less friends
into circles.

Hanging out on Google

The best feature of Google+ (in our humble opinions) is Google Hangouts, which allows you to talk with people via voice and video. Click the little Hangout icon, which is a double-quote icon that appears in the upper right corner of the Google+ window. Chapter 12 describes Google Hangouts in detail.

Chapter 11

Tweeting about Your Life

The Internet can let the world know the details of your life as it happens. How can you tell your friends right away that you found an outstanding purchase at the mall? Or that you have something stuck in your teeth? And how can you receive these vital messages from your friends even when you're not at home? Twitter (at www.twitter.com) is the answer. The service lets you post updates as often as you want, no matter where you are. This level of detail can, of course, be a mixed blessing. A friend of ours likens Twitter to a continuously updated Christmas letter.

When you create a free Twitter account, you create a micro-blog that allows only very short entries, no more than 140 characters each, known as *tweets*. You can send as many tweets as you want, and some people send many indeed. The simplest way is to log in to Twitter and type a line in the box at the top of the page, but you can also tweet from any of a vast number of Twitter-compatible programs, plug-ins on websites such as Facebook, as well as from your mobile phone. (See the section "Twitter on your phone or tablet," later in this chapter.)

Every user's tweets are visible on a web page; for example, President Barack Obama's tweets are visible at www.twitter.com/barackobama. Because it would be tedious to have to check every page of every person you're interested in, you can *follow* other Twitter users. Then on your Twitter home page, you see, in one chaotic list, all the tweets from everyone you're following. Twitter saves and indexes all tweets, and you can search for words and phrases to find recent tweets of interest.

Getting Started

To get started using Twitter, visit `www.twitter.com`. The website invites you to provide your name (which helps your friends find you on Twitter) as well as your password, and email address. When you click the Sign Up button, Twitter asks a few more questions and suggests a username based on the name you entered. Your username is your *handle* on Twitter, and other Twitter users refer to you by it. You can choose a username that's fun and different from your given name. In fact, unless your given name is rather unusual, you *have* to choose a different one because your username has to be different from the names of all 175 million existing Twitter accounts.

Don't forget to check the email address that you've provided during registration; Twitter sends an email to that address with a confirmation link.

Twitter in your browser

Figure 11-1 shows what Twitter looks like once you are logged in, including information about yourself, suggestions for other Twitter users that might interest you, and a series of recent tweets, most recent at the top. Remember that like all websites, Twitter may redesign its site at any moment, so it may not look or act exactly as we show and describe in this chapter.

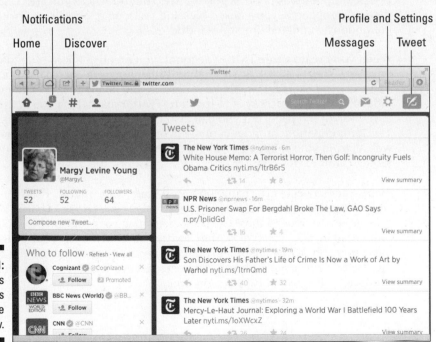

Figure 11-1: Twitter lists the tweets of people you follow.

Twitter on your phone or tablet

Web browsers are so 20th century — far too antiquated for today's modern twitterati. Mobile applications aim to make Twitter easier to use on your smartphone or tablet. They generally do not require you to use text messaging, but instead let you access Twitter by using simplified layouts designed for small screens.

Official Twitter apps are available for the iPhone (shown in Figure 11-2), Android, and other types of devices. Other apps and programs are also available if you want to monitor Twitter traffic and schedule outgoing tweets; see "Getting Serious about Twitter" at the end of this chapter.

Figure 11-2:
Reading
tweets on
the iPhone's
Twitter app.

Reading Tweets and Following Twitterers

To get started, read Twitter for a while to get the idea. Most people use Twitter to find out what's going on right now. Wait to tweet until you have the general idea and have something of interest to say. (We do a lot of reading and very, very little actual tweeting.)

Twitter can suggest what to read. *Trending* hashtags are hashtags that are very popular right now, so clicking them is a good way to find out what's current. Click the Discover icon (a hash or pound sign) on a Twitter web page to see what's trending (the list may also appear on your Twitter home page, if your screen is big enough). On a phone or tablet, brush the screen from right to left to switch to the Discover screen.

Searching the universe of tweets

You can search for people you know by entering their names into the Search box. (On a phone or tablet, you may need to click the magnifying-glass Search icon to see the Search box.) A surprising number of people and organizations use Twitter to send out announcements and updates. They range from pop stars (try username *LadyGaga*) to politicians *(SenWarren)*. Even the fictional Lord Voldemort, The Dark Lord of the Harry Potter series *(Lord_Voldemort7)*, is on Twitter.

You can also enter a keyword (such as *soccer* or *quilting*) into the Search box to find people who tweet about these subjects. Or you can click on the list of possible interests suggested by Twitter after you set up your account. For example, right after the Japanese earthquake and tsunami, you could read up-to-the-minute tweets from Japan by searching for *Japan, earthquake,* or *tsunami.* Try searching for the name or location of events in the news.

Click the Home icon in the upper left corner of the web page (or the Timeline icon at the bottom of your phone or tablet screen) to return to your Twitter home page (similar to Figure 11-1).

What's with all this weird punctuation?

As you read Twitter, you see a number of punctuation marks thrown in, apparently at random. Believe it or not, they mean something:

✔ **A hash mark (#),** (or what we still refer to as a sharp sign) appears at the beginning of a word to indicate that it's a *hashtag,* or a subject or keyword that people can search for. As you read tweets, look at their hashtags. If they appear in tweets that interest you, you can search for that hashtag to find other tweets about it.

✓ **An at-sign (@)** appears in front of someone's Twitter username. For example, mentions of the U.S. president look like *@BarackObama*.

Hey, I like this person's tweets

As you're browsing lists of twitterers, you may see a person or an organization whose tweets you want to receive. You can see a person's Twitter profile page by clicking their username. Or, go to `twitter.com/username` in your browser. If they look interesting and you want to see their future tweets, click the Follow button.

If you choose to follow a twitterer whose profile is private, she must approve your request before you can see her tweets. Otherwise, your request is approved automatically. Keep in mind that just because you're following someone doesn't necessarily mean that she's following you.

Another way to find your friends on Twitter is by using the Find Friends feature: Click the Home button in the upper left corner of the page of the Twitter web page, look at the Who To Follow list, and click Find Friends at the bottom of that list. Twitter displays a bunch of buttons for widely used webmail and social media accounts, such as AOL, Gmail, LinkedIn, and Facebook. You can click one to give Twitter access to your address book for that account and then identify people that you know on Twitter.

Twitter has a culture all of its own, but it's easier to simply watch the tweets scroll by and see the style rather than try to explain it.

How to Not Become Overwhelmed by All Those Tweets

After you read Twitter for more than about 15 minutes, you see that the volume is immense and that some of it is a lot more interesting than the rest.

Lists of your Twitter friends

When you log in to Twitter and view your home page, the Tweets section shows a list of all tweets from everyone you follow, with the tweets in reverse chronological order, most recent first. Eventually, you may be following so many other twitterers that it's hard to keep track of them all. This is when it's helpful to group Twitter accounts into lists.

For example, you may decide to have one list for your close friends, another list for your colleagues, and a third list for news organizations. The beauty of having lists is that they allow you to see all tweets from one group of people in one place.

To set up a list, go to your profile page by clicking your name on your home page, then More > Lists. You see the lists you've already created followed by a Create New List button. Choose a list name and description. You can also choose whether your list is public or private. Choose Private to make your list completely invisible to the outside world. For example, if you're setting up a list named My Real Friends, you can set that list to private so that no one else can see who is on the list, or even that the list exists. Then click Save List.

Many people enjoy creating public lists to help other people with similar interests. If you make your Favorite Mystery Authors list public, other mystery readers may come across the list and choose to follow it. If someone follows your list, your list is added to her collection of lists and she can easily visit it.

To add a twitterer to your list, visit your profile and then click the little gear-like Settings and Help icon. Click Add or Remove from Lists and select the list(s) to which you want to add them.

Saving your searches

Saved searches provide another way to sort through the avalanche of tweets and find the news you truly want. To create a search, enter one or more search terms into the Search box at the top of the page on Twitter. When viewing your search results, click the Save button in the upper-right corner. From any Twitter page, you can click in the Search box to see both your recent searches and your saved searches; select a saved search to see its latest results.

Preparing to Tweet

Reading tweets doesn't reveal much information about you to the world. But before you start tweeting, be sure to set your privacy settings, and others, to control who can see what.

Your Twitter profile

When you sign up for a Twitter account, you have the bare bones of a profile in place. But there's much more to add. To write additional information about yourself and to choose a look and feel for your profile, follow these steps:

1. **Click the Profile and Settings icon (your picture or a little gear) at the top of any Twitter web page (www.twitter.com) and choose View Profile.**

   If Twitter has redesigned its pages since we wrote this chapter, you might have to look around. And if you aren't logged in, you won't see it. Once you've located and clicked your link or icon, you see a page with your Twitter username and recent tweets (and retweets).

2. **Click the Edit Profile button on the right side of the page.**

   You see a page that looks like Figure 11-3. You can upload a photograph of yourself, upload a wide header picture to appear across the top of your page, enter your location, write a brief bio, and add the URL of your website, such as to your blog or Facebook profile. You can also change the background color of your profile. This information is available to any Twitter user, so don't include anything you'd want to keep private.

3. **Make your changes and click Save Changes.**

Figure 11-3: Fill out your Twitter profile before you start tweeting.

Private tweeting

Normally, your Twitter account is public, so anyone can view and follow your tweets. If you're one of the rare people who would rather not have every random person in the world watching what you say, click the Profile and Settings icon (your photo or a gear) in the upper right corner of any Twitter page and click Settings. Down the left side of the page is a list of the types of settings you can change. Click Security and Privacy and select the Protect My

Tweets check box to limit the visibility of your tweets to people you approve. Scroll down and click Save Changes.

Whether or not you approve someone to read your tweets, she can still see that your account exists. For example, if you follow someone, she can see you on her list of followers, along with your username, full name, photo, and bio.

How to Tweet

The simplest way to send a tweet is by visiting the Twitter home page at www.twitter.com or clicking the feather-pen Compose icon in the upper right corner of your mobile Twitter app. Type a message of 140 characters or fewer into the Compose New Tweet box and clicking the Tweet button to publish your tweet. That's it!

Be sure to proofread your tweet before publishing it. And never tweet in anger. After a tweet is out there, it's out there forever.

Hashtags identify keywords

To help people find a particular tweet, insert a *hashtag* (a word starting with the # pound sign character) into a tweet to specify that it's related to other tweets with the same topic tag. For example, include *#green* in your tweets about saving the planet.

Including a web address in your tweet

When all you want to do is share a few words, sending a tweet by way of Twitter is the simplest way. But what about when you want to include a link in your tweet?

Web addresses can be long, and tweets have to be short. What to do? Nothing, it turns out. Twitter automatically shortens nearly all URLs using their t.co shortener, so the shortened version is never more than 20 characters, no matter how long the original was. Paste a long URL into the Compose New Tweet box and see what happens.

Replying and retweeting

Figure 11-4 shows a series of tweets. Below each one are a series of icons:

✔ **Reply** (left-pointing arrow): Sometimes, you may want to reply to another user's message. If you start a message with the @ sign and the name of a user, the message is a reply to that user; clicking the Reply icon starts composing a new message with the user's username already entered for you. Or, you can insert *@user* in the middle of a tweet, as a mention. In either case, the user you reply to or mention sees your message whenever she clicks the Notifications icon (a bell, last we checked) on the Twitter home page.

✔ **Retweet** (two arrows making a square): If you see a tweet from a friend that you want to share with your own followers, go for it! Just give her credit by starting your tweet with `RT @username` and then repeating her words. Or click the Retweet button to do the same thing. Don't be shy about retweeting — people love that kind of shout-out.

✔ **Favorite** (star): If you particularly like someone's tweet, you can mark it as a Favorite by clicking the star. A star appears by the tweet, and the person who sent the tweet can see how many people "favorite" it.

Figure 11-4:
Reading,
replying
to, and
retweeting
your tweets.

If you want people to retweet your tweet, make it a little shorter than 140 characters to give them space to add "RT" and your username.

I'm talking only to you: direct messages

You can also send a *direct message* to someone, although it has to be someone who is following you. Click the Direct Messages icon (a little envelope) in the upper right corner of the page to see a list of the direct messages you've received and then click the New Message button. Type the person's Twitter username and your message. Then click the Send Message button. A direct message isn't visible to anyone else — only to the person that you sent it to.

Let's all tweet at the same time

A *tweetchat* is an event where a bunch of people tweet at the same time about the same subject using the same hashtag. It's a great way to have a public discussion on a topic. If you hear about a tweetchat, all you need to know to participate is the date and time to fire up your browser or Twitter app and the hashtag that will be included in all the tweets. At that time, search for that hashtag and follow along. If you want to chime in, reply to a tweet or compose your own tweet including the hashtag.

Getting Serious about Twitter

Twitter is so popular that many programs are available to make it simpler to send tweets, follow people, and find tweets on specific topics. Here are two:

- ✔ **HootSuite (www.hootsuite.com):** This popular Twitter application can be accessed from a browser window and used as a desktop application. You can use it to schedule a series of outgoing tweets.

- ✔ **TweetDeck (www.tweetdeck.com):** This program (provided by Twitter itself) runs on Windows and Macs (and on Google Chrome), and you can configure it to display tweets from people you follow, tweets that mention specific topics, tweets from Twitter lists, and more.

HootSuite and TweetDeck also let you view updates from your friends on Facebook, LinkedIn, and other social networks. To find more Twitter-related programs, search the web for *Twitter applications.* For more information about the Twitterverse, including the etiquette of tweeting and following, get *Twitter For Dummies*, by Laura Fitton, Anum Hussain, and Brittany Leaning (John Wiley & Sons, Inc.).

Tweets are not always what they seem

One of the best things about Twitter is that people can tweet really fast and really easily. This is usually good, but sometimes it's not so good.

Signing up for a Twitter account is very easy, and you don't have to provide anything more than a name and an email address (which of course, could be a webmail address you set up two minutes before.) So if you see tweets from someone famous, or someone you know, and they seem a little off, or totally out of character, perhaps it's someone else with an odd sense of humor.

Or it might not be someone else, it might be some*thing* else. Twitter makes it very easy to tweet automatically from other programs. Usually this is fine, as when John sends a tweet every time he adds an entry to his blog. But sometimes it's not, with tweets that are both odd and untouched by human hands.

Most tweets are fine, but as always, remember to apply common sense before reacting.

Chapter 12

Typing and Talking Online

• •

In This Chapter

▶ Typing to one friend at a time

▶ Talking to friends old and new, with a webcam

▶ Talking by telephone over the Internet

▶ Typing to a lot of friends at a time with chat rooms and mailing lists

• •

*E*mail is pretty fast, usually arriving in less than a minute. But sometimes that just isn't fast enough. Text chat or instant-message (IM) systems let you pop up a message on a friend's screen in a matter of seconds. You can also tell your messaging program the usernames of your friends and colleagues so that the program can alert you the instant that one of your buddies comes online and you can instantiate an instant message to them. (Excuse us — this topic gives us a headache. Wait just a moment while we get some instant coffee. Ahh, that's better.)

The good thing about instant messages is that you can stay in touch with people as fast as by talking to them on the phone. The bad thing about instant messages is that they also offer an unparalleled range of ways to annoy people. Use with discretion! Gregarious people can chat with a whole bunch of people at once, by either typing at the same time, like a party line, or sending messages to each other by email or web forum. Facebook Messenger is the most popular text chat system.

Of course, even better than typing messages to another person is talking right out loud. If your computer has a microphone and speakers, you can use text chat or other systems to talk to people online — even groups of people — with no toll charges. If you connect a digital video camera (or *webcam*) to your computer, your friends can even see you as you work or type. It's not hard to do! Google Hangouts, Viber, and Skype are popular options.

If you have a smart phone, don't confuse Facebook Messenger and other text chat programs with text messages; see the sidebar "Text messages vs. Internet messaging."

Text messages vs. Internet messaging (for cellphone users only)

If you have a cellphone, you may use it to send *text messages*, which are short (up to 140 characters) messages addressed to a phone number. Text messages, also called *SMS messages* (for Short Message Service), go from cell phone to cell phone and are not available on land-line phones. Depending on your contract with your cell phone carrier, you may pay for each text message, you may have a set number of free text messages per month, or you may have unlimited text messages. (If you have a teenager and don't want to go broke, choose the last option; costs per text message can be up to 25 cents for each message sent or received.)

Text messages do not require your phone to have a *data plan*, a smartphone contract feature that covers the data that goes between your smartphone and the Internet. A data plan includes all information *except* phone calls and text messages — stuff like email, reading Facebook, and watching videos on your phone.

The *text chat* programs we describe in this chapter are Internet services, so they use your data plan. They don't send or receive SMS text messages, so your cellphone company won't charge by the text for them. And they don't have the 140-character limit. But you do need a data plan to get the messages between your phone and the Internet. Smartphone and tablet apps like Google Hangouts do both Internet chat and SMS, which makes life both easier and more confusing.

Note: Some cellphone carriers enable you to email a text message to a cellphone. Okay, that's confusing, so we'll say it again slowly: You can send an email message that arrives on someone's cellphone as a text message. This feature is great for getting messages to people who don't have smartphones, but you have to know their cell phone carrier. In general you use the person's cellphone number as the username and the cellphone company's SMS gateway server as the domain. For example, someone with cellphone number 800-555-1212 on AT&T would have the email address `8005551212@txt.att.net`. For a list of SMS gateways for cellphone carriers, see `www.makeuseof.com/tag/email-to-sms`.

One-to-One Text Chat

This chapter describes how to use the most popular text chat system: Facebook Messenger, which is part of Facebook, described in Chapter 10. AIM (the initials of AOL Instant Messenger; the initials AOL used to represent America Online), iChat (which comes with Macs), and Yahoo! Messenger work similarly, and have similar features. Skype, Viber, and Google Hangouts, voice-and-video-over-Internet programs described in the section "Adding Voices and Faces," later in this chapter, also include text chat. Twitter's Direct Messages is another instant messaging system, described in Chapter 11. The sidebar "Which text chat system should I use?" helps you choose.

Chatting via Facebook

Originally, chat was part of the Facebook website and smartphone app. Then Facebook created a separate app called Facebook Messenger. When you install it, it asks to access your phone's or tablet's contacts list and send you notifications about incoming messages. Figure 12-1 shows what Facebook Messenger looks like on an iPhone.

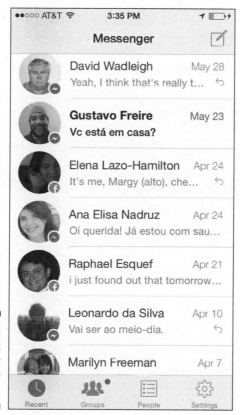

Figure 12-1: Facebook Messenger on your smartphone.

Facebook also has chat built into its website (www.facebook.com), so you can chat with any Facebook user who's online. Because Facebook users often are online just about 24/7 to fiddle with their pages and keep track of their friends, the chances of finding someone online for a chat are pretty good. In the lower-right corner of every Facebook web page is a little Chat icon showing the number of your friends who are online. Click it to see a list of potential chattees, pick a friend, and start typing. If someone chats with you, your Facebook page pops up a little chat window.

Text chat via Google

Google, the maker of Gmail (see Chapter 8), Google+ (covered in Chapter 10), and Google web search (described in Chapter 13), has built text chat into several of its websites. If you use any of these Google products, when you are looking at a message from another Google user, you may see a squarish speech bubble by their name. Click it to open a chat box, shown in Figure 12-2. Type a message and press Enter to send it. Your friend's replies appear in the same box.

Which text chat system should I use?

Unfortunately, text chat systems don't necessarily talk to one another. Because the goal of all these systems is to help you stay in touch with your friends, use whichever one they use. If you aren't sure who your friends are, Facebook Messenger is a good bet because it connects you with everyone on Facebook. AIM, Google Chat, Skype, and Yahoo! Messenger have similar features because when one adds a feature, the others tend to follow suit. All are free; support text, voice, and video; and allow more than two people to chat. (We've held meetings on Yahoo! Messenger with six people on voice and two on video and everyone typing snappy comments at the same time.) New messaging systems are appearing even as we update this book; consider WhatsApp (www.whatsapp.com, for smartphones only), Line (www.line.me), which originated in Japan; Viber (www.viber.com, described later in this chapter); and Telegram (www.telegram.org), an open-source messaging system with encryption.

Google Chat is based on an open standard known as XMPP (if you like acronyms) or Jabber (if you like names you can pronounce).

All Jabber systems can talk to each other, so if you know someone on a company or school or other Jabber account, you can talk to them with Google Chat. For example, Margy's work uses a private messaging system (HipChat) based on Jabber, and she can see her work messages on any chat program that supports Jabber.

The bottom line: Use whichever system your friends use. If you're message-mad or you have friends on more than one system, you can run more than one messaging program at the same time. Better yet, use a program that speaks all three IM languages. We know of and like three (all are free): Pidgin (www.pidgin.im), Adium (www.adium.im, the Mac version of Pidgin), and Trillian (www.trillian.im), simultaneously handle every IM system we've ever heard of. Trillian requires that you set up an account with it (separate from the accounts on the IM systems you're using) and tries to install a bunch of extra applications and toolbars when you install it; just say No. The pro version has more features for $20. Pidgin and Adium are plain old-fashioned freeware — no ads, no registration, no begging.

Figure 12-2:
When
you see
a speech
bubble next
to some-
one's name
in Gmail,
click it to
open a chat
box.

Abbreviations and Smileys for Chat

Typing is much slower than talking, so when people chat online, they tend to abbreviate wildly. Many chat abbreviations are the same as those used in email. Because text chat is live, however, some are unique. We also list some common *emoticons* (sometimes called *smileys*) — funky combinations of punctuation used to depict the emotional inflection of the sender. If at first you can't determine the meaning, try tilting your head to the left. Table 12-1 shows you a short list of chat abbreviations and emoticons.

Table 12-1		IM and Chat Shorthand	
Abbreviation	*What It Means*	*Abbreviation*	*What It Means*
AFK	Away from keyboard	RL	Real life (opposite of RP)
A/S/L	Age/sex/location (sample response: 35/f/LA)	ROTFL	Rolling on the floor laughing
BAK	Back at keyboard	RP	Role playing (acting out a character)

(continued)

Table 12-1 *(continued)*

Abbreviation	What It Means	Abbreviation	What It Means
BBL	Be back later	TL;DR	Too long; didn't read (followed by a summary)
BRB	Be right back	TTFN	Ta-ta for now!
CYBER	A chat conversation of a prurient nature (short for *cybersex*)	WB	Welcome back
IC	In character (playing a role)	:) or :-)	Smiling
IGGIE	To set the Ignore feature, as in "I've iggied Smart Mouth Sam"	;)	Winking
IM	Instant message	{{{{bob}}}}	Hugs for Bob
J/K	Just kidding	:(or :-(	Frowning
LTNS	Long time no see	:'(	Crying
LOL	Laughing out loud	O:)	Angel
NP	No problem	}:>	Devil
OOC	Out of character (an RL aside during RP)	:P	Sticking out tongue
PM	Private message (same as IM)	<----	Action marker that appears before a phrase indicating what you're doing (<----eating pizza, for example)
WTF?	What the heck?	*** or XOX	Kisses

Some chat programs convert these series of characters into little graphics, while others just show the text, but either way, the meaning should be clear. In addition to using the abbreviations in the table, chatters sometimes use simple shorthand abbreviations, as in If u cn rd ths ur rdy 2 chat. And don't forget your online manners, described in the sidebar "Some obvious rules of messaging conduct."

Some obvious rules of messaging conduct

Sending someone a text chat message is the online equivalent of walking up to someone on the street and starting a conversation. If it's someone you know, it's one thing; if not, it's usually an intrusion.

Unless you have a good reason to expect that the other person will welcome your message, don't send messages to people you don't know who haven't invited you to do so. Don't say anything that you wouldn't say in an analogous situation on the street.

Most text chat programs allow you to send and receive files. Unsolicited files from people you don't know are always spam or viruses, or both.

Most virus checkers don't monitor file transfers via messaging programs.

The messages you send with chat programs may appear to be ephemeral, but anyone in the conversation can easily store the messages. Most programs have a log feature that saves the series of messages in a text file, which may be embarrassing later.

Finally, if someone tells you to give a series of commands or to download and install a program, don't do it. And never tell anyone any of your passwords. Some chat systems, including Facebook Messenger, enable you to report anyone who sends abusive or criminal messages.

Adding Voices and Faces

If you don't want to talk with or see people while you chat — that is, if you don't mind being limited to typing back and forth with your friends — skip this section. If you want the audiovisual goodies, read on.

Google Hangout is the Google+ audio and video chat system. We also describe Viber, an up-and-coming app for smartphones, and Skype. Voice quality over most Internet connections is quite good, much better than that of a normal phone. The video ranges from poor to good, depending on the speed of the computer at each end and the speed of the Internet connection between them.

Say what? Hooking up the sound

Almost every computer comes with speakers that produce the various noises that your programs make. All Mac laptops and many Windows laptops have built-in microphones, and most desktop computers also have jacks for microphones, or a microphone built right into the monitor. (Check your computer manual or ask almost any teenager for help with this topic.)

If you don't have a microphone, you can get one that works with almost any computer. A mike should cost less than $20 at your local computer or office supply store. While you're there, also check the prices on computer headsets that have both headphones and a mike, because both you and the people you're talking to will sound much better over a headset than on the computer's built-in speakers. If you're thinking of getting a webcam (see the next section), many of them include microphones.

To test your mike and speakers on a Windows machine, run the Sound Recorder program; try recording yourself and playing it back:

1. **Choose Start⇨All Programs⇨Accessories⇨Entertainment⇨Sound Recorder or Start⇨All Programs⇨Accessories⇨Sound Recorder.**

2. **Click the red Record button to start recording, and click the square Stop button to stop.**

   Talk or sing or make other noises between your Start and Stop clicks.

3. **Click the triangular Play button to hear what you just recorded.**

   Click Record again to add to the end of your recording. Choose File⇨New to start over and throw away the sound you recorded.

4. **Choose File⇨Save to save it as a WAV (audio) file.**

   We like to make WAV recordings of our kids saying silly things and then email them (the recordings, not the kids) to their grandparents.

You can adjust the volume of your microphone (for the sound coming into the computer) and your speakers or headphones (for the sound coming out) by choosing Start⇨All Programs⇨Accessories⇨Entertainment⇨Volume Control or clicking the Volume Control icon on the right side of the Windows taskbar. If a volume control for your microphone doesn't appear, choose Options⇨Properties, select the Microsoft check box so that a check mark appears, and click OK. Or, the audio system on your computer may come with its own controls.

If you can record yourself and hear the recording when you play it back, you're ready for Internet-based phone calls or chats!

If you want to test how voices from the Internet sound on your computer, type the URL http://net.gurus.org/ngc.wav into your browser and see what happens. You may need to click an Open or Open with Default Application button after the sound downloads. (Yes, that's John's bass voice.)

I see you!

If you want other people to be able to see you during online conversations, consider installing a *webcam*. This small digital video camera can connect to a computer. Most laptops have built-in webcams above their screens; otherwise, you have to buy one. Webcams come in many sizes and shapes, and prices run from $30 to $100. More expensive webcams send higher-quality images at higher speeds and are supplied with better software. On the other hand, we've had great luck with a $36 webcam for chatting with friends and participating in videoconferences.

Most external webcams connect to your computer's USB port, a little rectangular plug on the back or side of the computer. Some cameras connect to special video-capture cards, which you have to open your (non-laptop) computer to install.

If you own a digital video camera for taking video of your family and friends, you may be able to connect it to your computer for use as a webcam. Check the manual that came with the camera.

Many webcam-related sites are, um, not, shall we say, family friendly. If you want to test your webcam with a total stranger, don't be surprised to see parts of the stranger that you wouldn't normally see.

Hanging out in Google Hangouts

If you have a Google ID (or use Gmail), you can use Google+ (Google's social networking site, described in Chapter 10) to open Google Hangouts' window. Point your browser at plus.google.com, log in if you aren't already (using your Google ID or Gmail address), and click the little double-quote icon in the upper right corner of the Google+ page. (Remember that Google may have redesigned this page since we wrote this, so look around for icons or links if need be.) You'll see an offer to start a new hangout, something like Start a Video Hangout. Click it (even if you don't plan to use video).

If your computer asks whether to trust the Google Talk Plugin, it's okay; that's how Google Hangouts does voice. After a second, you'll see your own face, and a window that looks like Figure 12-3.

Click the Join button to start the hangout, and then click Invite to invite other people to the conversation. You can type their email addresses, Google IDs, or even phone numbers to invite them.

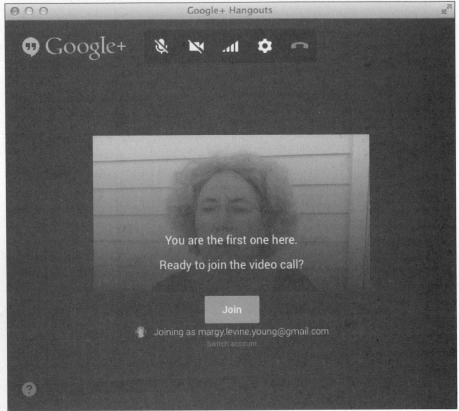

You are the first one here.

Ready to join the video call?

Join

Joining as margy.levine.young@gmail.com

Switch account

Figure 12-3:
Wanna
hang out
with Google
Hangouts?

Once you are chatting, a series of icons appear down the left side of the Google Hangouts window. (Move the mouse to the left side of the window if they don't appear.) Hover your mouse on an icon to see what it does. Click the Chat icon to start a text chat with the people in your hangout – very useful if you want to pass along web addresses or other written material. You can use the Screen Share icon to show what's on your screen to the other people in your hangout.

When you are in a video chat, if you are in a noisy place or have a microphone that picks up ambient noise, mute yourself except when you want to talk. Look for a little microphone icon and click it to mute or unmute.

Good Viber-ations

Viber is a newish voice program that runs on smartphones, Windows, and Macs. It started out as audio only, and then added video. You have to have a cellphone number to use it.

To download and install the Viber program onto your computer, visit www. viber.com, click the Get Viber or Download button, and follow the directions. (See Chapter 7 for more about how to download and install programs.) To install it on your phone, search the Apps Store or Google Play Store for "Viber".

When you run Viber the first time, you set it up:

1. **First, Viber asks whether you also have the app on your phone; if not, you can't use the system. Enter your cell phone number.**

2. **Viber sends a text message to your phone with a number.**

3. **Type the number into the Viber program on your computer, as a way to prove that the phone number is really yours.**

4. **Once you've done all that, you see the Viber window in Figure 12-4.**

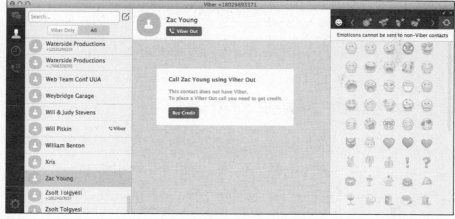

Figure 12-4: Viber shows your contacts from your computer and phone, including people who don't use Viber.

The first time you run Viber, it may already know about all your friends and coworkers, probably because it read them from the contacts list on your phone. On your Viber contacts list, you can see who else uses Viber by the purple "Viber" label. A phone number may appear under non-Viber users.

Click the name of the person you want to talk to, and then click Free Call (for a Viber-to-Viber call), Viber Out (to call their telephone number, which costs money), or Video. If you choose Viber Out, you'll have to buy Viber credit. These calls aren't free, but especially if you are calling overseas, they are a good deal.

Voice and video chat using Skype

You download and install Skype on your computer from www.skype.com. On their website, click the Download Skype or Get Skype button to download the program and install it as usual. You can also install it on your smartphone or tablet by loading the free program from the Apps Store or Google Play Store. The first time you run the program, you set up a free account with a username and password. Then you can start using the program to talk to other Skype users. Now that Microsoft owns Skype, you can log in with your Hotmail or Outlook.com address and password, too.

As with Viber, Skype isn't limited to talking to other Skype users. You can set up an account to which you add money — from a credit card or as a bonus included with certain computer headsets — and you can then call any normal phone in the world and pay by the minute. Rates are quite low, usually free for the United States and Canada, and about 2 cents per minute to Europe, and do not depend on where you're using Skype — only on where you're calling. John once called home using his laptop by way of a Wi-Fi connection in a hotel lobby in Argentina for 2 cents rather than the dollar a minute it would have cost from a pay phone. You can also use SkypeIn — a real phone number for your Skype phone so that people can call you — for a monthly fee.

Other Skype features

Skype lets you have conference calls of as many as five people and any combination of Skype users and SkypeOut calls to regular phones. It includes a text chat feature for typing with your friends while talking to them (or even when you aren't talking to them). And, it has a chat feature with SkypeMe, in which you set up a profile, set your online status to SkypeMe, and invite people to call. Skype users live all over the world, so with luck you may make some new, faraway friends.

Now You See It, Now You Don't: SnapChat

A completely different approach to chatting is to send pictures to friends – no video or text. Just in case the picture is, um, incriminating or embarrassing in some way, you can use SnapChat (www.snapchat.com), a smartphone app that enables you to take a picture with your phone, send it to a friend, and display the photo for only ten seconds before deleting it. Of course, the recipient can take a screenshot of the photo if she is quick enough (on an iPhone or iPad, press the power button and the round "belly button" at the same time to capture what's on the screen). SnapChat drives us crazy; if you want to send us a photo, either email it or text it!

Around the Virtual Town Pump

Typing or talking to a few people is fun and interesting, but for good gossip, you need a group. Fortunately, the Internet offers limitless opportunities to find like-minded people and discuss anything you can imagine. Clubs, churches, and other groups use the Internet to hold meetings. Hobbyists and fans talk about an amazing variety of topics, from knitting to *American Idol* and everything in between. People with medical problems support each other and exchange tips. You get the idea — anything that people might want to talk about is now under intense discussion somewhere on the Internet.

You can talk with groups of people on the Internet in lots of ways, including these:

- **Social networking sites,** such as Google+ and Facebook, described in Chapter 10.

- **Reddit,** a social sharing site, which we describe later in this chapter.

- **Email mailing lists,** in which you exchange messages by email.

- **Web-based message boards,** where messages appear on a web page.

- **Usenet newsgroups** (the original Internet discussion groups), which you read with a *newsreading* program. For a description of Usenet news- groups and how to read them, see our website at `http://net.gurus.org/usenet`, or go to `http://groups.google.com` on the web and search for topics that interest you.

This section tells you how to participate in Internet-based discussions using Facebook groups, Reddit, email mailing lists, and web message boards. These systems are not as instant as text chat: You post a message and, hours or days later, you receive a reply.

Participating in Facebook groups

You may already use Facebook to keep up with your friends, "like" famous people and brands, and post information about yourself. But you can also use Facebook to chat about specific topics of interest. *Facebook groups* are Facebook pages where people can post text, links, and picture about the topic of the group. Some groups are open to anyone, some require approval from the person who runs the group, and some are private.

Use the search box at the top of the Facebook page to search for topics that you'd like to discuss. You'll see a mishmash of people, organizations, and groups, so click the Groups link to narrow the list down. Click Join when you see one you like the looks of. If it's a closed group, you'll see a "Request Sent." You'll see a notification when (if) the group manager accepts your request. Figure 12-5 shows a Facebook group page.

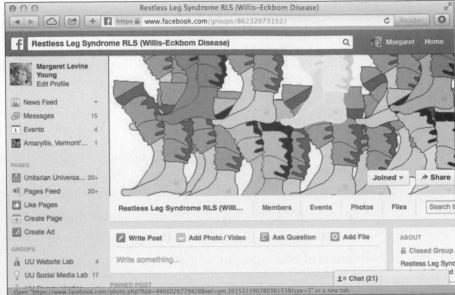

Figure 12-5: Facebook groups discuss anything and everything, from popular culture to medical issues.

You can create your own groups, too. Maybe your high school class needs a group? Or your reading or knitting group? To create a group, go to `www.facebook/browsegroups` (or click the More link next to the list of groups your are in) and click the Create Group button.

I read it on Reddit

Yes, that's why it's called "Reddit." You post a link to something interesting you saw or read on the Internet and then other people can comment on your posting, including voting the posting up or down. Comments can be upvoted or downvoted, too, so the most interesting, controversial, and funny items tend to rise to the top — literally to the top of the page.

Reddit is at `www.reddit.com`, and its home page (shown in Figure 12-6) shows the top-rated posts of the moment. But Reddit isn't one big discussion, it's thousands of *subreddits*, each on a specific topic. Along with topics you'd expect, like pets, television shows, and sports, subreddits include:

✓ **Today I Learned (TIL),** where you can post an interesting thing you learned today.

✔ **I Am A . . . (IAMA),** where you can identify yourself as a famous person or someone with an interesting talent or job, and offer to answer any question (Ask Me Anything, or AMA), sometimes for a limited amount of time.

✔ **WTF,** where people post astounding things they find on the Web.

Figure 12-6:
Reddit's home page describes itself as the front page for the Internet.

Each subreddit is its own community with its own rules, which are usually posted in the right-hand column of its pages.

Getting started on Reddit

You don't need an account to read Reddit, but an account allows you to subscribe to subreddits and to comment. Click the Login or Register link in the upper right area of the page and fill in a username and password. Include your email address so you can request a new password if you forget yours. That's all it takes.

Reddit's front page shows the top-rated postings from all the subreddits to which you are subscribed. Click the title or icon to see the original post, which can be a news story, any web page, or (frequently) an image. Click the Back button on your browser to return to Reddit. Below the title you can see how many comments the post has gotten; click that number to read the comments. When you particularly like or dislike a post or a comment, click the up-arrow or down-arrow to its left to *upvote* or *downvote* it. Reddit may not accept your vote if you are new to town; you earn Reddit *karma* by reading, commenting, and posting.

Reddit automatically subscribes you to some subreddits, just to get you started, but you can unsubscribe and find new subreddits to subscribe to. Click My Subreddits in the upper left corner to see and edit your list.

You can use the search box in the upper right corner of the Reddit page to search for topics that interest you. You see a list of the subreddits that include matching posts, and then a list of the posts themselves. Consider clicking a message that looks promising, reading it and its comments, and if you enjoy them, click the link at the top of the post to the subreddit to which the post was made. If the subreddit looks good, click the Subscribe button in the right-hand column.

Posting on Reddit

To post, click one of the links at the top of the right-hand column of the subreddit:

- **Submit a new link:** Most posts to Reddit are just links to other web pages or images on the web. You give your post a title to describe what it links to, and can choose which subreddits to post to.

- **Submit a new text post:** Some subreddits allow text posts, which are comments or questions you write yourself. You enter a title and the text of your post.

Don't try posting to Reddit right away. Browse the subreddit in which you want to post first, and be sure to read its rules. Posts that break the rules are removed by the subreddit's moderators. While most of Reddit is fairly benign, some parts are definitely Not Safe for Work, and are usually labeled "NSFW" so you won't be (too) surprised when you take a look.

Mailing lists: Are you sure that this isn't junk mail?

An email mailing list is quite different from a snail-mail mailing list. Yes, both distribute messages to the people on their lists, but the messages on most email mailing lists contain discussions among subscribers rather than junk mail and catalogs.

Here's how an email mailing list works. The list has its own, special email address, and anything someone sends to that address is sent to all people on the list. Because these people in turn often respond to the messages, the result is a running conversation. For example, if the authors of this book hosted the *chocolate-lovers* discussion about the use and abuse of chocolate, and if the list-server program ran at `lists.gurus.org`, the list of the address would be `chocolate-lovers@lists.gurus.org`. (We run a bunch of lists, but not one about chocolate. Yet.)

Different lists have different styles. Some are relatively formal, hewing closely to the official topic of the list. Others tend to go flying off into outer space, topic-wise. You have to read them for a while to be able to tell which list works which way.

Mailing lists fall into three categories:

- **Discussion:** Every subscriber can post a message. These lists lead to freewheeling discussions and can include a certain number of off-topic messages.

- **Moderated:** A moderator reviews every message before it's distributed. The moderator can stop irrelevant, redundant, or clueless postings from wasting everyone's time.

- **Announcement-only:** Only the moderator posts messages. Announcement mailing lists are essentially online newsletters.

Who handles all this mail?

Something or somebody has to take on the job of keeping track of who's on the mailing list and distributing messages to all its subscribers. This job is *way* too boring for a human being to handle, so programs usually do the job. (A few lists are still run by human beings, and we pity them!) Most lists are run by *list servers* or *mailing list managers*. Popular list manager programs include LISTSERV, Mailman, Majordomo, and many others, as well as web-based systems, such as Yahoo! Groups and Google Groups.

Talking to the human being in charge

Someone is in charge of every mailing list: the *list manager*. The list manager is in charge of helping people get on and off the list, answering questions about the list, and hosting the discussion. If you have a problem with a list, write a *nice* message to the list manager. Remember that most list managers are volunteers who sometimes eat, sleep, and work regular jobs as well as maintain mailing lists. If the reply takes longer than you want, be patient. *Don't* send cranky follow-ups — they just cheese off the list manager.

The list manager's email address is usually the same as the list address with the addition of *owner-* at the beginning or *-request* just before the @ character. For example, the manager of the list

```
chocolate-lovers@lists.gurus.org
```

would be

```
chocolate-lovers-request@lists.gurus.org
```

Getting on and off lists

To find out how to subscribe to a list, or how to unsubscribe to a list, take a look at the instructions that (with luck) accompanied whatever information you received about the mailing list. With most lists, you can subscribe, unsubscribe, and change your subscription settings from the web — you go to a web page and fill out a form. Generally, you enter your email address in a box on a web page and click either a Send or Subscribe button, and you're on the list. This strategy is often more convenient than sending a command by email.

Before you subscribe, be sure that you see a way to get *off* the list (an option that some marketing-oriented outfits neglect to provide).

You should receive a chatty, machine-generated welcoming message telling you that you have joined the list, along with a description of some commands you can use to fiddle with your mailing list membership. Usually, this message includes a request to confirm that you received this message and that it was indeed you who wanted to subscribe. Follow the instructions by clicking a link or replying to this message or doing whatever else the instructions say to do. Confirmation helps lists ensure that they aren't mailing into the void and keeps people from sticking you on lists without your knowledge. If you don't provide this confirmation, you aren't added to the list.

Save the chatty, informative welcome message that tells you about all the commands you can use when you're dealing with the list. For one thing, the message tells you how to get *off* the mailing list if it isn't to your liking. We have in our mail program a folder named Mailing Lists, in which we store the welcome messages from all the mailing lists we join, so that we don't have to embarrass ourselves by asking for help with unsubscribing later.

To remove yourself from a list, you again visit the web page for the list and follow the unsubscription instructions. Do *not* send a *Please unsubscribe me* message, because it only wastes the other subscribers' time.

Stupid mailing list tricks

Most list servers know plenty of other nonessential commands, including commands to hold your mail for a while, commands to send you a daily message that includes all postings for the day, and commands to see a subscriber list. For the exact commands, which vary depending on the list server software, refer to the instructions you received when you subscribed to the list. (You saved the welcome message, didn't you?)

Urrp! Computers digest messages!

Some mailing lists are *digested*. No, they're not dripping with digital gastric juices — they're digested more in the sense of *Reader's Digest*. All the messages over a particular period (usually a day or two) are gathered into one big message with a table of contents added at the front. Many people find this method more convenient than receiving messages separately, because you can easily look at all messages on the topic at one time.

We prefer to receive our messages individually and to tell our email program to sort our incoming messages into separate folders, one for each mailing list we subscribe to. Apple Mail, Windows Live Mail, and many other email programs can sort your messages.

Sending messages to mailing lists

Okay, you're signed up on a mailing list. Now what? First, wait a week or so to see what sort of messages arrive from the list — that way, you can get an idea of what you should or should not send to it. When you think that you have seen enough to avoid embarrassing yourself, try sending something in. That's easy: You mail a message to the list address, which is the same as the name of the list — `chocolate-lovers@lists.gurus.org` or `dandruff-l@ bluesuede.org` or whatever. Keep in mind that, because hundreds or thousands of people may be reading your pearls of wisdom, you shouldn't send anything until you have something to say, and try to spell things correctly. (You might think that this advice is obvious, but you would be sadly mistaken.) On popular lists, you may begin to get back responses within a few minutes of sending a message.

Some mailing lists have rules about who is allowed to send messages, so just because you're on the list doesn't automatically mean that any messages you send appear on the list. Some lists are *moderated:* Any message you send in is sent to a human *moderator* who decides what goes to the list and what doesn't. Although this process may sound sort of fascist, moderation can make a list about 50 times more interesting than it would be otherwise because a good moderator can filter out the boring and irrelevant messages and keep the list on track. Indeed, the people who complain the loudest about moderator censorship are usually the ones whose messages most urgently need to be filtered out.

Another rule that sometimes causes trouble is that many lists allow messages to be sent only from people whose addresses appear on the list, to prevent the list from being overrun with spam. If your mailing address changes, you have to resubscribe or else you can't post anything.

Boing!

Computer accounts are created and deleted often enough and email addresses change often enough that a large list always contains, at any given moment, addresses that are no longer valid. If you send a message to the list, your message is forwarded to these invalid addresses — and a return message (reporting a bad address) is generated for each of them. Mailing list managers (both human and computer) normally try to deflect error messages to the list owner, who can do something about them, rather than to you. As often as not, however, a persistently dumb mail system sends one of these failure messages directly to you. Just ignore it because you can't do anything about it.

Sometimes, you may see the message "I'm away on vacation" or "Click here if you're not a spammer" in response to list messages you send. *Do not respond to these messages, either —* vacation and antispam programs shouldn't even be responding to list mail. Forward the messages to the list manager, though, so that she can suspend those recipients' subscriptions until they get their software under control.

The fine points of replying to list messages

Often, you receive an interesting message from a list and want to respond to it. When you send your answer, does it go *only* to the person who sent the original message or to the *entire list?* It depends on how the list manager set up the list. About half the list managers set up their lists so that replies are sent automatically to just the person who sent the original message, on the theory that your response is likely to be of interest to only the original author. The other half set up the lists so that replies are sent to the entire list, on the theory that the list is a running public discussion. In messages coming from the list, the mailing list software automatically sets the Reply-To header line to the address to which replies should be sent. (Which way to set it up is a topic that can provoke endless, impassioned debate, so don't ever suggest that they change it.)

Fortunately, you're in charge of this feature. When you start to create a reply, your mail program should show you the address to which it's replying. If you don't like the address it's using, change it. Check the To and Cc fields to make sure that you're sending your message where you want. Don't run the risk of sending to the entire list a message such as "I agree with you — aren't the rest of these people idiots?" if you intend it for only one person.

While you're fixing the recipient's address, you may also want to fix the Subject line. After a few rounds of replies to replies to replies, the topic of discussion often wanders away from the original topic. Change the subject to better describe what is truly under discussion, as a favor to the other folks trying to follow the discussion.

How to avoid looking like a dimwit

After you subscribe to a mailing list, don't send anything to it until you read it for a week. Trust us — the list has been getting along without your insights since it began, and it can get along without them for one more week.

You can determine which topics people really discuss and the tone of the list, for example. Waiting also gives you a fair idea about which topics people are tired of. The classic newcomer gaffe is to subscribe to a list and immediately send a message asking a dumb question that isn't germane to the topic and that was beaten to death three days earlier.

The number-two newcomer gaffe is to send a message directly to the list asking to subscribe or unsubscribe. This type of message should be sent to the list manager or list server program, *not* to the list itself, where all the other subscribers can see that you screwed up.

One more thing not to do when you subscribe to a mailing list: If you don't like what another person is posting (for example, a newbie is posting blank messages or "Unsubscribe me" messages or is ranting interminably about a topic), don't waste everyone's time by posting a response on the list. The only thing more stupid than a stupid posting is a response complaining about it. Instead, email the person *privately* and ask him to stop, or email the list manager and ask that person to intervene.

Posting to message boards

Mailing lists are useful if you want to receive messages by email, but some people prefer to read messages on the web. These folks are in luck: A *message board* is a web-based discussion group that posts messages on a website. It's also known as a *discussion board, forum,* or *community.* Like mailing lists, some message boards are readable only by subscribers, some allow only subscribers to post, and some are *moderated* (that is, a moderator must approve messages before they appear on the message board). Other message boards are more similar to bulletin boards: Anyone can post at any time, and there's no continuity to the messages or feeling of community among the people who post.

Many websites include message boards. Some websites are dedicated to hosting message boards on lots of different topics. Some sites host message boards that can also send the messages to you by email, so they work as message boards and mailing lists rolled into one.

Here are some of our favorite web-based discussion sites:

- **Google Groups, at** `http://groups.google.com`: Google Groups started as a way for people to participate in Usenet newsgroups over the web. Then Google provided a way to set up new groups, too. You can search by topic for groups or messages of interest or create your own group.

- **Yahoo! Groups, at** `http://groups.yahoo.com`: Yahoo! Groups includes message boards and file libraries, and you can read the messages either on the website or by email — it's your choice when you join a group. Yahoo! Groups also features calendars for group events and real-time chats right on the website. To join, you must first sign up for a free Yahoo! ID, which also gets you a yahoo.com email address. You can also create your own Yahoo! group by clicking links — either a public group for all to join or a private group for your club or family.

Subscribing and participating

Most good message boards require you to register before you can subscribe, which means that you choose a username and password and possibly provide your email address and then respond to a message sent to that address. Registration makes it harder for spam-posting robots to take over the message board.

To subscribe to a community on this type of website, just follow the instructions on the site. Some community websites let you read messages posted to their lists without subscribing — you can click links to display the messages in your web browser.

Finding interesting online communities

Tens of thousands of communities — in the form of mailing lists or message boards or hybrids of the two — reside on the Internet, but there's no central directory of them. This is partly because so many lists are intended only for specific groups of people, such as members of the board of directors of the First Parish Church of Podunk or students in Economics 101 at Tech State.

You can find some communities by searching the web (as we describe in Chapter 13) and including the word or phrase mailing list, community, forum, or message board. Or, start at `http://groups.google.com` or `http://groups.yahoo.com` and search for your topic.

You can set up your own mailing lists or message boards, too. It's free because the sites display ads on their web pages and may even tack on ads to the postings on the list. If you have an unusual hobby, job, interest, or ailment, you may want to create a list to discuss it. Or, set up a list for a committee or family group to use for online discussions.

Look Who's Chatting

If mailing lists and message boards are too slow — if you want to chat with strangers right now — you might want to try a *chat room*, which is similar to CB radio. Chat rooms differ from the text chat described earlier in this chapter because they are public and you usually don't know the other people in the discussion.

You begin chatting by entering the *chat room*, where you can read onscreen what people are saying and then add your own comments by simply typing them and clicking Send. Although several people participating in the chat can type at the same time, every person's contribution is presented onscreen in the order it's received. Whatever people type appears in the general conversation window and is identified by screen name. On some chat systems, participants can select personal type fonts and colors for their comments.

If one of the people in a chat room seems to be someone you want to know better, you can ask to establish a *private room* or *direct connection,* which is a private conversation between you and the other person and not much different from instant messaging. And, of course, you might get this type of invitation from someone else. It isn't uncommon for someone in a chat room to be holding several direct conversations at the same time, although it's considered rude (not to mention confusing!) to overdo it.

You might also be asked to join a private chat room with several other people. We aren't quite sure just what goes on in those rooms because we've never been invited.

Where is everyone chatting?

Which groups of people you can chat with depends on which chat room system you connect to.

Many other websites include chat rooms, using a plug-in program that allows people to type at each other. Search the web for the word *chat* plus a topic that you want to talk to people about for a variety of chat venues.

Every chat room has a name; with luck, the name is an indication of what the chatters there are talking about or what they have in common. Some channels have names such as *lobby,* and the people there are probably just being sociable.

Who am I?

No matter which chat facility you use, every participant has a *screen name,* or *nickname,* often chosen to be unique, colorful, or clever and used as a mask. Chatters sometimes change their screen names. This anonymity makes a chat room a place where you need to be careful. On the other hand, one attraction of chatting is meeting new and interesting people. Many warm and wonderful friendships have evolved from a chance meeting in a chat room.

When you join a group and begin chatting, you see the screen names of the people who are already there and a window in which the current conversation often flies off the screen. If the group is friendly, somebody may even send you a welcome message.

As in real life, in a room full of strangers you're likely to encounter people you don't like much. Because it's possible to be fairly anonymous on the Internet, some people act boorish, vulgar, or crude. If you're new to chat, sooner or later you'll visit some disgusting places, although you'll find out how to avoid them and find rooms that have useful, friendly, and supportive conversations. Be extremely careful about letting children chat unsupervised (see Chapter 3). Even in chat rooms that are designed for young people and provide supervision, unwholesome goings-on can take place.

Type or talk?

The original chat rooms consisted entirely of people typing messages to each other. Newer chat systems include *voice chat* (which requires you to have a microphone and speakers on your computer) and even video (which requires a webcam if you want other people to be able to see you).

Getting used to chat culture

Your first time in a chat room can seem stupid or daunting or both. Here are some things you can do to survive your first encounters:

- Remember that when you enter a chat room, a conversation is probably already in progress. You don't know what went on before you arrived.

- Wait a minute or two to see a page full of exchanges so that you can understand some of the context before you start writing.

- Read messages for a while to figure out what's happening before sending a message to a chat group. (Reading without saying anything is known as *lurking.* When you finally venture to say something, you're *de-lurking.*) Lurking isn't necessarily a bad thing, but be aware that you might not always have the privacy you think you have.

- Some chat systems enable you to indicate people to ignore. Messages from these chatters no longer appear on your screen, although other members' replies to them appear. This strategy is usually the best way to deal with obnoxious chatters. You may also be able to set your chat program not to display the many system messages, which announce when people arrive or leave or are ejected forcefully from the chat room.

- Scroll up to see older messages if you have to, but remember that on most systems, after you scroll up, no new messages appear until you scroll back down.

Chatting etiquette isn't much different from email etiquette, and common sense is your best guide. Here are some additional chatting tips:

- The first rule of chatting is not to hurt anyone. A real person with real feelings is at the other end of the computer-chat connection. Don't insult people and don't use foul language, and don't respond to people who do.

- The second rule is to be cautious. You really have no idea who the other people are. Remember, too, that people might be people hanging out in a chat room and quietly collecting information, and you might not notice them because they never say anything. (See Chapter 2.)

- Keep your messages short and to the point.

- Create a profile with selected information about yourself. Most chat systems have provisions for creating *profiles* (personal information) that other members can access.

Don't give out your last name, phone number, or address. Extra caution is necessary for kids: A kid should never enter her age, hometown, school, last name, phone number, or address. Although you don't have to tell everything about yourself in your profile, what you do say should be truthful. The one exception is role-playing chat, where everyone is acting out a fantasy character.

  ✔ If you want to talk to someone in private, send a message saying hi, who you are, and what you want.

  ✔ If the tone of conversation in one chat room offends or bores you, try another. As in real life, you run into lots of people in chat rooms that you *don't* want to meet — and you don't have to stay there.

As in society at large, online chat involves a certain amount of contact with strangers. Most encounters are with reasonable folks. For the rest, common sense dictates that you keep your wits about you — and your private information private. See Chapter 2 for some guidelines for staying safe online.

Part IV
The Web Is Full of Cool Stuff

In this part . . .

- ✔ Find what you need on the Internet
- ✔ Play music and video on the web
- ✔ Go on an Internet shopping spree
- ✔ Manage your finances online

Chapter 13

Needles and Haystacks: Finding Almost Anything Online

"Okay, all this great stuff is out there on the Internet. How do I find it?" That's an excellent question — thanks for asking. Questions like that one are what make this country strong and vibrant. We salute you and say, "Keep asking questions!" Next question, please.

Oh, you want an *answer* to your question. Fortunately, quite a bit of stuff-finding stuff (that's a technical term) is on the web. More particularly, free services known as *search engines* and *directories* are available that cover most of the interesting material on the web. There's even a free encyclopedia, written by Internet users like you.

You can search in dozens or hundreds of different ways, depending on what you're looking for and how you prefer to search. Search can take some practice because billions of web pages are lurking out there, most of which have nothing to do with the topic you're looking for. (John has remarked that his ideal restaurant has only one item on the menu, but it's exactly what he wants. The Internet is about as far from that ideal as you can possibly imagine.)

To provide a smidgen of structure to this discussion, we describe several different sorts of searches:

- ✔ **Built-in searches:** Topic searches that a browser does automatically, which we aren't always thrilled about

- ✔ **Goods and services:** Stuff to buy or find out about, from mortgages to mouthwash

- ✔ **People:** Actual human beings whom you may want to contact, find out more about, or spy on

- ✔ **Topics:** Places, things, ideas, companies — anything you want to find out more about

To find topics, we use the various online search engines and directories, such as Google, Bing, and Yahoo!. To find people, however, we use directories of people — those are (fortunately) different from directories of web pages. If you're wondering what we're talking about, read on!

Search engine, directory — what's the difference?

When we talk about a *directory,* we mean a listing similar to an encyclopedia or a library's card catalog. (Well, similar to the computer system that *replaced* the card catalog.) A directory has named categories with entries assigned to them partly or entirely by human catalogers. You look up categories by finding one you want and seeing what it contains.

A *search engine,* on the other hand, periodically looks at every page it can find on the web, extracts keywords from them (all words except for *and* and *the* and the like), and makes a big list. (Yes, it takes a lot of computers. Google has several hundred thousand of them.) The search engine then tries to figure out which pages are most relevant, using factors such as how many other sites link to that page, and gives each page a score. You use the search engine by specifying some words that seem likely, and it finds all entries that contain that word, ranking them by their score.

We think of the index in the back of the book as a hard-copy equivalent of a search engine; it has its advantages and disadvantages, as do directories, which are more like this book's table of contents. Directories are organized better, but search engines are easier to use and more comprehensive. Directories use consistent terminology, and search engines use whichever terms the underlying web pages use. Directories contain fewer useless pages, but search engines are updated more often.

Some overlap exists between search engines and directories — Yahoo! includes a directory and a search engine; Google, which is mainly a search engine, includes a version of the Open Directory Project (ODP) directory.

Your Basic Search Strategy

When we look for topics on the Internet, we always begin with a search engine, usually Google. (The word *google* has now been "verbed," much to the dismay of the Google trademark lawyers.)

You use all search engines in more or less the same way:

1. **Start your web browser, such as Chrome, Firefox, Internet Explorer, or Safari.**

   Flip to Chapter 6 if you don't know what a browser is.

2. **Go to your favorite search engine's home page.**

   You can try one of these URLs (web addresses): www.bing.com, www.google.com, or www.yahoo.com. We list the URLs of other search sites later in this section.

   Or, just click in the Search bar in the upper-right corner of your browser window, to the right of the Address bar. (In Chrome, it's the same box.)

3. **Type some likely keywords in the Search bar (either your browser's Search bar or the Search bar that appears on the search engine's home page) and press Enter.**

   After a delay (usually brief, but after all, the web *is* big), the search engine returns a listing of links to pages that it thinks match your keywords. The full list of links that match your keywords may be way too long to deal with — say, 300,000 of them — but the search engine tries to put them in a reasonable order and lets you look at them a page at a time.

4. **Adjust and repeat your search until you find something you like.**

   One trick is to pick keywords that relate to your topic from two or three different directions, such as *ethiopian restaurants dubuque* or *war women song*. Here's the secret: Think of words that would be on a page containing the information you want. After some clicking around to get the hang of it, you find all sorts of good stuff.

5. **If the search engine is producing results too scattered to be useful and you can't think of any better keywords, try the Yahoo! Directory at dir.yahoo.com.**

   When you see a list of links to topic areas, click a topic area of interest. In the directory approach, you begin at a general topic and follow links to subtopics. Each page has links to pages that become increasingly specific until they link to actual pages that are likely to be of interest.

The lazy searcher's search page

You may feel a wee bit overwhelmed by all the search directories and search engines we discuss in this chapter. If it makes you feel any better, so do we.

To make a little sense of all this stuff, we made ourselves a search page that connects to all the directories and search engines we use — call it

one-stop searching. You can use it, too. Give it a try at `net.gurus.org/search`.

In the not unlikely event that new search systems are created or some existing ones have moved or died, this page gives you our latest greatest list and lets you sign up for emailed updates whenever we change it.

Search, Ho!

Once upon a time in an Internet far, far away, lots of search engines and directories battled with each other to see which would be the favorite. Participants were AltaVista and Dogpile and lots of other sites you can find in earlier editions of this book. Well, it seems that the first pan galactic search war is pretty much over, with Google the victor — at least for now. However, Microsoft is fighting back with its Bing search engine. Visit `net.gurus.org/search` for all the exciting developments.

Google, our favorite search engine

Our favorite web search engine is Google. It has little (software) robots that spend their time merrily visiting web pages and reporting what they see. It makes a humongous index of which words occurred in which pages; when you search for a topic, it picks pages from the index that contain the words you asked for. Google uses a sophisticated ranking system, based on how many *other* websites refer to each page in the index. Usually, the Google ranking puts the best pages first, right after a few sites that have paid to be listed at the top.

Refining your search

Using Google or any other search engine is an exercise in remote-control mind reading. You have to guess words that will appear on the pages you're looking for. Sometimes it's easy — if you're looking for recipes for Key lime pie, *key lime pie* is a good set of search words because you know the name of what you're looking for. On the other hand, if you have forgotten that the capital of France is Paris, it's sometimes hard to tease a useful page out of a search engine because you don't know which words to look for. (If you try searching for *France capital,* some search engines show you information about capital gains taxation in France, or Fort de France, which is the capital of the French overseas département of Martinique. Many people must ask this question, because Google takes pity on you and tells you at the top: "Best guess for France capital is Paris.")

Now that we have you all discouraged, try some Google searches. Direct your browser to www.google.com. You see a screen like the one shown in Figure 13-1.

Figure 13-1: Google, classic style.

The number-one reason a search doesn't find anything

Well, it may not be *your* number-one reason, but it's *our* number-one reason: A search word is spelled wrong or mistyped. John notes that his fingers insist on typing *Interent,* which doesn't find much — other than web pages from other people who can't spell or type. Google often catches spelling mistakes and helpfully suggests alternatives. We sometimes use a Google search to check the preferred spelling of words that haven't made it into the dictionary yet. (Thanks to our friend Jean Armour Polly for reminding us about this problem.)

Type some search terms and Google finds the pages that best match your terms. That's "*best* match," not "match" — if it can't match all the terms, it finds pages that match as well as possible. Google ignores words that occur too often to be usable as index terms, both the obvious (ones such as *and,* *the,* and *of*) and merely routine (terms such as *internet* and *mail*). These rules can sound somewhat discouraging, but in fact it's still not hard to get useful results from Google. You just have to think up good search terms. Try the recipe example by typing *key lime pie* and clicking the Search button. You see a response like the one shown in Figure 13-2.

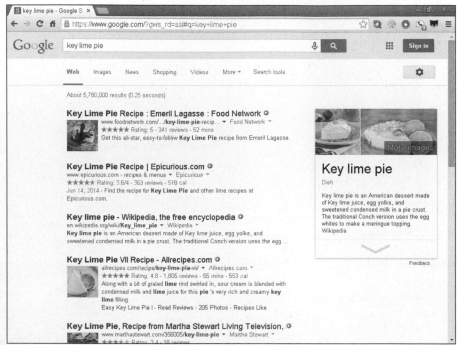

Figure 13-2:
Plenty of pages of pie.

Handy search engine targeting tips

Google makes it easy to refine your search even more specifically to target the pages you want to find. After every search, your search terms appear in a box at the top of the page so that you can change them and try again. Here are some tips on how you may want to change your terms:

✔ If two or more words should appear together, put quotes around them, as in `"Elvis Presley"`. You can do that with the pie search (`"key lime pie"`) because,

after all, that's the pie's name, although in this example, Google is clever enough to realize that it's a common phrase and pretends that you typed the quotes anyway.

✔ Use + and – to indicate words that must either appear or not appear, such as `+Elvis +Costello -Presley` if you're looking for Diana Krall's husband.

✔ Capitalization doesn't matter. We use all lowercase for our search terms.

Your results won't look exactly like Figure 13-2 because Google will have updated its database since this book was published. (These results have gotten a lot better since we started using this example in earlier editions of this book. Now it understands that you're probably looking for a recipe.) Most of the pages that Google found do, in fact, have something to do with Key lime pie — many have good recipes. Google says it found 1,130,000 matches (yow!), but in the interest of sanity it shows you about 100 of them, 10 at a time. Although that's still probably more than you want to look at, you should at least look at the next couple of screens of matches if the first screen doesn't have what you want. Because the list includes a lot of restaurants with Key lime pie on the menu and a hair salon named Key Lime Pie, you can simply narrow the search to only recipes by adding the keyword *recipe*. Search engines are dumb; you have to add the intelligence. At the bottom of the Google screen are page numbers; click Next to go to the next page.

The links in the right column and sometimes at the top of the results are *sponsored* links — that is, paid ads, ranked by how much the advertiser was willing to pay. Often they're worth clicking, but remember that they're ads. Google identifies paid ads with a little Ad icon or label.

The I'm Feeling Lucky button searches and takes you directly to the first link, which works, well, when you're lucky.

Even more Google options

Although Google looks very simple, it has plenty of other options that can be handy. You can

✔ **Get there from here.** Type a street address, and Google offers a link to a map. Type a person's name and a full or partial address, at least the state abbreviation, and Google gives you addresses and phone numbers. Type a phone number, and it often gives you the name and address. (Try typing *202-456-1414*). The information is all collected from public sources, but if you find this process a bit too creepy, look yourself up and if it finds you, it includes a link to a page where you can have your information removed.

✔ **Fly there from here.** Type something like `fly new york hong kong feb 7 feb 14` and Google's first result is a table of airline flights and prices, calculated by their flight search subsidiary. Click on any of the results in that box and you'll get more result pages that you can use to book a trip through an airline or travel agent web site. (For more info on buying airline tickets online, see Chapter 15.)

✔ **Search for images and videos as well as for text.** Often, Google shows relevant images or videos in with its search results. You can click any of them, or to see more images or videos, just click the Image or Videos links on any Google results page. Google has no idea what each image or video is but looks at the surrounding text and the filename of the image or video and does a remarkably good job of guessing. If you search for a *key lime pie* image, you indeed see dozens of pictures of tasty pies, and a video search finds a lot of videos of pie preparation. The SafeSearch feature omits pictures of naked people and the like. If you turn it off, you can find some impressively unsafe pictures.

✔ **Read the news.** Google News (click the News link or start at `news.google.com`) shows a summary of current online news culled automatically from thousands of sources all over the world. *Warning:* If you're interested in current events, you can easily waste 12 hours a day following links from here.

✔ **Limit your search to a specific website.** If you know what site has the information you want, include *site:* and the website address in the search. For example, if you want to know what the *New York Times* says about a subject, include *site:nytimes.com*.

✔ **Do painless arithmetic.** Google is even a calculator. Type *2+2* and Google says `2 + 2 = 4`. It knows units, so if you type *4 feet 8.5 inches,* Google says `4 feet 8.5 inches = 1.4351 meters` and tells you why that's an interesting width. It can also convert currencies and metric measurements.

Google does more than search

Here are a bunch of other services that Google offers. (As far as we can tell, all these services are part of the Google Grand Plan for Global Domination, but the services are free and good, so we use them.)

You can see a map of almost anywhere. At Google Maps, you type an address and see a map of the area or a satellite photo of the same area or both superimposed. Try it at `maps.google.com`. Or, if you're tired of hearing about Google all the time, try MapQuest, at `www.mapquest.com`, another excellent map site, or Yahoo! Local Maps at `maps.yahoo.com`. Even cooler is Google Earth (at `earth.google.com`), which displays 3D maps and images.

You can create and store word processing documents and spreadsheets. Why buy Microsoft Word or Microsoft Excel or WordPerfect when Google Apps can do the job? Google Docs (`docs.google.com`) is an online word processor and Google Sheets (`sheets.google.com`) is a browser-based spreadsheet program. If you don't already have a Gmail account, which works with all of these services, visit `docs.google.com`, create a free Google account, and go to it. All you need is your browser or the Google Docs and Google Sheets apps on your phone or tablet. Neither the word processor nor the spreadsheet program is as powerful as PC-based programs such as Word and Excel, but for basic documents, they do the job and they're getting better. One of the nicest features is that you can share your documents and spreadsheets with your co-workers and friends so that they can see and edit the documents, too. See the section in Chapter 17 about sharing documents and calendars for more information.

You can store files online. Google Drive (`drive.google.com`) provides free storage for your files, via your browser or the Google Drive app on your phone or tablet. If you install the optional Google Drive program on your computer it can synchronize the files in a folder on your hard disk with the files in your Google Drive website, automatically uploading and downloading files as needed.

You can send and receive email. We tell you about Google Mail (Gmail) in Chapter 8.

You can organize and display your digital photos. Google offers the Picasa program (at `picasa.google.com`), which helps you organize your photos, provides a photo editor, and enables you to upload them to your own photo website. You can also download the free Picasa program to organize and identify the photos on your computer.

Google adds more features almost every week. To see what they offer, start at `www.google.com`, click the little pattern of nine dots, then More, and choose Even More from the menu that appears.

Bing!

Microsoft never cedes any part of the computer business without a struggle to the death, and web search is no exception. After many false starts over many years, its Bing search engine, shown in Figure 13-3, shows promise.

(Bing's background images changes daily.) Its basic operation is a lot like Google: You type some search terms and it finds you some web pages. If you would rather see images or videos, look at the clickable Images and Videos links at the top of the page (unless Microsoft moves them), just like Google. If you want maps and satellite images, use the Maps link, just like the one at Google. If you're looking for news stories, well, you get the idea, even though Bing is reputed to mean Bing Is Not Google. If imitation is the sincerest form of flattery, Google must be feeling extremely flattered.

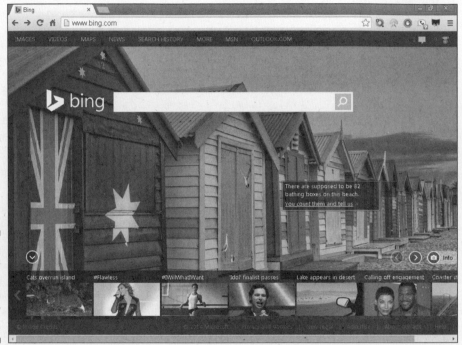

Figure 13-3:
Bing, ready to go, with a bonus geography lesson.

Bing isn't exactly the same as Google. In most cases, in its results, it suggests related searches you might want to try. The video search runs previews of the videos it found if you mouse over any of them, which is kind of cute. Its satellite images are different from Google's, so you might see a clearer view in one than in the other. Overall, we don't find any overwhelming reason to prefer Bing, but it's worth a look.

One significant difference in Bing is that Microsoft has made it easy to embed Bing searches into other websites, including a split of the money from any ads in the search results, so you can expect to find Bing lurking in lots of other places on the web.

Browsing with Directories

Sometimes a web search just doesn't find what you're looking for. Coming up with the right search terms can be tricky if no specific word or phrase sums up what you want to know. This is the moment to try a web directory. If you know in general but not in detail what you're looking for, clicking up and down through directory pages is a good way to narrow your search and find pages of interest.

Yahoo! for directories

Yahoo! is one of the oldest directories — and still a good one. You can search for entries or click from category to category until you find something you like. Start at `dir.yahoo.com`. As with all web pages, the exact design may have changed by the time you read this section. A whole bunch of categories and subcategories are listed on the left; click any of them to see another page that has even more subcategories and links to actual web pages. You can click a link to a page if you see one you like, or click a sub-subcategory, and so on. Figure 13-4 shows the Yahoo! Directory page for Games in Recreation.

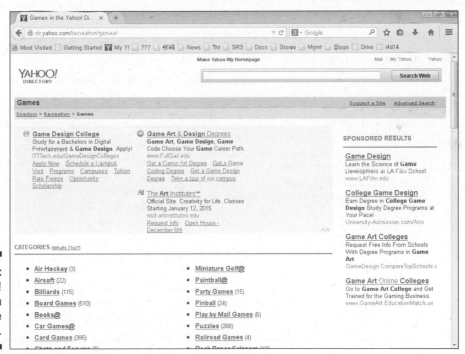

Figure 13-4: Yahoo! shows you how to have fun.

Early on, you could easily submit a web page to Yahoo! by simply entering a page description and web address of the page into the Submissions page and waiting a week or so for the editors to look at the new page. Submitting pages is now so popular that normal submissions take a *long* time (months) before anyone on staff looks at them, unless you pay them $299 per year for the "express" service. You can draw your own conclusions about how the fee affects what information gets into Yahoo! (and what doesn't).

Yahoo! also has a search engine, but it's actually Bing underneath.

The 404 blues

More often than we want to admit, when you click a link from a search results page, you see — rather than the promised page — a message such as 404 Not Found. What did you do wrong? Nothing. Web pages come and go and move around with great velocity, and the various web search engines were designed as delivery vehicles (not garbage trucks), so they do a lousy job of cleaning out links to old, dead pages that have gone away.

At least the search engines are a bit better in this regard than the manual directories. That's because search engines have software robots (called *spiders* because they roam the web) that revisit all indexed pages every once in a while and note whether they still exist. Even so, many lonely months can pass between spider visits, and a great deal can happen to a page in the meantime. Google *caches* (stores) a copy of most pages it visits, so even if the original has gone away, you can click the Cache link at the end of a Google index entry to see a copy of the page as it was when Google last looked at it.

Here are some other ways to chase down a tantalizing link that has wandered off into nowhere:

✔ The Internet Archive operates a nifty service, the Wayback Machine, that can retrieve older versions of websites. Enter your broken link in its Search bar at www. archive.org. (Yes, this site owns a lot of computers too.)

✔ Sometimes websites try to tidy up a bit and move their files around in the process. If the broken link is a long one — say, www.frobliedoop. org/glompty-dompty/snrok/ amazingtip.html — try its shorter versions: www.frobliedoop.org/ glompty-dompty/snrok or www. frobliedoop.org/glompty- dompty or even www.frobliedoop. org to find clues to where they put that tip. Also try a Google search on just the filename, such as amazingtip.html. You might find a copy at another website.

✔ Finally, we should mention that websites sometimes shut down, because of either equipment failure or periodic maintenance. (Late nights, Sunday mornings, and major holidays are favorite times for the latter.) Your 404 link just might magically work tomorrow.

Bad links are all just part of life on the online frontier — the high-tech equivalent of riding your horse along the trail in the Old West and noticing that there sure are a lot of bleached-white cattle skulls lying around.

For facts, try Wikipedia first

TIP

Wikipedia, at `en.wikipedia.org`, is an encyclopedia you can use for free over the Internet. The site looks like Figure 13-5. *Wiki* means fast in Hawaiian (actually, *wikiwiki* does, best known before the Internet as the name of the interterminal bus at the Honolulu airport), and Wikipedia has earned its name. The Wikipedia project, which started in 2001, has grown to more than 3 million articles in English, covering almost every conceivable topic, from the Battle of Dunkirk to *For Dummies* books. Yes, it even has a Key lime pie article, where you read this: "Key lime pie is made with canned sweetened condensed milk, since fresh milk was not a common commodity in the Florida Keys before modern refrigerated distribution methods." Also, since 2006, it has been the Florida state pie.

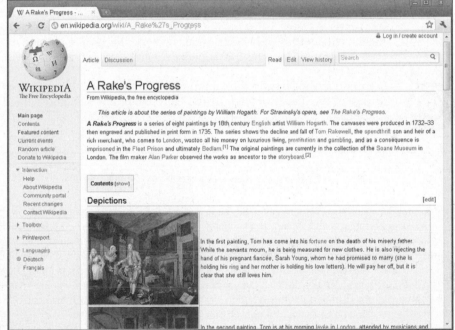

Figure 13-5: Anyone can edit the Wikipedia online encyclopedia.

If you're looking for the scoop on most topics, Wikipedia is a helpful place to start. You can search for article titles or article text. Words in the article body that are highlighted in blue link to other articles in Wikipedia. Many articles also have links to external websites that have more information on the topic. Articles are created and edited by a volunteer team of more than 300,000 active contributors. Wikipedias exist in dozens of other languages as well. (Adding the `en` characters at the beginning of its web address gets you the English version. Check out `is.wikipedia.org` if you've ever wondered what the Icelandic language looks like.)

Anyone can edit most Wikipedia articles whenever they want. This concept might seem to be a prescription for chaos, but most articles are watched over by interested volunteers, and inappropriate edits are quickly reversed, so the overall quality remains remarkably high. If you add information, you are expected to include a link to your source; like all encyclopedias, Wikipedia is not the place for original research or personal anecdotes.

If the idea of editing encyclopedia articles on your favorite subjects sounds appealing, talk to your family first. Wikipedia can be extremely addictive.

Articles are supposed to reflect a neutral point of view (NPOV, in Wikispeak), but a few topics — such as abortion, creationism, and Middle East politics — are continually debated. Wikipedia isn't as authoritative as conventional works, like *Encyclopædia Britannica,* but its articles are usually up to date and to the point, with side issues dealt with by links to other articles. One particularly cool Wikipedia feature is its collection of comprehensive lists, `en.wikipedia.org/wiki/Category:Lists`, on all sorts of arcane subjects. One of our favorites is the list of countries with electric mains power plugs, voltages, and frequencies; type *mains power systems* in Wikipedia's Search box to find it.

If you do a Google search on a topic, a Wikipedia article is likely to show up as one of the links Google returns. That link might be a good place to start reading.

Who pays for all this stuff?

You may be wondering who pays for all these wonderful search systems. Advertising supports all except two of them. On every page of most search systems, you see lots and lots of ads. It used to be that ad revenue was skimpy — hence the dot-com bust of 2000 — but then the search sites discovered an important secret: When you enter keywords, you're telling the search site something about your interests at the moment. This information turns out to be *extremely* valuable to advertisers. An automobile company might pay a lot to have its ad near the top of the results page when you search for *automobile dealer Kansas.* Some sites (notably, Google) auction off prime ad placement. Google marks these ads as `sponsored` links. Usually, they're on the right side of the results page, but sometimes they're on top with a colored background. (Surprise — this type costs more.) Other search sites may not be as scrupulous. Advertisers pay Google when you click their links.

Wikipedia works on the open source model. The vast majority of contributors are unpaid volunteers, but the substantial bills for running the site are paid for by grants and donations. If you use Wikipedia much, you should kick in a few bucks.

The Usual Suspects: Other Useful Search Sites

After you surf around Yahoo!, Google, and Bing for a while, you may want to check out the competition. Here are some sites that provide specialized types of searches:

- ✔ **DuckDuckGo:** This quirky search engine (at `duckduckgo.com` or `ddg.gg`) promises not to collect personal information, as all the other search engines do, but does a respectable job of searching anyway. It fetches results from a wide range of other sources (with permission) ranging from Bing to the Pokemon Encyclopedia.

- ✔ **About.com:** This directory (at `www.about.com`) has several hundred semiprofessional "guides" who manage the topic areas. The guides vary from okay to very good (Margy knows a couple of very good ones), so if you're looking for in-depth information on a topic, check About.com to see what the guide has to say. The site was purchased by the _New York Times_ in 2005.

- ✔ **Ask.com:** Originally named Ask Jeeves, this site's (at `www.ask.com`) original gimmick was that you could ask your question in English and it'd try to answer it. When you're typing text into a little box, it turns out to be easier to type some keywords than a long polite sentence, but the underlying search engine is worth a try. It was purchased by the media conglomerate IAC (InterActive Corp.) in 2005.

The ten-minute challenge

Our friend Doug Hacker (his real name) claims to be able to find the answer to any factual query on the Internet in less than ten minutes. We challenged him to find a quote we vaguely knew from the liner notes of a Duke Ellington album whose title we couldn't remember. He had the complete quote in about an hour but spent less than five minutes himself actually searching. How? He found a mailing list about Duke Ellington, subscribed, and asked the question. Several members replied in short order. The more time you spend finding your way around the Internet, the more you know where to go for the information you need.

Finding People

Finding people on the Internet is surprisingly easy. It's so easy that, indeed, sometimes it's creepy. Two overlapping categories of people-finders are available: those that look for people's email and web addresses and those that look for people's phone numbers and street addresses.

Looking for email addresses

The process of finding email and web addresses is hit-and-miss. Because no online equivalent to the telephone company's official phone book has ever existed, your best bet is to type into Google a person's name and a few other identifying words (such as the town where the person lives and the company where the person works) to see whether any of the matches it finds includes an address. Finding addresses by searching used to be pretty easy, but in recent years, as spammers have taken to scraping off the web every address they can find, a lot of websites now *munge* (obscure) or delete email addresses.

You can search online all you want, but there's no substitute for calling someone up and asking, "What's your email address?"

Googling for people

Type someone's name and address at Google (for the address, type at least the state abbreviation, but more is better), and it shows you matches from phone book listings.

If you're wondering whether someone has a website, use Bing or Google to search for the person's name. If you're wondering whether you're famous, use Bing or Google to search for your own name to see how many people mention you or link to your web pages. (If you do it more than once, you're *ego surfing*.) If you receive email from someone you don't know, search for the email address — unless the message was spam, the address is bound to appear on a web page somewhere.

Using other people-search sites

Here are some other sites that search for people:

- ✔ **Canada 411:** Canada 411 (canada411.ca) is a complete Canadian telephone book, sponsored by the major Canadian telephone companies. *Aussi disponsible en français,* eh? For several years, the listings for Alberta and Saskatchewan were missing, leading to concern that the two provinces were too boring to bother with, but they're all there now, proving that they're just as gnarly as everyone else.

- ✔ **Yellow pages directories:** Quite a few "yellow pages" business directories, both national and local, are on the web, like those at www.superpages.com and www.yp.com.

We're from Your Browser, and We're Here to Help You

Every search engine wants to be your best friend, which, no doubt by coincidence, will increase its market share. (Who? Us? Opinionated?) To cement this friendship, browser makers go to great effort to arrange things so that when you type some search words, the search happens on its own search engine rather than on anyone else's.

Internet Explorer, Firefox, and Safari all have the Search bar to the right of the Address bar, as shown in Figure 13-6.

Figure 13-6: Shortcut Search bars in Internet Explorer, Firefox, and Safari.

If you type a word or phrase in the Search bar, your browser opens your pre-ferred search engine and displays the results of a search for whatever you typed. Or, if you type on the Address bar an entry that doesn't look like an address, it pretends that you typed it on the Search bar and searches anyway. (Google Chrome has only one box where you type something, and it decides what you want.) How convenient is that! You can specify which search engine you want this feature to use:

- ✔ **Firefox:** Choose a search engine from its short list by clicking the Search Engine icon to the right of the Address bar (and to the left of the Search bar). Click the icon and choose a different site. Or, choose Manage Search Engines to display a list of search engines that Firefox knows about and add your favorites.

- ✔ **Google Chrome:** Click the Customize (little wrench) icon to the right of the Address bar, select Options, click the Basics tab if it isn't already selected, and set Default Search to your favorite search site. Click the Manage button if you want to choose a site that isn't on their list.

- ✔ **Internet Explorer:** Choose Tools⇨Internet Options, click the General tab if it isn't already selected, and click the Settings button in the Search section.

- ✔ **Safari:** Click the little magnifying glass in the Search bar, where the menu offers a choice between Google and Yahoo!.

Too Many Toolbars

Every search engine vendor offers a *toolbar* that you can add to your browser. The *toolbar* is a bar above your browser's main window with the Search bar and some other stuff on it, such as links to relevant websites and sometimes browser tools such as pop-up blockers. Back when browsers were young and had no Search bars or built-in pop-up blockers, the toolbars were somewhat useful. These days, they're mostly a way to force another search-engine-specific Search bar into your browser, taking up space on your screen that would other-wise be available to look at web pages (refer to Figure 13-7).

We generally recommend that you decline any invitations to install browser toolbars, because their value is negligible. If a specific toolbar has a specific feature you want that isn't otherwise available in your browser, such as the page rank display on the Google toolbar, it doesn't hurt to install it, other than losing that half-inch of screen real estate.

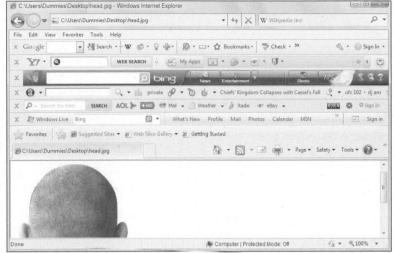

Figure 13-7:
Toolbar
mania:
Don't let this
happen to
you.

To get rid of unwanted toolbars in Internet Explorer, right-click in a blank part of any menu or toolbar to open a menu where you can deselect the ones you don't want. To get rid of toolbars in Firefox, choose Tools⇨Add-Ons (which shows all add-ons, including the toolbars), click the one you don't want, and then click the Uninstall or Remove button that appears.

Stumbling upon something interesting

John doesn't like it, but Margy enjoys using StumbleUpon (www.stumbleupon.com) to find websites. Rather than allow you to specify what you're looking for, StumbleUpon tries to guess which web pages you might find interesting and shows one to you. You can click a button to say whether you like the site and then click the Stumble button to see another web page. StumbleUpon adjusts its guesses based on what you say you like.

Chapter 14

Music and Video on the Web

A thousand years ago, when we wrote the first edition of *Internet For Dummies*, Internet content consisted almost entirely of text. (It was 1993, but it sure *feels* like a thousand years ago.) You could download a few archives of pictures, and there was this weird thing, the World Wide Web, that could mix together pictures and text on the same page, but for the most part, it consisted of text: People's connections were so slow, downloading pictures took so long, and computer screens were so fuzzy that we stuck to text. The pictures you could download were single images, such as cartoons and snapshots. Audio was nearly unheard of (so to speak), and video files were so bulky that even if you could find a clip and wait a week for it to download, it wouldn't fit on your computer's disk. By the late 1990s, Internet connections had sped up enough and screens had improved enough that pictures were normal fare — and audio was entering the mainstream enough that we put a twelve second voice message on our website, in case any of our readers had sound cards. (It's still there, at net.gurus.org/ngc.wav.)

Things have advanced a little since then. Ordinary users now have Net connections that run at several million bits per second — faster than the main backbones of the early 1990s — and computer disks have gotten enormous beyond imagining. Passing around audio and video over the Net has become practical and widespread. In fact, the amounts of available audio and video are now so vast that you could spend your entire life looking at online commercials without ever finding anything worth watching. This chapter tries to bring a little order to the vast wasteland of online media.

To avoid writing *audio and/or video* a hundred more times in this chapter, henceforth we use the concise (albeit imprecise) term *media* to refer to them.

Seven Ways to Get Media and One Way Not To

You can get your media fix in approximately ten zillion different programs and formats. Fortunately, they fall into a modest number of categories: free, streaming, purchased, shared, rental, and outright stolen.

Receiving media as a gift

The simplest approach is to download media offered for free and then play it. Visit www.nasa.gov/multimedia, where NASA has lots of free little movies on topics ranging from dust storms on Mars to how a roller coaster ride feels like taking off in the space shuttle. You can also find independent movies and videos from producers more interested in letting people see their work than in charging for it. Visit epitonic.com for an eclectic collection of music by artists, some well known and some obscure, released so that people can listen to it and make their own mixes.

Borrowing media by streaming it

Even on a broadband connection, downloading a whole media clip can take a while. Rather than download first and play later, *streaming* media downloads as it plays, thereby re-creating (in a complex digital manner) the way that radio and TV have worked since the 1920s. As with TV and radio, after it's streamed, it's gone — and if you want to play it again, you have to stream it again. Streaming audio can work over a dialup connection, but streaming video needs a broadband connection.

Most streaming media is provided *on demand:* You click a link and they send you whatever it is, sort of like a jukebox. Alternatively, sometimes streaming media is a single program to which you can listen in and hear what's playing at any moment. Not surprisingly, it's named *Internet radio,* and in many cases the audio stream is an actual radio program, such as our local public radio stations at wrvo.fm in upstate New York and www.vpr.net (click Listen Live) in Vermont. We say more about Internet radio in the section "Listening to Internet radio" later in this chapter.

Buying media

Apple iTunes makes buying music and video easy. Go to www.apple.com/itunes to listen to the first little bit of any song in its catalog. If you like it, you can buy your own, permanent copy (usually for 99 cents) that you can copy to your iPod, play on your computer, or burn on a CD. You don't have to be a Mac user to use iTunes; you can play the tunes by using the Windows version of the iTunes program. (See the section "Organizing your music with iTunes," later in this chapter.) It's no surprise that people buy in droves, making iTunes the biggest online music store. Likewise, many more websites sell music either from a web-based store or as an add-on to a rental service, most for about the same price as at iTunes.

Apple makes it easy to listen to and watch your iTunes music and videos on an iPhone, iPod, or iPad. If you have an Android or other smartphone or tablet, programs are also available for transferring your music and videos to your phone.

Amazon.com (www.amazon.com), the world's largest bookstore, also sells downloadable tunes in MP3 format. The sale catalog is considerably larger than the streaming catalog for Amazon Prime customers (customers who pay about $100 a year for free two-day shipping and other perks).

Playing media from CDs or DVDs you already own

You probably own a whole lot of digital music in the form of music CDs. Copying your music CDs to your computer is known as *ripping*, and it's easy to do. Windows Media Player, iTunes, and other music programs can copy all tracks from a CD and put the songs into your music library so that you can play them from your computer (without the CD) or copy them to your MP3 player. See "Copying music from your own CDs," later in this chapter.

Subscribing to media services

You can subscribe to audio programs over the Internet. A *podcast* is an audio file distributed over the Net for listening to on an iPod or another type of MP3 player or any computer with speakers. Many radio shows are available as podcasts; go to www.npr.org to find many of them. Lots of organizations and people make podcasts, too. See the section "Subscribing to podcasts with iTunes," later in this chapter, for instructions.

Sharing media

The original version of Napster was the first well-known music exchange service, allowing members to download MP3 music files from each other for free. The system was the first large-scale *peer-to-peer* (*P2P*) information exchange, where people exchange files with each other rather than download them from a central library. Eventually, the big record labels sued and shut it down because most of the material that people exchanged was in flagrant violation of the music's copyright. Napster was later reincarnated as a site for music rental and free online music streaming — but no free downloading.

The popular file-sharing system BitTorrent (www.bittorrent.com) has thus far been able to fly under the legal radar, unlike LimeWire (www.limewire.com), which was shut down by a court order. They resemble an earlier Napster — a network from which you can download music for free, a certain amount of which is provided against the wishes of the owners of said music. While you're downloading music from other people's computers, they are in turn downloading music from you, so they can significantly slow down your computer and your Internet connection. The music industry insists that these folks are morally reprehensible, but people use BitTorrent in particular to share large amounts of entirely legal and legitimate material along with the dodgy stuff. We suggest that you stay away from it — as legal music gets cheaper and cheaper, why risk breaking the law to save a few bucks?

Renting media

A great deal of music isn't available for free, but it's available for cheap. Services such as Real Networks Rhapsody (www.real.com/rhapsody) offer monthly subscriptions that let you listen to large libraries of recorded music. Amazon (www.amazon.com) offers streaming music as part of their $99/yr Prime package. Spotify (www.spotify.com) offers a basic service with ads for free, or premium with no ads and some extra features for $10/mo ($5 for students.)

These rental services have enormous catalogs of music, and each one claims to be the largest. They really *are* large: While checking out Rhapsody, we were finally able to do a side-by-side comparison of Desi Arnaz's muscular late-1940s version of *Babalu* and his mentor Xavier Cugat's more elegant 1941 recording. (You'll just have to decide for yourself which one you like better.) However, when you stop paying rent, your music vanishes. Remember — you never owned it.

You can find video rental websites too — not just for renting a DVD but also for downloading the video over the Internet and watching it on your computer. For example, Netflix, at www.netflix.com, is known for its DVD-rental-by-mail service, but you can also stream videos on demand. Not all its DVDs are available for streaming, but for the ones that are, you see a Play button on the website. Amazon Prime includes video on demand, too.

Downloads for the post-literate

Not all downloadable audio files contain music. A thriving market exists for what used to be called "talking books." You can download books and magazines and just about anything else you might otherwise read, as well as radio programs you might have missed. Although listening to downloaded books on your computer works fine — and it can be an essential tool for the visually impaired — it's kind of pointless if you can read the paper book faster than you can listen to it (and kick back on the patio while you're at it). But if you drive to work or go jogging, a talking book on CD in the car player (or copied to your phone or the iPod on your belt) is just the ticket.

The largest source of talking books is Amazon's Audible.com (www.audible.com). You can buy individual books for book-like prices or subscribe and listen to one or two books a month cheaper than you can by paying individually. Either way, the books you buy are yours to keep. They have apps for iPhones and Android devices, and have also made deals with many other media programs, so you can find an Audible plug-in for iTunes that lets you copy your books to an iPod, as well as a plug-in for Windows Media Player for all the MP3 devices it handles, and so forth. For the traditionally minded, they provide an iTunes plugin you can use to burn them to CDs (*lots* of CDs — about 15 for a full-length book). If your phone or tablet does Bluetooth (all recent ones do), and your car radio also does Bluetooth (ditto), it's not hard to play the books on your phone, with the sound coming from the car speakers.

Audible usually offers a trial subscription with a couple of free books, and its catalog includes public-interest stuff (such as presidential inaugural speeches) available for free if you want to try it out. ***Warning:*** John tried it out and ended up inventing errands that involved driving to faraway stores so that he could listen to the last chapter of *The DaVinci Code.* On the other hand, Margy's husband survived a long commute thanks to his Audible subscription.

A non-commercial alternative is Librivox (librivox.org), which provides free audio recordings of books that are in the public domain, recorded by volunteers. Margy's son is working his way through the complete works of H.P. Lovecraft, listening to the Librivox recordings.

Stealing media — um, no

Plenty of pirated stuff is still on the Net, and probably always will be. We expect that our readers, because they're of good moral character, wouldn't want to look for it, but if you do, you have to do so without our help.

What Are You Listening With?

The two most popular programs used for playing web-based online media are Windows Media Player and Apple iTunes. These include separate player programs and plug-ins for web browsers so that web pages can embed little windows that show movies or play music.

iTunes

`www.apple.com/itunes`

Apple iTunes, shown in Figure 14-1, has become insanely popular because you have to use it if you have an iPhone or iPod. In addition to playing and organizing music, iTunes is the way to load music from your computer onto the iPod or iPhone. You may have heard of it as a music store and a way to organize music, but iTunes can play all sorts of media, including videos. iTunes supports streaming video as well as audio in most popular formats.

Ripping CDs to your computer and keeping your music organized in iTunes are described later in this chapter.

Figure 14-1:
You can use
iTunes to
buy music,
rip and
burn CDs,
organize
songs into
playlists,
subscribe
to podcasts,
and maybe
even wash
the dishes.

Windows Media Player

`www.microsoft.com/windows/windowsmedia`

Microsoft has its own streaming audio and video formats, and it bundles a player for them with Windows. The Windows Media Player program, shown in Figure 14-2, can play files in Advanced Systems Format (with the extension .asf or .asx), in addition to most other formats. More recent versions added useful new features, so if you don't have Media Player version 11 or later, it's worth your time to visit Windows Update or the Media Player site to download it. (Media Player itself may nag you to upgrade, if you have an older version.)

Figure 14-2:
Organizing
your
music with
Windows
Media
Player.

Click the Music and Videos tabs on the left side of the Media Player window to see which audio and video files you have. Click Media Guide to browse links to popular music. When you put an audio CD into your computer's CD or DVD drive, it displays the list of tracks on the CD and you can click Rip CD to *rip* (copy) tracks from the CD to your hard drive and to your Windows Media Player library. You can also burn music CDs by clicking the Burn tab.

Okay, How about Some Music?

Two hot activities on the Internet are downloading and exchanging music files with your friends in the MP3 file format. MP3 stands for *MP*EG level *3* (acronyms within acronyms — how technoid) and is simply the soundtrack format used with MPEG movies. Because this format is widely available and does a good job of compressing music to a reasonable size for downloading, it has been adopted by music lovers on the Net. As you may already have guessed, MP3 players (similar to the iPod and little, less-expensive devices from Sandisk and Rio) can play MP3 files, too, which is the main reason for their popularity. Many cellphones can play MP3 files, too.

You can play MP3 files by using many different programs, including iTunes and Windows Media Player. This section explains how to use iTunes to organize music, subscribe to podcasts, make playlists, and listen to radio stations over the Internet because all the programs are fairly similar. If you use Windows Media Player, you get the general idea.

Naturally, Microsoft has the competing file format WMA, with the extension .wma. iTunes can also handle WMA files.

Copying music from your own CDs

You already own tons of music on those racks of CDs that will soon be obsolete. You can rip (copy) the tracks from an audio CD by using iTunes. When you put an audio CD into your computer's CD drive, iTunes asks whether you want to import the tracks into your iTunes library. Click Yes to begin copying. iTunes looks up the CD using an online database so that you can see the titles of the tracks and even the album artwork.

When you rip music from CDs, you can specify which format to store the files in. We use the MP3 format because the files are smaller than some other formats and because every music player can handle MP3s. In iTunes, choose Edit⇨Preferences or iTunes⇨Preferences, click the General tab if it isn't already selected, click the Import Settings button, click the Import Using option, set it to MP3 Encoder, and click OK twice. You can also choose the quality, where you trade off file size against sound quality.

Organizing your music with iTunes

Apple iTunes (www.apple.com/itunes) lets you buy legal, downloaded songs for a reasonable price, 99 cents apiece and up, based on popularity. Both Mac and Windows users can buy and play songs from iTunes by downloading the free iTunes program, which is excellent for keeping your songs organized even if you don't have an iPod or buy from the iTunes store. Click iTunes Store to browse the store — iTunes turns into a web browser to enable you to click around to find audio and video files. Apple iPhones and iPads come with an iTunes app pre-installed.

Making playlists

In iTunes, you can organize your music into playlists, which are your own customized albums. One playlist can be music you like to listen to while washing the dishes, and another playlist might be for your fabulous oldies collection. Or, each user of your computer can have her own playlists. You can have as many playlists as you like. (Margy has one playlist of the baritone parts she needs to learn for her women's barbershop group, Maiden Vermont, and another playlist of instrumental jazz, 1960s rock, and Hindu chanting to listen to while working.)

You create a new playlist by choosing File⇨New Playlist or by pressing Ctrl+N. In the iTunes app, touch Playlists at the bottom of the screen and then New Playlist. You can name the playlist whatever you want and then drag in music from your library. Dragging a song from the library to a playlist doesn't remove it from the library or copy the file — you can put the same song into multiple playlists, and all the while it continues to be stored in your general iTunes library just once. You can also create a "Genius playlist" by specifying a song that you like; iTunes shows you a playlist of similar songs.

Subscribing to Podcasts

Podcasts are audio magazines that deliver MP3 files of talk or music directly to your computer (see the section "Subscribing to media services," earlier in this chapter). The word is a combination of i*Pod* and broad*cast,* but you don't need an iPod to listen to them — any computer or MP3 player will do. Radio programs, companies, musicians, comedians, and just plain people produce podcasts about a huge variety of different subjects, everything from "The Twilight Saga" to the stock market.

Video podcasts are the same idea, but you receive video rather than audio files.

Subscribing to podcasts on the web

Several websites provide directories of podcasts, including LearnOutLoud's directory at `www.learnoutloud.com/Podcast-Directory` and `Podcastdirectory.com`. They enable you to find podcasts by topic, subscribe to them, and listen to them from the website.

Or, go to the website of the program you want to subscribe to. National Public Radio at `www.npr.org` originates dozens of podcasts. We enjoy:

- Radiolab, at `www.radiolab.org`, with science-based stories
- Serial, at `serialpodcast.org`, from the makers of This American Life (another great podcast, at `thisamericanlife.org`)
- The TED Radio Hour, at `www.npr.org/programs/ted-radio-hour`
- Welcome to Night Vale, at `www.commonplacebooks.com`, a weird drama for young hipsters
- Wait Wait Don't Tell Me, at `www.npr.org/programs/wait-wait-dont-tell-me`, a weekly news quiz

Subscribing to podcasts with iTunes

To subscribe to a podcast, click the iTunes Store link in iTunes and then click the Podcasts link. When you find a podcast that looks interesting, you can click an episode to listen to it on the spot or click the Subscribe button to receive all future episodes automatically. Most podcasts are free, and iTunes downloads the latest episodes every time you start the program.

Playing Music and Podcasts

If you want to listen to music or podcasts while you're sitting in front of your computer, you're all set — fire up iTunes or Windows Media Player and listen. But we hear that some people actually have lives and want to listen to music in other places.

More threats and promises

Folks ripping their favorite tunes from CDs or download services and emailing them to their 50 closest friends comprise a hideous threat to the recording industry, not to mention that they're violating copyright law. (The previous hideous threats, for readers old enough to remember, were cassette tapes and home VCRs, which totally destroyed the music and movie industries. What — they didn't? Uh, well, *this* time it's different because, um, just because it is.) The industry's efforts to shut down websites that offer ripped songs for free downloading has been moderately successful, but private email is hard to stop.

The recording industry came up with the Secure Digital Music Initiative, a music file format of its own. The SDMI was intended to let you download but not share music. It flopped, partly because it had technical defects quickly analyzed and reported by enterprising college professors and students and partly because nobody wanted crippleware music. The recording industry has been filing lawsuits against the most visible music sharers, on the peculiar theory that if it threatens and sues its customers, their attitudes will improve and they will buy more stuff. Maybe someday the industry will figure out, as Apple did, that if it sells decent music at reasonable prices and lets customers listen to it the way they want to, people will pay for it.

There's CDs, and then there's CDs

Although all CDs look the same, they don't all play the same. Normal audio CDs contain a maximum of about 74 minutes of music and work on every CD player ever made. When you burn a CD-R (the kind of CD you can write to only once), you're making a normal audio CD. Because blank CD-Rs are cheap (about 20 cents apiece if you buy them in quantity), the main disadvantage of this approach is that you end up with large stacks of CDs.

MP3 files are much smaller than audio CD files, so if you burn a CD full of MP3s, you can put about ten hours of music on each disc. DVD players and many recent CD players, including the one in your car, can play MP3 CDs. If you're not sure whether your player can handle MP3 CDs, just make one on your computer and try it in your player. It doesn't hurt your player, although you might see some odd error messages. Although rewritable CD-RWs don't work in normal CD players, players that can handle MP3 CDs can usually handle CD-RWs. Again, if you're not sure, try it; it doesn't hurt anything if it doesn't work.

You can buy a portable MP3 player — an iPod, a cheaper alternative from another manufacturer, or a phone that includes an MP3 player — and take thousands of MP3 cuts to listen to while you jog, travel, or just hang out. Your smartphone probably has an MP3 player app, like iTunes on the iPhone. (Android users can search the Google Play Store for an app; there are dozens, including DoubleTwist and Google Play Music.) You hook your MP3 player to your computer whenever you want to download new tunes. These players can hold *weeks* of music and podcasts. The most popular is the ubiquitous Apple iPod, but other players are cheaper and work fine. Only iPods and other i-devices can play M4P (copy-protected) music and only files to which you own a license.

Listening to Internet Radio

If you like to listen to music while you work, check out real radio stations or Internet-only radio stations. Most radio stations now *stream* their talk and music on the Internet in addition to broadcasting it over the air. Go to a radio station's website and click the Listen Now or similarly named link — for example, we're listening to a show about backyard chickens at wbur.org as we write this section. Many radio stations have MP3 players built into their websites.

Tuning in to a station

Like real radio stations, Internet-only stations offer a mix of music and talk and sometimes commercials. Unlike real (broadcast) radio stations, they're extremely cheap to set up, so lots and lots of people do — providing lots of quirky little niche stations run by people all over the world. You listen to them in a streaming program, usually iTunes or Windows Media. Most are available for free, some require a subscription, and some have a subscription option to make the ads go away.

If you use iTunes, click the Radio link in iTunes to get started. You see a menu of different types of stations, and after choosing one, you can peruse stations from across the country at your leisure for free. Double-click a station to listen to it.

To get started, here are some directories of Internet radio stations:

- ✔ SHOUTcast Radio Directory, at `shoutcast.com`, gives you a choice of its website or your existing player. (This website lets you know that they use cookies, described in Chapter 7, to remember what kinds of stations you've requested.)
- ✔ `StreamFinder.com` has an audio player right on the web page.
- ✔ Live 365 Internet Radio, at `http://www.live365.com`, streams several thousand stations with every possible kind of music.

Either way (broadcast radio or Internet-only radio), you can listen to talk and music from all over the United States — or the world.

Making your own station

Every radio station — Internet or broadcast — chooses a range of styles of music to play. Why should you be limited to the musical tastes of existing radio stations? Instead, you can create your own musical mix, including music you don't even own!

Enter Pandora Radio, at `www.pandora.com` (shown in Figure 14-3). As its website states, it's a new kind of radio station, one that plays only music you like. Type the names of a musician or group or the name of a song and Pandora finds, in its huge musical database, music that's similar to what you specify. You can't play the exact song you want, but you can play similar music, displaying information about the artist and album. When Pandora guesses wrong about what it thinks you like, you can click the thumbs-down icon to kill the song. When it guesses right, click the thumbs-up icon to tell it to play more songs like that one.

You can name your "radio station" and have several stations for different kinds of music — maybe one for working and another for paying bills. You can also share your radio station with other people so that they can listen to the mix you have created.

Jango, at `www.jango.com`, and last.fm (at `last.fm` — no *.com*) work like Pandora. Many of these sites also have apps for iPhones, Androids, and other smartphones and tablet computers.

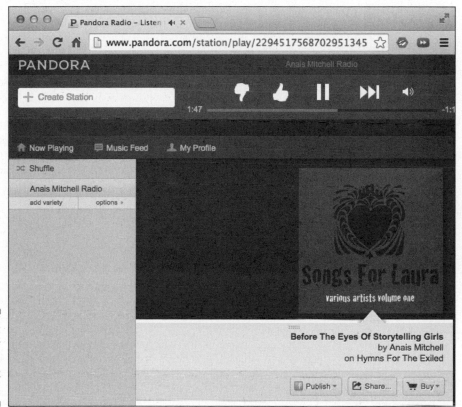

Figure 14-3:
Make your own radio station at Pandora.

Watching Movies on the Web

Now that most people have fast Internet connections, watching video over the Net has become possible and popular. You can watch short videos at YouTube, television shows, or entire movies or upload your own videos for others to watch.

Older web browsers can't play videos — you need to get a player program. You also need a reasonably fast computer to display movies in anything close to real time. Flash, the most widely used player, plugs into your web browser (download it for free from `get.adobe.com/flashplayer`). iTunes and Windows Media Player also handle movies (and are described earlier in this chapter). No popular mobile devices — not the iPhone, iPod touch, iPad, nor any Android device — supports Flash, the technology that web browsers use to display video, so not all these options will work on these devices. Fortunately, most video providers have apps you can use on mobile devices.

The YouTube thing

Probably the largest Internet video phenomenon is YouTube (www.youtube.com). It's a site like Google (which owns YouTube), but rather than an Internet search engine for information at large, it's only for videos. On YouTube you can find everything from *Saturday Night Live* clips to previews for upcoming movies to strange homemade Lego flicks. According to the *New York Times*, people post more than 100 million videos on YouTube every *day* – 48 hours of video uploaded every minute, with over 3 billion video views every day. Unfortunately, Google is losing an amazing amount of money on YouTube every day because few advertisers want their ads displayed alongside such a weird and unpredictable collection of videos.

In the Search bar, you can type a word or phrase related to the video you're looking for and YouTube displays a list of links of possible videos, as shown in Figure 14-4. Click the image or title to play the video. Video-playing software is embedded in the website, so you need nothing but an Internet connection to watch videos on YouTube. (See the later sidebar "Too many video file formats.") If you see a video you like a lot and want to share with your 50 closest friends, you can click the Share link below the video to email a link, post a tweet on Twitter (see Chapter 11), or write it on your Facebook wall, as described in Chapter 10.

Figure 14-4: Millions of weird and occasionally wonderful videos are available on YouTube.

Other YouTube-like websites include Vimeo (www.vimeo.com), Metacafe (www.metacafe.com), and Bing Videos (bing.com/videos). Justin.tv (at www.justin.tv, with no *.com*) shows live video — stuff that's happening right now. The Online Video Guide (www.ovguide.com) can help you find TV and movies on the web.

If you have an iPhone, iPod, iPad, or Android device, you can't display YouTube in its web browser. Instead, they come with a YouTube app preinstalled.

Putting the "You" in YouTube

You can upload a video to YouTube as long as it's on your computer, you own the copyright (YouTube deletes stolen videos), it's neither defamatory nor pornographic, and it's no longer than ten minutes. To upload, follow these steps:

1. **Create a free YouTube account by clicking the Sign In link in the upper right corner of any YouTube page.**

   Or, sign in to your existing account. If you have a Google account, use it.

2. **Click the Upload button.**

   Or, click the Post a Video Response link below an existing video.

3. **Select the video file on your computer and follow the instructions.**

   You can choose whether to make the video public or private, name the video, add a description and keywords, and specify which category it's in. YouTube uploads your video and converts it to the Flash format for streaming. Uploading can take a while (ten minutes or more) depending on the speed of your Internet connection.

After your video is on YouTube, you can share it with your friends.

If a video is public on YouTube, it's really, really public. Think twice about including personally identifying information about yourself or your kids unless the video is something you're truly proud of. After you upload a file, you can click your account name in the upper right corner of the web page, choose My Videos, click the Edit button below a video, and change the Broadcasting and Sharing Options from Public to Unlisted (anyone with the link can view) or Private (only people you choose can view).

Too many video file formats

The original standard digital-movie format is Moving Picture Experts Group (MPEG). MPEG was designed by a committee down the hall from the JPEG committee that defined file formats for scanned photos and (practically unprecedented in the history of computer standards efforts) was designed based on earlier work. MPEG files have the extension .mpeg or .mpg.

Microsoft, responding to the challenge of emerging standards that it didn't control, created its own formats. Audio/Visual Interleave (AVI) format is for nonstreaming video, with the extension .avi. Advanced Streaming Format (with the extension .asf or .asx) is for both streaming audio and video data. They also created Silverlight, which is a lot like Flash, only different. It's available on Windows and Macs. The mostly compatible open source package Moonlight is available for Linux.

These formats were mostly replaced by Flash because it's what YouTube uses — files that end with .flv and a few variations. The Flash player (a free download from `get.adobe.com/flashplayer`) plugs into your web browser and plays streaming video in several qualities, including one that's similar to HD television. For reasons more political than technical, Flash doesn't work on Apple or Android mobile devices.

All these problems are supposed to go away when web browsers support the latest version of the HTML web coding language, HTML 5, available in most recent browsers. Unlike its predecessors which needed video plugins, HTML 5 will have its own built-in nonproprietary video player, which means there'll no good reason for every video site not to support it. They're still working the bugs out, so it'll still be a few years until HTML 5 works everywhere.

Watching movies

You can stream movies from the web, although usually not for free (at least, not legally). If you have a Netflix account to receive DVDs by mail, you can add streaming videos from its website (`www.netflix.com`) for a little extra, or turn off the DVDs-by-mail subscription and just pay for streaming. Netflix has a huge inventory of videos available for streaming, although some titles are available only on DVD. On the website, you add movies to your queue if you want to watch them later or receive the DVD by mail. Or, click the Watch Instantly tab to find a movie and watch it now.

Amazon.com offers a Video On Demand service, which enables you to stream movies for a fee. You can save movies for later after you pay for them or watch previously purchased videos again. Choose the Movies Music & Games department and then click Amazon Instant Video. Their Amazon Prime service requires an annual fee, includes instant video, and is cheaper than individual rentals if you watch more than two movies a month (as well as the streaming music described earlier in the chapter, rental e-books, faster package delivery, and 20% off your diaper subscription.)

Sharing media around the home and dorm

Microsoft Windows 7 and newer have a feature that lets you set up all your computers, at least the ones running Windows, as a *HomeGroup* that can easily share resources on all your computers and other networked devices. Open Windows Media Player, switch to the Library page, and click Stream⇨Turn On Media Streaming. If your computer isn't already in a HomeGroup, it undergoes the process to join an existing group and set one up. After you do that, the Library page shows an icon for the libraries of everyone else, on your computer and others, who has turned on media streaming, and you can play their stuff just like you can play your own. You're also supposed to be able to play from your computer onto networked players and other devices; if your Windows computer can see them on the network, it sets up icons so that you can access them.

You also have the option to allow streaming to the Internet, which we do *not* recommend because, unless you set up your system file protections very carefully, you can allow random strangers on the Net into your computer. We expect the most enthusiastic use of network media streaming will be in "homes" that are college dormitories, where everyone in the dorm is already on the same network, so now they can all share each other's music at the click of a mouse.

Watching TV

Missed your favorite television show? Didn't record it on your TiVo? You might be able to catch it on Hulu, at www.hulu.com or the Hulu app on your mobile device. It's supported by ABC, Fox, NBC, and others, so it shows entire episodes, not ten-minute clips, and has copyrighted shows that aren't available anywhere else online, at least not legally. YouTube has responded with YouTube Shows, at www.youtube.com/shows, which is different from the regular YouTube site; like Hulu, it has commercial video, with no amateur uploads.

Blip.tv (at blip.tv — no *.com* at the end) hosts shows you may never have heard of because they're made by independent creators. Link TV at www.linktv.org shows educational programs from around the world.

Netflix has television shows as well as movies, so if you have a Netflix account, you can stream TV, too.

Chapter 15

More Shopping, Less Dropping

In This Chapter

▶ Discovering the pros and cons of shopping online

▶ Using your credit card online without fear

▶ Shopping step-by-step

▶ Finding the lowest price

▶ Finding airline tickets, books, clothes, computers, food, and mutual funds online

▶ Lots of opinions about what you should buy

*W*e've gone shopping on the Internet, and we've gone shopping in the *souq* in Marrakech. The experiences were surprisingly similar except that the *souq* smelled more interesting and probably had more live snakes. The Internet is the world's biggest bazaar, with stores that carry everything from books to blouses, from DVDs to prescription drugs, from mutual funds to musical instruments, and from plane tickets to, uh, specialized personal products. (Don't read too much into that one.) Shopping online is convenient — no parking or standing in line — and you can compare prices easily. But is online shopping safe? Well, we've bought all kinds of products online, and we're still alive to tell the tale. (We got a nice rug in the *souq*, too.)

Shopping Online: Pros and Cons

Here are some reasons for shopping online:

✔ Online stores are convenient and open all night, and they don't mind if you aren't wearing shoes or if you window-shop for a week before you buy something.

✔ Prices are often lower online, and you can compare prices at several online establishments in a matter of minutes. Even if you eventually make your purchase in a brick-and-mortar store, the information you find online can save you money. Shipping and handling is usually the same as you pay for mail order (although some sites offer free shipping for large orders or customers in a "Prime" program), and you don't have to drive or park.

✔ Online stores can sometimes offer a better selection. They usually ship directly from the warehouse rather than keeping stock on the shelf at dozens of branches. If you're looking for an item that's hard to find — for example, a part for that vintage toaster oven you're repairing — the web can save you weeks of searching.

✔ Sometimes, stuff just isn't available locally, and buying online can save you a trip. (The authors of this book live in small rural towns. Trumansburg, New York, is a wonderful place, but if you want to buy a new toaster, you're out of luck. And Margy couldn't find a harmonium anywhere in the Champlain Valley.)

✔ Some online stores offer smartphone apps. When someone tells Margy about an interesting book, she's likely to order it on the spot, using an online bookseller's iPhone app.

✔ Unlike malls, online stores don't have Muzak. (A few websites play background music, but we don't linger on those sites.)

On the other hand, here are some reasons that you shouldn't buy everything on the Net:

✔ You can't physically look at or try on stuff before you buy it, and in most cases, you have to wait for it to be shipped to you. (We haven't had much luck buying pants online, f'rinstance.)

✔ Your local stores deserve support so that they'll be there when you need something right now or need their help in picking something out.

✔ You can't flirt with the staff at a web store or find out the latest town gossip.

The Credit Card Question

How do you pay for products you buy online? Usually, you pay by credit card, the same way you pay for anything else. Isn't it incredibly, awfully dangerous to give out your credit card number online, though? Well, no.

When you use "plastic" at a restaurant, you give your physical card with your physical signature to the server, who takes it to the back room, does who-knows-what with it, and then brings it back. Compared with that, the risk of sending your number to an online store is pretty small. A friend of ours used to run a restaurant and later an online store and assures us that there's no comparison: The online store had none of the credit card problems that the restaurant did.

Cookie alert

You may have heard horrible stories about the cookies that web sites reputedly use to spy on you, steal your data, ravage your computer, inject cellulite into your hips while you sleep, and otherwise make your life miserable. After extensive investigation, we have found that most cookies aren't bad; when you're shopping online, they're quite helpful. (See the section "Cookies can be good" in Chapter 2 for more on cookies.)

A *cookie* is no more than a little chunk of text that a website sends to a browser with a request (not a command) to send the cookie back during future visits to the same website. The cookie is stored on your computer in the

form of a tiny snippet of text. That's all it is. For online shopping carts, cookies let the web server track the items you have selected but not yet bought, even if you log out and turn off your computer in the interim. Stores can also use cookies to keep track of the last time you visited and what you bought, but they can keep that data on their own computers, so what's the big deal?

So called *third party* cookies are less harmless, often used to track ads shown to you on different sites, but most browsers block them automatically. For more info on blocking web sites from storing cookies on your computer, see how in Chapter 7.

Many books (including earlier editions of this one) made a big deal about whether a website has a security certificate, which means that it shows a little lock in the corner of the web browser window. The lock is nice to have, but the problem it solves — bad guys snooping on the connection somewhere between your PC and the seller's web site — isn't a likely one unless you're using a public wireless network connection at a coffee shop or the like. We think you should worry more about whether a store selling something is run well enough that it ships you the item you bought. Recent security breaches that revealed credit card numbers to crooks came about when those crooks broke into a store's database, not snooped on your Internet connection.

Credit cards and debit cards look the same and spend the same, but credit cards bill you at the end of the month whereas debit cards take the money right out of your bank account. In the United States, consumer protection laws are much stronger for credit cards. The important difference is that in case of a disputed transaction, *you* have the money if you used a credit card but *they* have it if you used a debit card. Use a credit card to get the better protection, and then pay the bill at the end of the month so that you don't owe interest.

If, after this harangue, you still don't want to send your credit card number over the Internet, most online stores are happy to have you call in your card number over the phone (although, likely as not, an operator halfway around the globe then enters your credit card number by using the Internet). If you're one of those fiscally responsible holdouts who doesn't "do plastic," send a check or money order.

Paying at the Store

Buying stuff at an online store isn't much different from buying it at a regular store. Most stores hope you will buy several items at a time, so they use *shopping carts*. As you click your way around a site, you can toss items into your cart, adding and removing them as you want, by clicking a button labeled something like Add Item or Buy Now. When you have the items you want, you visit the virtual checkout line and buy the items in your cart, at which point you tell them where to send them and how you're paying. Until you visit the checkout, you can always take the items out of your cart if you decide that you don't want them, and at online stores they don't become shopworn, no matter how often you do that.

Figure 15-1 shows the shopping cart at an online book store we like, with two items in it. When you click the Secure Checkout button, the next page asks for the rest of your order details.

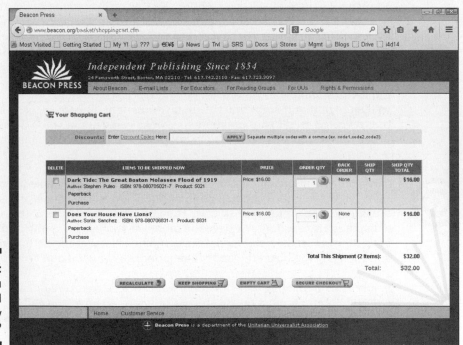

Figure 15-1:
Have you finished your holiday shopping?

Some stores even have the online equivalents of layaway plans and gift registries. For example, some web shopping sites let you add items to a wish list that you can share with your friends so that you or someone else can buy the item for you later. Some sites offer gift certificates, too, for shopping online. Most online stores encourage you to create an account with a password so that if you return to the site it can remember your name, address, and payment method.

Be sure to look for a checkbox or link that allows you to decline to receive offers and notices from the retailed, unless you really want them.

How Little Do You Want to Pay?

As little as possible, of course. About 15 minutes after the second online store appeared, someone realized that you could look at the stores to find who charges how much for which item and then report back on your own website. Price comparison sites work well *if* you can exactly identify the products you want to buy. For books, consumer electronics, computers, and computer parts, it's always worth a look. But if you're looking for khaki pants, no two pairs are the same, and most of us would rather pay an extra ten bucks to avoid a pair that makes us look like a spandex-wrapped potato.

Comparison sites now work two ways. One is to visit store sites and *scrape* (copy) the prices. The other is to make a deal with interested stores and let them upload their prices directly, typically in return for a commission when users click through. Both methods work okay, but we have seen comparison sites showing different prices from the ones you see if you visit the store site directly. Here are a few of our favorites:

- ✔ **Google Shopping** (www.google.com/products) is the latest incarnation of the Google price comparison site that was originally named Froogle. Stores upload prices, but Google doesn't charge them. (The search pages have ads on the right.) The searching is helpful, but the inventory is spotty.

- ✔ **ISBN.NU** (isbn.nu) checks prices for new books at a dozen online stores and tells you which one has the best price. The site scrapes the prices and then uses the stores' affiliate programs to get paid.

- ✔ **MySimon** (www.mysimon.com) compares prices from a wide variety of online stores. Owned by CBS Interactive which also owns tech news site Cnet.

- ✔ **Shopping.com** (www.shopping.com) is eBay's comparison site, which compares many online stores including, of course, eBay.

✔ **Nextag** (www.nextag.com) also covers a wide range of products. Stores pay to be listed, so you should check other sites, too.

✔ **Pricegrabber** (www.pricegrabber.com) has good coverage of everything from musical instruments to computer parts.

✔ **Red Laser** is an iPhone and Android app (available from the App Store or Google Play Store) that enables you to scan a barcode while you are standing in a store. It then displays a list of online stores that sell it, with prices. It's owned by eBay.

If you are ordering from an online store for the first time, you may want to check its reputation at www.resellerratings.com and read reviews from past customers.

Up, Up, and Away

We buy lots of airline tickets online. Although the online travel sites aren't as good as the very best human travel agents, the sites are now better than most agents and vastly better than bad travel agents. Even if you have a good agent, online sites let you look around to see your options before you get on the phone. Some airlines offer on their own websites some cheap fares that aren't available any other way. The airlines know that it costs them much less to let the web do the work, and they pay you (sometimes in the form of a hefty discount) to use their web sites.

The theory of airline tickets

Three giant airline computer systems in the United States — Sabre, Galileo/Worldspan (two formerly separate systems that merged), and Amadeus — handle nearly all airline reservations in the United States. (A site such as this is known as a *CRS,* or a computer reservations systems, or a *GDS,* for global distribution system.) Google's ITA Software, which we discuss below, is trying to get into the GDS business, although so far their only GDS customer is Cape Air, a small regional airline.

Although every airline has a "home" GDS, the systems are all interlinked so that you can, with few exceptions, buy tickets for any airline from any GDS. Some low-price, start-up airlines are available by way of GDS, but others — notably, Southwest — don't participate in any of these systems but have instead their own websites, where you can check flights and buy tickets.

In theory, all these systems show the same data; in practice, however, they get a little out of sync with each other. If you're looking for seats on a sold-out flight, an airline's home system is most likely to have that last, elusive seat. If you're looking for the lowest fare to somewhere, check all three systems (using different travel websites) because a fare that's marked as sold out on one system often mysteriously reappears on another system. Also check Orbitz (`www.orbitz.com`) which has direct-connect access to many airlines, bypassing GDS altogether.

Some fare categories are visible only to travel agents and don't appear on any websites, particularly if you aren't staying over a weekend or you're taking a complicated international trip, so check with a good agent before buying if you're taking a short expensive trip during the week or an international trip more complex than a round trip. On the other hand, many airlines offer some special deals that are *only* on their websites and that agents often don't know about. Confused? You should be. We have been.

The confusion is even worse if you want to fly internationally. Official fares to most countries are set by way of the IATA (International Air Transportation Association) cartel, so computer systems usually list only IATA fares for international flights. If you need to buy tickets sooner than a month ahead, you can often find entirely legal *consolidator tickets* for considerably less than the official price, so an online or offline agent is extremely useful for finding the best price. International airlines also have some impressive online offers, most notably from Cathay Pacific, which usually has a pass that includes a ticket from the United States to Hong Kong and then unlimited travel all over Asia.

Here's our distilled wisdom about buying tickets online:

- ✔ **Check online systems.** See which flights are available and the range of prices. Check sites that use different GDSs. (We list some sites at the end of this section.)

- ✔ **After you find a likely airline, check that airline's site.** Look for special, web-only deals. If a low-fare airline flies the route, be sure to check that one, too.

- ✔ **Check prices on flights serving all nearby airports.** An extra 45 minutes of driving time can save you hundreds of dollars.

- ✔ **For a trip more complicated than a simple round trip, check with a travel agent.** You can check by phone, email, or the agent's website to see whether he can beat the online price, and buy your tickets from the agent unless the online deal is better.

- ✔ **For international tickets, check for consolidator tickets.** Do everything in this list and check both online and with your agent, particularly if you don't qualify for the lowest published fare. For complex international trips, such as around the world, agents can usually find routes and prices that the automated systems can't.

- ✔ **Don't overbid.** If you bid on airline tickets at a travel auction website, make sure that you already know the price at which you can buy the ticket.

Before looking at online agents, check out ITA Software (`www.itasoftware.com`). This company produces the fare search engine used by Orbitz and many airline sites. ITA's own site has a version that just searches and doesn't try to sell you any tickets, with more search options than most of its clients offer. They've been bought by Google, and their results are also integrated into some Google searches.

If you hate flying or would rather take the train, Amtrak and VIA Rail Canada offer online reservations (`www.amtrak.com` and `www.viarail.ca`). If you're visiting Europe, a Eurailpass at `www.raileurope.com` can make sense if you plan to take a whole lot of trains, or check schedules and fares for most European railways at the excellent Loco2 at `https://loco2.com` or Capitaine Train at `https://www.capitainetrain.com`. You can also book cruises online. (If a travel site is in another language, look around for an "English" link, or an America, Canadian, or U.K. flag to switch it to English.)

Major airline ticket sites, other than individual airlines, include

- **Expedia** (`www.expedia.com`): The Microsoft entry into the travel biz is now a part of the Interactive media empire.

- **Hotwire** (`www.hotwire.com`): This multi-airline site offers discounted leftover tickets and rental cars and hotels.

- **Orbitz** (`www.orbitz.com`): Orbitz is the high-tech entry into the travel biz, with most airlines' weekly web specials.

- **Priceline** (`www.priceline.com`) Priceline has cheezy TV ads with the guy who no longer looks much like the captain of the Starship Enterprise. They now offer discounted tickets like Hotwire, the "name your own price" reverse auction for which they're best known, and regular tickets like other agents.

- **Travelocity** (`www.travelocity.com`): Travelocity is the Sabre entry into the travel biz. Yahoo! Travel and the AOL travel section are both Travelocity underneath.

Fare-comparison sites abound, including Kayak (`www.kayak.com`), Mobissimo (`www.mobissimo.com`), Hipmunk (`www.hipmunk.com`) and FareCompare (`www.farecompare.com`). We don't find any of them comprehensive enough to depend on, but they're worth a look if you want to try to find that elusive last cheap seat. Most can also help you book hotels and rental cars, too.

More about online airlines

Because the online airline situation changes weekly, anything more we print here would be out of date before you read it. One author of this book is an air travel nerd in his spare time; to see his current list of online airline websites, web specials, and online travel agents, visit `http://airinfo.travel`.

Even More Places to Shop

Here are a few other places for you to shop on the web. We have even bought stuff from most of them.

Auctions and used stuff

You can participate in online auctions of everything from computers and computer parts to antiques to vacation packages. Online auctions resemble any other kind of auction in at least one respect: If you know what you're looking for and know what it's worth, you can find some outstanding values; if you don't, you can easily overpay for junk. We've found replacement parts for a blender, and plates in bowls in our discontinued china pattern.

Many auctions — notably, eBay (as shown in Figure 15-2) — also allow you to list your own stuff for sale, which can be a way to get rid of some of your household clutter a little more discreetly than in a yard sale. The PayPal service (www.paypal.com), now owned by eBay, lets you accept credit card payment from the highest bidder by email. (See Chapter 16 for more information about PayPal.)

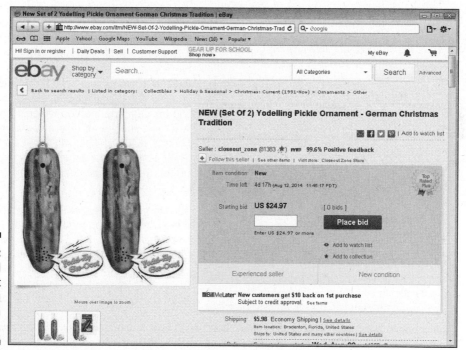

Figure 15-2: You can find just about anything for sale on eBay.

Online auction sites include

- **eBay** (`http://www.ebay.com`): This auction site is the most popular one on the web, and people flock there to sell all sorts of stuff, from baby clothes and toys to computer parts to cars to the occasional tropical island. You can sell stuff, too, by registering as a seller. eBay charges a small commission for auctions, which the seller pays. Searching the completed auctions at eBay is also a terrific way to find out how much an item is worth — you can see what people end up paying for items. If you're thinking of selling that rare Beanie Baby, search the completed auctions for the bad news that it's worth slightly less than it was when it was new and for ideas about how to write an effective description.

- **Half.com** (`www.half.com`): This division of eBay is more like a consignment shop than an auction. Sellers list used items they want to sell at a fixed price, such as books (including textbooks), CDs, movies, video games, electronic equipment, and trading cards. eBay maintains that it'll merge this site into its main eBay site, but it never does.

Don't fall for these online scams

Online commerce, like any other commerce, has a few bad apples. Here are some rotten spots to avoid, particularly on eBay and Craigslist, where you're often buying or selling from individuals, not established companies. Our key piece of advice is that every site has a normal way to do business, and anything out of the ordinary is a red flag. On eBay, the normal way to pay is by using Paypal. Unless you happen to buy from a seller close enough that you can pick up the goods and look at them before you pay, don't pay any other way. On Craigslist, the normal way to buy stuff is for the buyer and seller to meet in person to look at the goods and pay.

The nonresident landlord: A Craigslist ad shows a fabulous apartment at a low price. When you write to the landlord, he explains that he had to move to a faraway city for a new job, he still needs to sublet his old apartment, he's too far away to come back, so just send him the paperwork and the deposit. Uh, no, unless you never want to see your deposit again. The apartments are usually real, ads copied from real ads, but the "landlord" is not.

The large cashier's check: You sell something on eBay for $100. The buyer explains that he has a $1,000 cashier's check that he'll send you, deposit it, wait a few days for it to clear, and you can just wire back $850 and keep an extra $50 for your trouble. What could go wrong? A forged check can take a week or more to bounce, by which time you're out the $850 and the scammer is long gone. A similar oil rig scam targets restaurants; see `dirtcandynyc.com/?p=82`.

The too-good-to-be-true deal: An eBay seller or a website offers an iPhone for $20, or a similarly fabulous deal. Your $20 may be real, but the iPhone isn't. Now and then you can get a great deal on eBay from a seller who underprices an auction on an obscure item, but we all know what an iPhone costs, and it isn't $20.

Craigslist

Craigslist (`craigslist.org`), Figure 15-3, is the website that your local newspaper hates the most, because it's just like the classified ads, only free. It has subsites for cities large and small all over the world, where you can find everything from a used car to a new apartment, job, or boyfriend. Unlike eBay, Craigslist listings are supposed to be local, so the two parties (we'd say buyer and seller, but some of the ads are for personals) can meet in person to complete the deal. Nearly all ads are free; they only charge for real estate ads in a few large cities, which brings in enough money to pay for everything else.

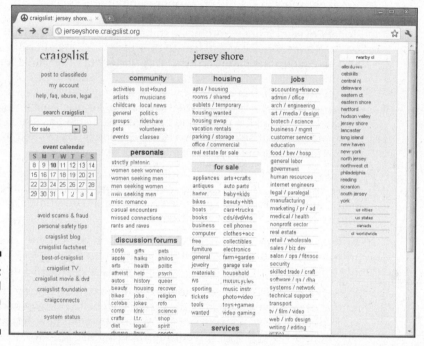

Figure 15-3: Buy and sell locally with Craigslist.

We've had good luck buying and selling appliances, cars, and even an elderly Sunfish sailboat on Craigslist. They do a good job of policing bogus ads, but see the earlier section "Don't fall for these online scams" to know what to watch out for.

Books, music, and more

You can't flip through the books in an online bookstore as easily as you can in person (although Amazon.com comes close by offering a selection of pages from many books). However, if you know what you want, you can find good deals.

Here are some top sites:

- **AbeBooks:** This site, formerly Advanced Book Exchange, offers the combined catalogs of thousands of secondhand booksellers at `www.abebooks.com`. You pay the same price as you would in a used-book shop (plus shipping, of course), and you save hours of searching. Whether you're looking for a favorite book from your childhood or a rare, first-edition *For Dummies* book, this site is worth visiting.

- **AddALL:** AddALL (`www.addall.com`) is another good used-book site offering titles from thousands of used-book stores as well as a price comparison service for new books.

- **Amazon.com:** One of the great online-commerce success stories (at `www.amazon.com`) sprang up from nothing — if you call several million dollars of seed money nothing — to become one of the Net's biggest online stores. Amazon.com has an enormous catalog of books and CDs and an equally enormous and growing variety of other junk, much of which can get to you in a few days. It also has an affiliates program in which other websites can refer you to their favorite books for sale at Amazon, creating sort of a virtual virtual-bookstore. Amazon sells most books at less than list price, and in most cases also has used copies from independent sellers. It also has used books, DVDs, and just about everything else from pogo sticks to underwear.

- **Barnes and Noble:** Barnes & Noble (`www.bn.com`) is the biggest bookstore chain in the United States, and its online bookstore is big, complete, and well done. You can even return online purchases at any of its stores. It also has a large selection of music.

- **Kobo**: Kobo supports your local bookshop, so you can buy books online without guilt. When you sign up for an account, Kobo asks you to identify your favorite independent bookstore and give them a cut.

- **Powell's Books:** The largest independent (nonchain) bookstore in the United States has a correspondingly large website (`www.powellbooks.com`) offering new and used books. We like its email newsletter with new and rediscovered books and author interviews.

Clothes

This section points out a few familiar clothing merchants with online stores. A little Googlage can find hundreds of other stores, both familiar and obscure:

- **Eddie Bauer:** This site (`www.eddiebauer.com`) has way more stuff than is available in its stores. (John gave up on the stores about the third time they said, "Oh, you have to order that from the website.")

✔ **The Gap:** This site (www.gap.com) has the same stuff you find in its stores, but for people of unusual vertical or horizontal dimension, it also has jeans in sizes the stores don't stock, as well as links to Banana Republic and Old Navy, its upscale and downscale divisions.

✔ **Lands' End:** Most of this catalog is online (www.landsend.com), and you can order anything you find in any of its individual printed catalogs along with online-only discounted overstocks. It also has plenty of the folksy blather that encourages you to think of the company in terms of a few folks in the cornfields of Wisconsin rather than a corporate mail-order colossus belonging to Sears Roebuck. (It's both.)

✔ **REI:** This large sports-equipment and outdoor-wear co-op is headquartered in Seattle. Members receive a small rebate on purchases. The whole catalog is online (www.rei.com), and you can find occasional online specials and discounts.

Computers

When you're shopping for computer hardware online, be sure that the vendor you're considering offers both a good return policy (in case the computer doesn't work when it arrives) and a long warranty.

Here are a few well-known vendors:

✔ **Apple Computer:** The Apple site (store.apple.com) has lots of information about Macintosh computers, and now it offers online purchasing of the iPad, iPod, and iPhone, too.

✔ **Best Buy:** This site (www.bestbuy.com) is the online version of the ubiquitous big-box store. Orders can be shipped, or you can pick them up at your local store.

✔ **CDW:** CDW (www.cdw.com) has a good selection of hardware and software, and we've found it to be reliable.

✔ **Dell Computers:** This site has an extensive catalog with online ordering and custom computer system configurations (www.dell.com).

✔ **Newegg** (www.newegg.com) We have no idea where the name came from, but we've found them to be a reliable source of computer and electronic equipment.

✔ **Other World Computing** (www.macsales.com) is great for Macs and accessories.

✔ **PC Connection and Mac Connection:** For computer hardware, software, and accessories, PC and Mac Connection (www.pcconnection.com and www.macconnection.com) is one of the oldest and most reliable online computer retailers. And, you can specify overnight delivery within the continental United States even if you order as late as 2 a.m.!

An online shopper's checklist

Here are some questions to keep in mind when you're shopping online. Astute shoppers will notice that these questions are the same ones to keep in mind wherever you're shopping:

✔ Are the descriptions clear enough to know what you're ordering?

✔ Are the prices competitive, with other online stores *and* with mail-order and regular retail?

✔ Does the store have the products in stock, or does it offer a firm shipping date?

✔ Does the store display reviews from customers who have bought and used the item?

✔ Does the store have a good reputation?

✔ Does the store have a clearly written privacy policy that limits what it can do with the data it collects from you?

✔ Can you ask questions about your order?

✔ Does the store use a shipping method that allows you to track the shipment?

✔ How can you return unsatisfactory goods?

Food

To show the range of edibles available online, here are some of our favorite places to point, click, and chow down:

✔ **Bobolink Dairy**: A recovering software nerd and his family in rural New Jersey make and sell their own cheese — a rich, gooey, French-style cheese. Its URL (www.cowsoutside.com) refers to cows out in the pasture rather than tied up in the barn.

✔ **Cabot Creamery:** This site (www.cabotcheese.coop) sells some of the best cheddar in Vermont. (Don't tell anyone that a lot of the milk comes from New York.)

✔ **Gaspar's** (www.linguica.com): If you weren't aware that Portuguese garlic sausage is one of the four basic food groups, this site will fix that problem. Oddly, online orders incur steep shipping charges, but phone or fax orders are shipped free, so we print and fax the order form. Also check out the competition at www.amarals.com. Both have Autocrat Coffee Syrup, which will inspire gasps of recognition from anyone who grew up in Rhode Island.

✔ **Gimme Coffee:** This site (www.gimmecoffee.com) features highly opinionated coffee from the wilds of upstate New York. Gimme Coffee has online orders and lots of advice on what to do with your coffee after it arrives; follow the Gimme Locations link to find pictures of the place John goes when he's in need of literary inspiration, also known as *caffeine*.

✔ **The Kitchen Link**: Search this site (www.kitchenlink.com) for the perfect recipe and then shop for the ingredients.

✔ **Peapod:** Peapod (www.peapod.com) lets you shop for groceries online and then delivers them to your home. You have to live in an area that the parent grocery chains serve — the northeast (Stop and Shop), Washington DC and Philadelphia (Giant), and Chicago areas. If you live somewhere else, Netgrocer (www.netgrocer.com) delivers nonperishables by rather pricey overnight express, and perishables in a limited area near its New Jersey headquarters.

More Opinions Than You Ever Imagined

With all the products available to buy on the web, how can you decide what to get? Fortunately, you aren't on your own. Lots and lots of websites offer you advice on everything from cruise ships to restaurants to used cars. Many of these sites are part of *Web 2.0*, a jargonful way to say that most of what's on the website was contributed by the users. This concept has two helpful benefits: You get the combined experience of all those users, and the website gets all that stuff for free. In many cases, sites show a combination of professional reviews and user comments, which would be Web 1½. Here are some review sites we've found useful.

Travel and food

Travel guidebooks have been around since Baedeker in the 1820s, and restaurant guides at least since Michelin in 1900. Now they've moved online, so you can check out the advice and then let them know if you disagree:

✔ **Yelp:** (yelp.com) Yelp, Figure 15-4, is the most comprehensive city guide around, with geographically organized reviews of everything from car dealers to restaurants to botanical gardens. It's a good spot to look for places to eat.

✔ **TripAdvisor:** (tripadvisor.com) As its name suggests, it's a site for travelers. Type a place name, and it tells you where to stay, what to see, and perhaps how to get there. The site is aimed more at people visiting an area, as opposed to Yelp, which is more for people who live there. The company has an empire of related travel websites including seatguru.com (where to sit on a plane) and flipkey.com (vacation house rentals.) Hotel owners take their reviews seriously and often respond directly to particularly good or bad ones.

✔ **Zagat:** Zagat (zagat.com) made the leap from printed guides to online quite successfully. Everything in the printed guides is on the website, and web reviews are now the main material for the printed guides. Basic information is available for free, and access to full reviews requires a subscription. If you contribute reviews, the site often comps subscriptions or sends you the next printed guide. Recently sold to Google, who say they plan to integrate its reviews into their local searches.

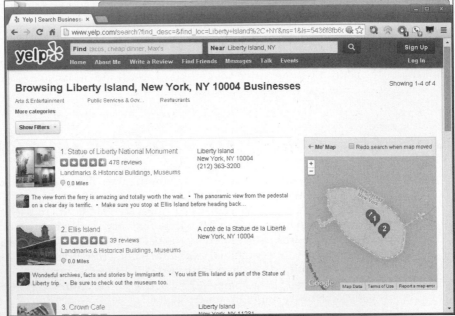

Figure 15-4:
Yelp reviews
just about
everything

✔ **OpenTable:** (opentable.com) The largest site for making restaurant reservations, it also has reviews from both their own users and Zagat. We use it to quickly find out who has a table and at what time tonight.

✔ **Via Michelin:** (viamichelin.com) The famous Michelin guides made the transition to online as well. It has restaurant reviews for much of Europe, New York, Chicago, and San Francisco, and hotel and sightseeing guides for nearly everywhere. Reviews show both their professional reviews and user comments.

Vroom, vroom

A car is one of the biggest purchases most of us make. Now you can do your research so that by the time you reach the dealer, you probably know more about the car you want to buy than the salesman does. Let these sites help you:

✔ **Edmunds:** (edmunds.com) This site is where we start looking for a car. It has reviews of new and used cars (both professional and user contributed), listings of vehicles for sale, and typical sale prices so that you have a good idea of how much you should pay.

- **Cars.com:** (`cars.com`) Remember back when you looked for a car in the classified ads in the paper instead of pointing and clicking? The papers have realized that the ads aren't coming back to the paper, so five large newspaper chains jointly run Cars.com. Its original purpose was to be the online version of the classifieds so that the papers could compete with online markets such as Craigslist. Now the site has expanded to become a full-service car info site. If you want to buy or sell a used car, be sure to check the suggested Kelly price on Cars.com and the Edmunds price, because they're often quite different.

- **Dealerrater:** (`dealerrater.com`) This site just has ratings of car dealers, for both sales and service. The dealers take their ratings quite seriously, so it's worth letting the world know when you have a particularly good or bad experience.

For that even bigger purchase, a place to live, Yelp has reviews of real estate agents and apartments.

Real Estate

Imagine you're walking the dog along the street, you pass a house with a "For Sale" sign, whip out your smartphone, check the asking price, and say, "Hah! They'll never get that much." We'd never do anything that crass, but, uh, we know some people who do, that's it.

Are these reviews real?

If anyone can write a review, what keeps ethically challenged businesses from writing fake favorable reviews for themselves, and unfavorable reviews of their competitors? Nothing, unfortunately. All the legitimate review sites try to police their reviews (look at the page of conditions at Dealerrater, saying that that if you or a relative work in the car business, you absolutely, totally, cannot review anything go away don't even think about it), but some fake reviews show up, particularly on TripAdvisor. Most of the people writing fake reviews aren't good at it, so if you see a place with five favorable reviews and one that hated it, or vice versa, it might be a fake. It's also possible that the place is inconsistent, but after you read reviews for a while, you can tell.

Also, quite a lot of "review" sites are completely fake. Any site purporting to compare credit cards other than Bank Rate (`www.bankrate.com`) is a fake, trying to sell you whichever card it reviews favorably. Again, it isn't hard to tell, if you stumble across a review site you never heard of and it generously offers to sell you whatever item has the most stars, now you know why.

Since real estate sales and tax assessments are public information, recorded with the local government, and real estate offered for sale is almost always published online by the selling agent, there are impressively comprehensive databases of prices. The two major public sites are Zillow and Trulia:

- ✔ **Zillow** (www.zillow.com) is our favorite real estate info site. They have maps of most of the country so you can pick an area and it'll show you a map with all of the local real estate for sale, Figure 15-5. If you zoom in, you can see individual lots. Real estate voyeurs enjoy their Zestimates of how much a property listed for sale will really sell for, and their estimated values of every other house, as well. If you're in the market, they have info about taxes and schools, and links to agents who can show you the house. They have nice apps for smartphones and tablets that can automatically show you the map for where you are right now.

- ✔ **Trulia** (www.trulia.com) is a lot like Zillow, and will become even more similar, since they're planning to merge. But their maps are a little different, and it's worth looking at both to see which you prefer.

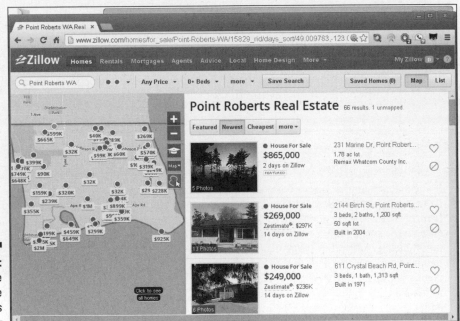

Figure 15-5:
Looks like some nice houses

Many county and city assessment departments put all or part of their information online, which can provide an amazing amount of detail both for seeing if your assessment is in line with the neighbors, or looking at what the housing is like in a place you might want to move.

Real estate, temporary version

Zillow and Trulia also show real estate for rent, both for long term living and in some areas for short term vacations. Vacationers and other travelers also have these options, offering short term rentals direct from the property owners:

- **Airbnb** (www.airbnb.com) offers everything from a couch in someone's spare room to fully furnished houses for short term visits, both in the US and other countries. We've found a cute little studio in Paris (up four narrow flights of stairs, but that's Paris for you) and a beautiful apartment in Montreal.

- **HomeAway** (www.homeaway.com) has vacation rentals from all over the world.

- **FlipKey** (www.flipkey.com) is part of TripAdvisor, with vacation rentals.

Questions and Answers

Several sites match people with questions and people with answers. Ask anything, and as likely as not you'll get answers. Often the answers are even correct. (This problem is a chronic one.) All of them organize questions by topic, so you can browse existing answered and unanswered questions and write your own questions and answers. The usual suspects include

- **Answers.com:** The largest Q-and-A site has a huge range of topics. The questions range from middle schoolers who want you to do their homework ("What was the cold war?") to complex questions about science and finance. The system does a good job of guessing when a new question is the same as an old one and linking them.

- **Quora:** A more recent entry in the Q and A biz, Quora (quora.com) appeals to a more business-oriented and professional audience. Rather than put questions into categories, they tag questions with keywords so that you can look for questions about Bank and New Jersey or the like. A surprising number of real world experts participate, such as Burton Malkiel, the father of index mutual finds, who answers a lot of investment questions.

- **Yahoo! Answers:** (answers.yahoo.com) This site is similar to Answers.com but has a younger crowd and an unfortunate tendency for the answers to be wrong.

Where'd all this spam come from?

Merchants know that people who've bought stuff from them before are likely to buy from them again. To help this process along, most of them will start sending you ads after you buy anything. Often those ads come with startling frequency, like the day after you order and every three days thereafter.

Usually there is a pre-checked box on the order form that you can un-check to avoid the spam. Or if not, or you forget, every legitimate merchant has an "unsubscribe" link in every ad, which works. (This isn't because they're nice; it's because the law requires it.) If you buy something, and you uncheck the box and they spam you anyway, or you tell them to stop and they don't, now you know they're not legit, but by then it's too late. Oh, well.

Chapter 16

Banking, Bill Paying, and Investing Online

In This Chapter

▶ Managing your checking and savings accounts online

▶ Looking at your credit card statements online

▶ Emailing payments with PayPal

▶ Managing your investments online

▶ Keeping track of your home budget

*O*nce upon a time, money was substantial stuff that glinted in the sun and clinked when you dropped it on the table. Investments were engraved certificates that you kept in your safe-deposit box if they worked out, or used as bathroom wallpaper if they didn't. Well, that was then. Now, money and investments are mere electronic blips scampering from computer to computer, and if you do any banking or investing, one of the computers they scamper through might as well be yours.

You can do just about any banking online that doesn't require physically handling pieces of paper, which means everything except withdrawing cash and, at some banks, depositing checks. For these tasks, you have to use an ATM or, if you're truly retro, physically visit a bank branch and talk to a human being. But we help you avoid the last option as much as possible.

Going to the Bank Without Ever Leaving Home

Nearly every bank in the United States now offers online banking. They don't do it to be cool; they do it because online banking is vastly cheaper for them than ATMs or tellers. Because both you and your bank have a strong interest in making sure that the person messing around online with your accounts is *you,* the sign-up process is usually a bit complicated — the bank either calls you to verify that you signed up or mails you a paper letter specifying your password. After you're signed up, you visit the bank's website and log in with your new username or number and password. Every bank's website is different, but they all show you an account statement along the lines of the one from John's bank, shown in Figure 16-1.

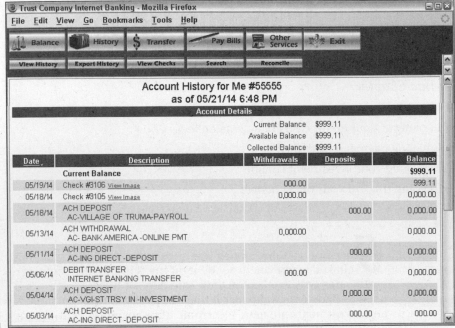

Figure 16-1:
A week of bank stuff, give or take a few details.

As you can see, deposits and withdrawals look like they do on printed statements you receive in the mail. If you click the View Image link next to a check number, it shows you a picture of the canceled check. The Automated Clearing House, or ACH, lines are described in the nearby sidebar "ACH! It's better than a check!" You can also download a PDF of your bank statements.

If you use an accounting program such as Quicken or Microsoft Money, banks invariably offer a way to download your account info into your program. Look for a link labeled Download or Export. In Figure 16-1, it's the small Export History button, near the upper-left corner.

Details differ, but beyond the capability to check your statement, all banks offer roughly the same services, including transfers and bill-paying and sometimes check deposit by taking a picture of the check.

ACH! It's better than a check!

For the past 150 years or so, the usual way to move money from one person's account at a bank to a second person's account at another bank has been for the first person to write a check and give it to the second person, who takes it to her bank and deposits it. (At least, that's the system in the United States — in Europe, the first person writes out a bank transfer and gives it to his bank to set up the payment.) Now that we're in the computer age, we have a high-tech replacement for this process: ACH transfers.

Automated Clearing House, or *ACH,* transfers can do anything a check can do. Rather than print payroll checks, companies can use ACH to deposit money directly into employees' bank accounts. The U.S. government uses ACH to make Social Security payments. You can use ACH to pay bills or to move money between accounts at different banks. For most purposes, ACH transactions are better than paper checks because they're faster and more reliable.

To identify the account to use for an ACH transfer, you need to provide the *routing number,* which identifies the bank, and the account number at that bank. The easiest way to find the routing number for your own checking account is to look at the line of funny-looking numbers printed along the bottom of one of your checks. The routing number consists of nine digits, usually printed at the left end of the line. The account number also appears on that line, and a check number (which ACH doesn't use) may appear, too. Savings accounts also work for ACH transfers; to find the routing number, look at a check from the same bank or call the bank and ask.

You may be wondering, "Can anyone who knows my account number suck money from my account by using ACH?" Well, yes. But when you receive your statement, you can challenge any bogus ACH transaction just as you can challenge a forged check and get your money back. In practice, ACH is safe and reliable, and we use it for our own accounts all the time.

Transferring money between bank accounts

If you have more than one account at a bank, a checking and savings account, some CDs, or a mortgage, you can usually move money from one account to another. In the account shown in Figure 16-1, the line that says *Internet Banking Transfer* indicates that money has been transferred from the checking account to a mortgage account, to make the monthly mortgage payment. To get a better idea of how this transaction works, here are the steps for transferring money from a checking account to a mortgage account (again, specific steps vary among banks):

1. **Click the Transfer button (or whatever your bank's website calls it).**

2. **Enter the amount you want to transfer in the box labeled Amount (or similar wording).**

3. **Select the account that the transferred money is coming from, generally from a list of possible From accounts.**

4. **Select the account number the transferred money is going to, generally from a list of possible To accounts.**

5. **Click the button labeled Transfer or Do It (or similar wording) — it's done.**

It's that easy. Most banks handle transfers within the bank the same day; at John's bank, you can enter a transfer as late as 7 p.m., which is handy when you remember at dinnertime that the mortgage is due today.

Many banks also let you make transfers to and from accounts at *other* banks, using ACH. To set up transfers, you provide the other bank's routing code and account number. Depending on the bank, you may be required to provide a voided check from that account, verify that the account name is the same as your account name, or make a couple of tiny deposits into the account and answer correctly when they ask you for the amounts. After you set up a transfer, it resembles a transfer within your own bank: You specify the accounts and the amount and then click. You can also transfer money between your bank and your mutual fund or brokerage account. In Figure 16-1, for example, the ACH deposits from ING Direct are from another bank, and the ACH deposit from VGI-ST TRSY is from a Vanguard mutual fund.

Transfers to other banks have two important differences: time and price. Even though the transfer is handled entirely electronically, the money takes anywhere from two days to a week to show up at the other end, depending on the other bank. The time it takes for any particular bank is consistent, so if the transaction took three days the last time, expect it to take three days the next time. If you must have the money available so that you can write checks on it, allow a week and keep an eye on your balances until you've made enough transfers to know how long they take.

The price for transfers varies from zero to two bucks, with no consistency among banks. A transfer can be started from either the sending *(push)* or receiving *(pull)* end; often, Bank A charges you a dollar if you tell it to *send* money to Bank B, but if (instead) you tell Bank B to *receive* exactly the same amount of money from Bank A, it's free. All else being equal, pushing gets the money there faster.

You can use PayPal to move money from just about any bank account to any other bank account for free. It's a handy way to make online transfers (and we describe it later in this chapter).

Paying bills online

Writing checks is *so* 20th century; our young-adult kids have never written a check. Now you can pay most of your bills online. In many cases, you can arrange for automatic payments from your bank account for routine monthly bills. (In Figure 16-1, *Bank America* refers to the MasterCard bill.) We've arranged automatic payments for credit card, electric and gas, and mobile phone bills — a typical mix. Most banks offer a *bill-pay* service, using one of a handful of specialized companies in this field. Some banks provide bill-pay for free, some charge, and some provide it for free as part of a package. Even if your bank doesn't offer bill-pay, utility and credit card companies often can arrange for you to pay their bills automatically from your checking account.

When the bank pays the bill, it sends an ACH transfer if it recognizes the payee (generally larger companies); otherwise, it mails a paper check. If the bank pays by ACH, the payment is usually received the next day; otherwise it's mailed the next day — and the mail takes however long it takes.

Each of these companies has its own procedure. We use a credit card example to show how this process usually works. Figure 16-2 shows the online payment page at American Express. When logged in to its website, you set up payments by entering your bank account's routing code and account number, which ACH needs. (See the preceding sidebar, "ACH! It's better than a check!") After the payment info is set up, you visit the website and specify how much you want to pay and when, and the bill is then paid from your bank account. Usually, you get credit the same day, which is a big help to avoid paying credit card interest when you remember at the last minute that the bill is due. Some cards, including American Express, also offer the option to pay every month automatically on the due date — just the thing for thrifty card users who pay off their bills every month.

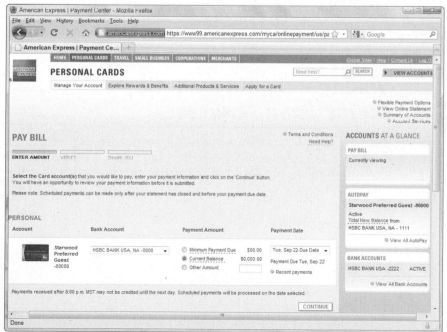

Figure 16-2:
Pay the credit card bill with one click.

Figure 16-3 shows the bill payment service from John's bank. To set it up, you pick the companies to pay and then enter your account number and the name and address of the company to pay, if the bank doesn't already have it on file. Some bill-pay systems offer the option of *electronic presentment,* in which you see your bill on the web rather than receive it by paper mail. You also tell the system which bank account you want to pay the bills from. Then, to pay your bills each month, you just visit the bank's website and enter the amounts to pay and the date. The bank automatically moves the money out of your account on the date for each payment. Some banks offer recurring payments so that you can tell them to pay the same amounts every month.

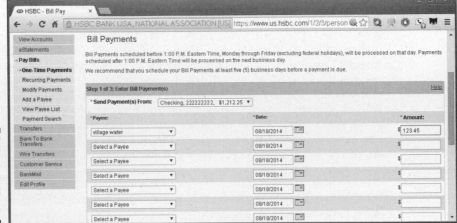

Figure 16-3:
Point, click, and pay the water and electric bills.

Taking advantage of other online bank services

Because doing business over the web is much cheaper than doing it in person, banks are putting all sorts of other services online. Visit your bank's website to see what it offers. Among some of the services we've seen offered are

- Loan applications
- New accounts
- Retirement accounts
- Checkbook-balancing calculators

Checking out a few recommended banks

These days, any bank you pass while driving down the street offers online banking, but some specialist banks do everything online. Although it's possible to do all your banking online, we prefer to have our main account at a local bank, where we can drop by and argue with the staff, and to use an online bank for a high-interest savings account that you can't get at a local bank.

To give you a flavor of what's available, here are some banks we use and recommend:

- ✔ **Simple** (www.simple.com): A new online-only bank.
- ✔ **Gobank** (www.gobank.com) Another new online-only bank,
- ✔ **Capital One 360** (http://home.capitalone360.com): A large regional bank.

All three offer free online checking accounts; Capital One also offers savings accounts that pay relatively high interest. Capital One has branches mostly in the northeast and Texas, but their best deals are online.

To open an account at any of these banks, you fill out a form on its website, usually including the ACH info about your existing checking account to link to your new account. After it's set up, you can move money back and forth between the accounts as needed. Each will send you a MasterCard or Visa debit card you can use to pay for stuff, and also to take cash out of ATMs. Each has a network of ATMs you can use for free, mostly at stores and gas stations. To get money into your account, each has a mobile phone app that lets you deposit checks by taking pictures of them, or you can use ACH or payroll direct deposit. Gobank also has arrangements with Walmart and 7-11 to accept cash deposits.

Money you put into your savings account has to stay there for a week before you can get it back, and you can only make six online withdrawals per month. (Accounts at other banks have similar rules.) Capital One also offers certificates of deposit, mortgages, home equity loans, and retirement accounts. These are full-service banks, and offer everything else a bank offers, all available online if you want it.

We've used all of these banks quite happily, but we give the nod to Capital One because it offers a wider range of services and has been around longer.

 To squeeze the last bit of interest out of your money, visit www.bankrate.com where you can find a listing of banks paying the highest rates on online savings accounts or certificates of deposit. Search for _MMA_ (money market account) for an online savings account.

How real are these banks, anyway?

When you open a bank account in person, you visit the bank and then look around to see that the bank looks like a bank, with tellers, people in suits, and a vault, which is good — or, you see a couple of people in a Winnebago with card tables and some money in cooler chests, which is bad. When you visit a bank's website, it's hard to tell a good one from a bad one. But it's not hard to do a little research.

Every real bank in the United States is a member of the Federal Deposit Insurance Corporation (FDIC). The FDIC has a nice-looking website at www.fdic.gov that has, among other things, detailed reports on every member bank. On the home page, click the Deposit Insurance link near the upper-left corner, and then click Bank Find, at the top of the list. On that page, you can search by name or location. For example, to check out Capital One, enter Capital One, and

search. (For this particular bank, an alternative route to the same information is to click the FDIC icon on the bank's home page.) Either way, you see a reassuring page indicating that yes, it's insured. For more information, click Financial Information to see the bank's latest balance sheets. In this case, it says that the bank has $236 billion in assets and $34 billion in capital. Looks like a bank to us. Simple and Gobank are a little harder to find; if you look at the small print at the bottom of the screen, you'll find that Gobank is a brand name of Green Dot Bank, and Simple's accounts are really at The Bancorp Bank.

Credit unions (joining one isn't a bad idea if you're eligible) are insured by the National Credit Union Association at www.ncua.gov. You can search for the name of your credit union to check its status.

Trying out combo banking

If you have an account with a stockbroker, such as the ones we list later in this chapter, it generally offers a check-writing option, which makes it act like a checking account, usually at low cost. If you don't have a local bank you like, this option can be a good one.

Dealing with Credit Cards

Just about every credit card in the country offers online access for the same reason that bank accounts do — online transactions are a lot cheaper for them than calls to the toll-free number.

Online credit card services start with applying for the card. Search your fave search engine for credit cards and you find a phantasmagoria of offers. They change daily, but you can look for various goodies — no annual fee, bonuses and rebates, and low interest rates. Most sites that appear to compare cards are in fact selling one bank's cards, so treat their claims of unique and superior features with skepticism.

After you have your card, typical online conveniences include these:

- ✔ Check your balance and recent transactions.

- ✔ Pay your bill from your checking account.

- ✔ Apply for a credit line increase.

- ✔ Ask for copies of sales slips for charges you don't recognize, or challenge ones you think are bogus.

- ✔ Download account information into Quicken and other personal finance programs.

- ✔ Manage rebate and bonus programs related to the cards.

Different credit-card-issuing banks have somewhat different versions of these services, but comparing them without getting the credit card first is difficult. For example, some banks let you set up automatic payments to pay each bill in full on the due date, getting the maximum use of your money without paying interest. At others, you have to visit their website every month to schedule the month's payment. We would make a list of features, but it would be out of date before it was printed, so visit some bank websites to see what they're offering. (We compared two different banks in the tenth edition of this book, but then they merged, keeping the worst features of each one. Sigh.)

Pay for Your Stuff with PayPal

Credit cards are easy to use — if you're *spending* money. Until recently, it has been all but impossible for individuals (rather than companies) to receive payments by credit card. Even small businesses found it expensive and time consuming to accept credit card payments. PayPal (www.paypal.com) has changed all that, and it also provides an easy way to move money among accounts at different banks.

PayPal is a boon to individuals who buy and sell at auction sites such as eBay (which owns PayPal), but it has many other uses, too. PayPal helps you start a small business on the web: Small organizations can use PayPal to collect payments for events such as dinners and amateur theater, nonprofits can accept donations, and it's just about the only way to make payments to individuals in other countries without paying a service charge larger than the amount you're paying.

If you plan to accept PayPal for your business, be sure to heed PayPal's warnings regarding shipping *only to verified buyer addresses.* Be sure to comply carefully with all the fine print to protect yourself against fraud. Most first-time sellers learn the hard way that it's they who pay the cost of fraud — and even the cost of their customers' innocent errors. The PayPal fraud rate is lower than that of most credit card fraud, but it's a case of *merchant beware* — know your customer and take appropriate steps to safeguard your transactions.

To use PayPal, you set up an account, which is quite easy. It wants your name, mailing address, phone number, and email address. The basic personal account is all you need unless you plan to sell a whole lot of stuff on eBay. (If your plans change, you can upgrade your account.) PayPal encourages you to provide it with your bank account number so that when you pay somebody, PayPal can take the money directly. That way, they don't have to pay the credit card companies, and you can move any money you receive into your account with minimum hassle. You should also link a credit card if you have one.

When you first tell PayPal to link your account to a bank account, PayPal verifies your bank account number by making two random deposits of less than a dollar. You then have to tell it the amount of the deposits to complete your registration. You can link several bank accounts to your PayPal account and then move money out of one account and into PayPal, wait a few days for the transaction to be complete, and then move the money out of PayPal and into a different account — all for free. If you live in the United States, you can link only U.S. bank accounts; if you live anywhere else, you can link both U.S. accounts and accounts in your own country.

After you open an account, you can send money to anyone who can receive email. If that person doesn't already have a PayPal account, she opens one when "cashing" your email. The money you send can come from the balance in your PayPal account or from a bank account or credit card that you link to your PayPal account. After you have money in your account, you can use it to pay other people, move it to your linked bank account, or spend it with a debit card linked to your PayPal account. Check the list of fees carefully. Payments marked *Personal* and made without using a credit card are generally free. Everything else has about a 3 percent fee. Every time you set up a payment, PayPal deducts it from your balance, if any, and then from your linked bank account. If you want to pay with your credit card instead, usually a good idea for eBay and other commercial payments, you have to click a little Change link and change it before completing the payment.

PayPal is usually the easiest and cheapest way to send moderate (less than $1,000) amounts of money to people in other countries. It charges a few percent to change money from one currency to another, but compared to the alternatives, such as bank wires, foreign currency checks, or Western Union, it's a bargain.

Criminals send out spam claiming to be from PayPal and claiming that you "must" provide them with your account number and password right away to clear up an account problem. Don't fall for it. PayPal will *never* ask you for your password or account information in an email message — or anywhere other than on its website. If you receive a message that seems to be from PayPal and are unsure whether it's real, don't click on any links in the message — instead, manually type **www.paypal.com** into your web browser and log in. If anything's wrong, the website tells you. If you get a suspicious email from PayPal, forward the entire email to spoof@paypal.com.

Send Money to Your Pals

Although you can use PayPal to send money to your friends, if you do it very often, it's more convenient and usually cheaper to use peer payment systems such as Venmo and Dwolla. The good news is that they are really cheap, often free, but the bad news is that they don't offer the buyer protection that credit cards and PayPal do. They warn you to pay only people you know, so in practice this isn't a problem if you use them that way.

To use any of them, you first set up an account, which they usually call a wallet, and link it to some combination of bank accounts, debit cards, or credit cards. Then you can send money to other people, or ask them to send you money. When you send money, it comes out of your wallet, or if there isn't enough, out of a linked bank account or card. When you receive money, it goes into your wallet where you can pay other people, or move it to a linked bank account.

All of these systems have web sites, listed below, which are the easiest places to set up an account. They also all have apps for mobile devices, which is the easiest way to use them. If you're out with friends, and someone else has just paid for the pizza, you can use the app right there to pay for your share, or she can send you a payment request, as in Figure 16-4. They all provide a wide range of ways to identify your payees, including email address, mobile phone number, and often Facebook or Twitter account names.

The three systems we describe here are more similar than different, so the one to use is the one your friends use. They're all free to sign up, so if your friends use different ones, you can join them all.

- ✔ **Dwolla:** (www.dwolla.com) Accounts can link only to bank accounts, not cards. Payments under $10 are free, above cost 25¢. Payments only to other Dwolla members. Can also be used for some business payments.

- ✔ **Venmo:** (www.venmo.com) Accounts can link to bank accounts, credit and debit cards. Payments from your wallet or bank account are free, while credit cards may be free or may cost about 3%. Can pay anyone; nonmembers get email encouraging them to join and collect their payment, which is returned if they don't do so.

- ✔ **Google Wallet:** (wallet.google.com) Google's wallet is a peer payment system as well as being the way to pay for downloads on Android devices and a payment system that competes with PayPal. You need a Google account to use Google Wallet. Anyone with an Android device has a Google wallet as part of their Google account, although they often don't realize it can be used for more than downloads. Gmail users already have Google accounts, too. Accounts can link to bank accounts, credit, or debit cards. Peer payments are free unless the money comes from a credit card.

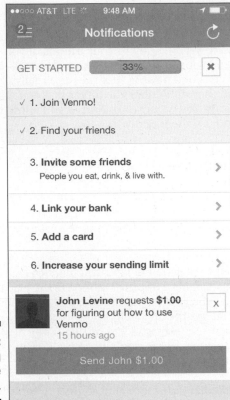

Figure 16-4:
Requesting
money in the
Venmo app.

Investing Your Money Online

If you invest in mutual funds or the stock market (something that's difficult to avoid these days unless you anticipate dying at an early age), you can find a remarkable range of resources online. An enormous amount of stock information is also available, providing Net users with research resources as good as professional analysts had before the advent of online investing.

The most important thing to remember about *all* online financial resources is that everyone has an ax to grind — and wants to get paid somehow. In most cases, the situation is straightforward; for example, a mutual fund manager wants you to invest in her funds, and a stockbroker wants you to buy and sell stocks with him. Some other sites are less obvious: Some are supported by advertising, and others push certain special kinds of investments. Just consider the source (and any vested interests they may have in mind) when you're considering that source's advice.

Mutual funds

Mutual funds are definitely the investment of the baby boomer generation. The world now has more mutual funds than it has stocks for the funds to buy. (Kind of makes you wonder, doesn't it?) Most fund managers have at least descriptions of the funds and prospectuses online, and many now provide online access so that you can check your account, move money from one fund to another within a fund group, and buy and sell funds — all with the money coming from and going to your bank account by way of ACH.

Well-known fund groups include

- **American Century:** A broad group of funds at www.americancentury.com
- **Fidelity Investments:** The 500-pound gorilla of mutual funds; specializes in actively managed funds at www.fidelity.com
- **Vanguard Group:** The other 500-pound gorilla; specializes in low-cost and index funds at www.vanguard.com

The online brokers listed in the following section also let you buy and sell mutual funds, although it almost always costs less if you deal directly with the fund manager.

Stockbrokers

Most well-known, full-service brokerage firms have jumped onto the web, along with a new generation of low-cost online brokers that offer remarkably cheap stock trading. A trade that may cost $100 with a full-service firm can cost as little as $8 with a low-cost broker. The main difference is that the cheap firms don't offer investment advice and don't assign you to a specific broker. For people who do their own research and don't want advice from a broker, the low-cost firms work well. For people who need some advice, the partial- or full-service firms often offer lower-cost trades online, and they let you get a complete view of your account whenever you want. The number of extra services the brokerages offer (such as retirement accounts, dividend reinvestment, and automatic transfers to and from your checking account) varies widely.

Online brokers include

- **Charles Schwab:** The original discount broker (www.schwab.com) offers somewhat more investment help than E-Trade and TD Ameritrade, but at a slightly higher price. Kathleen Sindell, the author of *Investing Online For Dummies,* 5th Edition (John Wiley & Sons, Inc.), recommended this site to us.

- **E-Trade:** This low-cost, no-advice broker (`www.etrade.com`) also offers bank accounts, credit cards, boat loans, and just about every other financial service known to humankind.

- **Scottrade:** Another low-cost, no-advice broker, Scottrade (`www.scottrade.com`) also has offices with live brokers, for people who want extra help at extra cost.

- **TD Ameritrade:** The low-cost, limited-advice broker (`www.tdameritrade.com`) is affiliated with Toronto-Dominion Bank, one of the largest Canadian banks that also has extensive US operations. It has good online research tools.

Most fund groups, including the ones in the preceding list, have brokerage departments — which can be a good choice if you want to hold both individual stocks and funds.

Portfolio tracking

Several services let you track your portfolio online. You enter the number of shares of every fund and stock you own, and the service can tell you — at any time — exactly how much they're worth and how much money you lost today. Some of them send, by email, a daily portfolio report, if requested. These reports are handy if you have mutual funds from more than one group or both funds and stocks. All tracking services are either supported by advertising or run by a brokerage that hopes to gain your trading business:

- **Google Finance:** This tracking service (`www.google.com/finance`) offers multiple portfolios with a minimalist Google style. Google is, at the moment, the only site that offers real-time, as opposed to 20-minute delayed, stock quotes for people who think they can beat the market. You need a Google account to use Google Finance.

- **MSN Money:** This service (`money.msn.com`) also has portfolios and lots of information, although we find it cumbersome to set up and more of a pain to use than My Yahoo!. To use all its features, you have to use Internet Explorer.

- **Yahoo! Finance:** Enter multiple portfolios and customize your screens with related company and general news reports at finance.`yahoo.com`. You can also see lots of company and industry news, including some access to sites that otherwise require paid subscriptions. It's advertiser supported, comprehensive, and easy to use.

- **Marketwatch:** This online part (`www.marketwatch.com`) of the *Wall Street Journal* lets you track portfolios, automatically linking accounts at many online stockbrokers, and read news stories. Although the site wants you to subscribe to the magazines, the free portfolio tracker isn't bad. Click the Portfolio link at the top to get started, and remember that you don't have to sign up for its email newsletters if you don't want to.

Budgeting Tools

Sites to help spend, pay, and invest your money are useful, assuming that you have money to spend, pay, and invest. Toward that end, some websites help you make and follow a budget. They link to your bank and credit card accounts so that they can track the money coming in and out and let you know how reality compares to your budget. We've found some significant bugs in the ones we've tried that made them misreport our financial situation, so if your finances are complex, check their numbers before you trust them. However, if your finances are simple (and all in one currency), these sites can be useful for categorizing your spending and comparing it to your budget.

Mint (www.mint.com), the site that many people use, tracks your budget against your bank accounts, with frequent offers from their sponsors. It's strong in budgeting tools, suggestions about how your budget compares with its other million users, warnings of upcoming bills, and lots of pretty charts and graphs. They're a subsidiary of Intuit, makers of popular finance package Quicken, but you don't need Quicken in order to use the Mint site. John finds that the features that are supposed to collect information from your other online banks and investment accounts don't work very well, and it totally botches accounts in anything but US dollars. (He has an account in Canada.) But if your financial life happens to consist of things that Mint is good at, it may work well for you.

Are account aggregators safe?

Many of the sites we describe can *aggregate* your accounts, which just means that you can give them your login credentials from one site to a second site, and the second site can read the account info from the first site. This can be very handy — Marketwatch uses it to analyze your investments, and Mint uses it to track your entire financial life as far as you'll allow, with banks, credit cards, investments, real estate, and car loans.

While this is without a doubt really convenient, are you setting yourself up to for disaster if your information leaks? As far as we can tell, no. A company called Yodlee handles most of the connections to other institutions. They've been doing this for 15 years, and it appears that they've never screwed up, which is pretty impressive. While there's always some risk to anything you do online, if a reputable site offers account aggregation, it's okay to use it.

Part V
Putting Your Own Stuff on the Web

In this part . . .

- ✔ Explore some ways to put yourself out there online
- ✔ Get to know the ins and outs of blogging

Chapter 17

Making a Splash Online

*B*ack at the dawn of the World Wide Web (in 1989), the plan was that people all over the world would communicate among themselves — a virtual rustic global village. That isn't exactly how it turned out, with giant megamalls like Amazon.com making the web a distinctly nonrustic experience. But after you've browsed the web for a while, you'll probably think of putting your own material online. Hey, you've got interesting things to say, probably more interesting than a lot of websites you've surfed past!

Yes, it's time to stop just browsing the web and start putting yourself out there in various ways. This chapter walks you through a bunch of ways to post information on the web and explains how to start with ones that are easy.

Ways to Go Public on the Web

You can post information on the Internet in lots of different ways. Some require more start-up effort than others. Here's an overview of the best methods for putting your own information online:

✔ **Join a social network:** Websites such as Facebook, LinkedIn, and MySpace started as glorified personal ads and have expanded to include photos, video, email, blogs, polls — you name it. See Chapter 10.

✔ **Create photo galleries:** Many sites enable you to create an online gallery of photos or other pictures. Make your gallery public or share it with only friends and family. See the later section "Say 'Cheese!'"

- ✔ **Share videos:** If you have home videos, animated movies, or other digital video you created or edited using software on your PC or Mac, you can post it on a number of video sites. See Chapter 14.

- ✔ **Share documents, spreadsheets, and calendars:** Post word processing documents or spreadsheets that select personnel can view or edit, and create calendars that others can see and change. See the section "Sharing Documents and Calendars," later in this chapter.

- ✔ **Write a weblog (blog):** Create an online diary or journal with chronological entries. Chapter 18 describes how to read blogs and write your own blog.

- ✔ **Use Twitter to let your friends know what you're up to:** Twitter is a little, tiny blog where you post short messages *(tweets)* and read other people's messages. See Chapter 11.

- ✔ **Build a handcrafted website:** You can use Google Sites, Homestead, Weebly, or a web page editor to create a website with pages of your choosing. See the section "Making Your Own Website," later in this chapter, to find out how.

- ✔ **Sell stuff:** Sell goods or services in an online storefront or auction. See the section "Setting Up an Online Shop," at the end of this chapter.

Say "Cheese!"

We love sharing our family photos with other people, and the web makes it easy. Also, sharing over the web saves you the cost of making extra prints of your snapshots, and it's quick. Several websites enable you to upload your digital pictures to the sites and share the pictures with your friends and family. These free photo-sharing sites make their money by selling prints — after your family sees that gorgeous shot of little Daisy finger-painting with pudding, they'll *have* to have a copy for the fridge!

Of course, the most popular way to share pictures is on Facebook.

You can try one of these photo-sharing sites:

- ✔ **Flickr** (part of Yahoo!) at `flickr.com` is probably the biggest photo-sharing site. Upload pictures from your computer, email them, or send them from your phone — videos, too. Flickr gives you the choice of making photos public to all Flickr users, accessible only to specific groups of people, or completely private.

- ✔ **Picasa** (from Google) at `picasa.google.com` combines a free photo-organizing program with a web-based picture-sharing site and photo editing tools, at `picasaweb.google.com`.

✔ **Photobucket** (owned by Fox) at `photobucket.com` hosts both pictures and video.

✔ **Snapfish** at `www.snapfish.com` lets you set up online photo albums using either photos you upload or rolls of film you mail in to the site. You can share the albums and order prints.

After you create an account at one of these sites, you can upload photos into online photo albums by filling out forms on the website. Then you can share your albums with your friends. If you want, you can make your photos on these sites invisible to the general public — only to the people with whom you share the album.

You (and your friends) can also order prints of your uploaded photos — that's how these sites make their money. The prices for prints are reasonable, and we find these systems convenient. You can print your photos as calendars, cards, books, and even postage stamps.

Another way to share photos is to include them on a blog, as described in Chapter 18. Blogs are useful if you want to use your photos to illustrate a narrative, such as the story of your trip to Spain. **Tumblr** at `www.tumblr.com` is nominally a blog site, but many people use it to host photos and video.

Picture formats

Pictures come in dozens of formats. Fortunately, only three picture formats are in common use on the web: GIF, JPEG, and PNG. Many lengthy — er, *free* and *frank* — discussions have occurred on the Internet concerning the relative merits of these formats. John, who is an Official Graphics Format Expert, by virtue of having persuaded two otherwise reputable publishers to publish his books on the topic, suggests that photographs work better in JPEG format, whereas clip art, icons, and cartoons are better in GIF or PNG. If you're in doubt, JPEG files are smaller, and they download faster. PNG is a superior, new replacement for GIF, and its only disadvantage is that people with truly ancient browsers (Netscape 3.0 and older, for example) can't easily view PNG files.

If you have a picture in any other format, such as BMP or PCX, you must convert it to GIF, JPEG, or PNG before you can use it on the web. Windows comes with Paint, which you can run by choosing Start⇨All Programs⇨Accessories⇨Paint. Or, try Paint. Net at `www.getpaint.net`, an excellent freeware paint program that can convert file formats. Picasa can also convert file formats. For the Mac, consider GraphicConverter at `www.lemkesoft.de`; click the Sprache tab for the English version of the site.

Organizing Your Photos, Too

Several programs help you organize the pictures on your computer as well as upload and share them online. Picasa is the Google photo management program, which you can download from www.picasa.com or picasa.google.com. The program finds the photos on your computer (identifying them by their filename extensions) and helps you organize, caption, and edit them. You can then upload the photos or albums to the website for sharing with your friends and family. Figure 17-1 shows the Picasa photo sharing website.

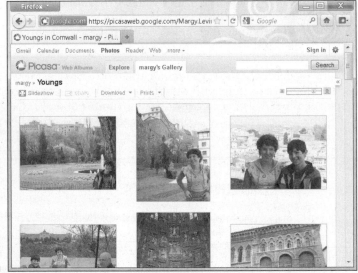

Figure 17-1: Picasa helps organize your photos and upload them to its website for sharing.

Sharing Documents and Calendars

Have you ever wished that you could share a spreadsheet or word processing document with other people, and maybe even let them make changes? Suppose that you're the commissioner of a fantasy football league and you want to share a spreadsheet of players and their statistics with the other players. Yeah, you can email a spreadsheet to everyone, but what if you make updates? Instead, you can upload the spreadsheet to a document-sharing site and share it with the other players.

Or, a document or spreadsheet might be just for you, but you may need to be able to edit it from more than one computer. Our kids use a document sharing site to work on their school papers both at home and at school — it's much easier than copying their files to a thumb drive or disk, which they'd probably forget on the kitchen counter, right next to their lunch.

Document sharing sites let you use the web as your word processing, spreadsheet, or presentation program, storing your files online. You can see, edit, and print your documents, spreadsheets, and presentations from any computer that's on the Internet. In fact, these sites are so good that some people use them for all their documents and spreadsheets, even if they have word processing and spreadsheet programs on their computers.

Creating a Google document

The most popular document sharing site is Google Drive, at `drive.google.com`. Its applications, called Docs (word processor), Sheets (spreadsheet), and Slides (presentations) don't support every advanced feature of Microsoft Word and Excel and Powerpoint, but they handle all the basics. Figure 17-2 shows a Google Docs word processing document. The toolbar just above the document provides formatting options, much like a "real" word processor, and the menu bar (File, Edit, View, and so on) provides other features. You can print your spreadsheet, presentation, or document or export it to your computer as a normal document file that office programs such as Microsoft Office or the freeware LibreOffice can handle.

Figure 17-2:
A group of people can view and edit a Google Doc, unless they're too hungry to concentrate.

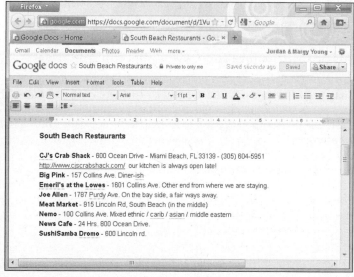

To get started with Google Drive, follow these steps:

1. **Sign in at `drive.google.com` with your Google account username and password.**

   Or, if you're already signed in at another Google site, click Drive on the list of Google services at the top of the screen. Either way, you see the Google Drive screen, with a list of the files you can view or edit.

2. **To upload a word processing document, presentation, or spreadsheet from your computer, click Upload, click Browse, and select the file or folder to import. Then click Upload File.**

   Google Drive uploads the file and creates a new document, presentation, or spreadsheet you can edit and share.

3. **To create a new document, presentation, or spreadsheet from scratch (rather than upload it), click Create and choose the kind of file you want to create.**

   Hey, the Create menu has a bunch of other options, too (maybe more since we wrote this chapter), such as Drawing, which is a simple paint program.

   Google creates a new file of the type you chose and displays it on the screen, with the appropriate menu bar and icons for editing.

4. **If you created the file from scratch, give it a name. Click on the default name which will be something like "Untitled document" and type a better name.**

5. **Type information in the document, presentation, or spreadsheet as usual.**

   If you made a spreadsheet, click in a cell and then type in it. To edit a cell, double-click it or click it and press F2.

6. **Google Drive automatically saves what you type, usually within a few seconds.**

   Google saves your data in the *cloud* — in one of the innumerable web servers that Google maintains and that you never have to see or worry about. Your changes are saved as you edit, so you're unlikely to lose your work.

Google has Drive, Docs, and Sheets apps for Windows, Mac, and most mobile devices. The Drive app for Windows and Mac make your Drive folders appear to be on your computer. The ones for mobile devices have an app for Drive, and separate apps for Docs, Sheets, and Slides so you can view and (with some difficulty) edit files on your device.

Sharing the wealth

After you have a document or spreadsheet or presentation in Google Drive, you can share it with other people. Choose File⇨Share and cut-and-paste or type email addresses into the People box. Click Can Edit if you want to allow them to make changes to your document or spreadsheet, or Can Comment to let them add comments, or Can View if they can look but not touch. Enter the text of the email message that Google Drive will send to invite them to look at your document or spreadsheet, and click Share.

Your invitees receive a message explaining how to access the information you're sharing.

You can also give people a web address they can use to view the document or spreadsheet (no editing). Click Share, click Get Sharable Link, and choose whether the link lets people Edit, Comment, or View. You'll see a rather long URL that you can email or IM to people so that they can take a look.

Making and sharing an online calendar

A handy kind of information you can share is an online calendar. Maybe your club, church, theater, or another organization holds public events. Or, maybe it has a schedule of meetings to share with a small group of people. Either way, you can make an online calendar, enter events or meetings on it, and make it available for viewing or editing.

Google Calendars, at `www.google.com/calendar`, enables you to make one or more calendars, share them with other people, and make them public. You can display more than one calendar, overlaid in different colors, so that you can see your own events alongside your friends' or co-workers' events. Microsoft has a similar service at `calendar.live.com`.

Margy's family has a Google calendar for tracking family events. On the computer in her kitchen, family members refer to the online calendar rather than to the traditional, coffee-stained, paper wall calendar. They sync their family Google calendar with the calendars on their smartphones or other devices, such as the iPhone, iPad, and Android phone. (Okay, we *are* geeks, but having a shared family calendar with us all the time sure is convenient! John, on the other hand, thinks that a Google calendar is no substitute for a paper calendar with pictures of Japanese anime cartoons.)

Looking beyond Google Docs

Not surprisingly, Microsoft has decided to play this game, too. If you go to Microsoft Office Online, at `products.office.com/en-us/office-online`, you can create (surprise!) documents, presentations, and spreadsheets, saved in your OneDrive account. To get started, sign in with your Windows Live account, such as your Hotmail account (or make one for free).

Microsoft also offers Office 365, which is a subscription version of their desktop office software suite. For $100/year, you can run Office on up to five PCs and Macs, and up to five mobile devices. Files can be stored either on the computer or in the cloud. If you have a bunch of PCs, the pricing is often cheaper than buying software separately for each.

Plain Old Files in the Cloud

Sometimes you don't want all the help that Google Drive offers, editing and reformatting files, you just want to stash files somewhere that lets you and perhaps your friends download them, exactly as you uploaded them, with less hassle than trying to mail everything around as attachments. We use cloud storage for collections of full resolution photos from a camera, and audio recordings we've made of events. The most popular service is Dropbox. To store or share files in Dropbox, follow these steps:

1. **If you don't already have a Dropbox account, create one.**

   Visit www.dropbox.com, click Sign Up, and create an account. Choose the free basic account which is plenty for most people; you can always upgrade to a paid account if it turns out you need more space.

2. **Log in at www.dropbox.com if you aren't logged in already.**

3. **Upload files to your Dropbox account.**

   Usually you can just drag files into the Dropbox browser window, and they'll upload automatically. Failing that, click the Upload icon (a rectangle with a small plus sign) to get an upload menu. Uploading large files can take a while, so look at the progress meter at the bottom of the screen to see what's going on.

4. **To download files, log into your Dropbox account from the computer where you want to download them, and click on the files you want.**

   They download to your computer.

5. **To share a file or folder with someone else, mouse over the file and click the little Share icon that appears.**

   The first time you do this, they'll ask you to confirm your email address by clicking in a link they send you. Once you've done that, they show you a URL you can copy and paste into email or instant messages, or they offer to send mail for you. When the recipient clicks on the URL, they see your Dropbox file or folder, which they can download.

Dropbox has a lot of other useful features. Most notably, they have download-able applications for Windows, Mac, Linux, and Android and Apple mobile devices that make the Dropbox folders appear as folders on your computer or device. If you use Dropbox very much, it's worth installing and using these.

Although Dropbox is the most popular cloud storage provider, there are plenty of others:

✔ **Microsoft OneDrive** (`https://onedrive.live.com`) provides upload and download features similar to Dropbox, and is also integrated with Office, so you can use OneDrive files directly from Office programs.

✔ **Amazon CloudDrive** (`https://www.amazon.com/clouddrive/`) provides similar features to Dropbox, with free storage of photos.

It's important to keep backups of your files, and Dropbox or another cloud storage service can keep backup copies in the event of a hard disk failure, power surge, fire, or flood.

Making Your Own Website

At the beginning of this chapter, we list a bunch of ways you can put infor-mation on the web. These ways are terrific, just terrific — we love them all — but they may not be enough for you. What if you want more? What if you need a website with a bunch of pages, with titles you choose, about topics you choose, and maybe even with your own domain name? Okay, you're ready for the next step.

Page creators abound

You have (as usual) several ways to create a website, beyond using Facebook, photo sharing sites, and blogs. The simplest is to use a *page creator site*. At these sites, you can design the look of your site, create a home page for the site, and create as many other pages as you want. Different pages can have different layouts. You don't have to learn to use HTML, the formatting language used by all web pages; see the later sidebar "Why you don't care (much) about HTML."

Page creator sites offer a variety of features, so look carefully before choosing one:

✔ **Cost:** The site may be free or may incur a monthly charge. Free sites often display ads over which you have little control.

✔ **Customization:** Some page creator sites allow more customization of the design than others. Some let you see the HTML (web page code) that makes up your pages and tweak it so that your pages look just right. Others don't allow it.

✔ **Subdomain:** Your site can be a *subdomain* of the page creator site, where your web address is the main site's address with www replaced by a name you choose. You might want your website to have its own domain name (that web address ending in .com or whatever) to give it a little extra cachet. You can find more information about best practices regarding domain names and the various technical details of acquiring one in *Building Websites All-in-One For Dummies,* by David Karlins and Doug Sahlin (John Wiley & Sons, Inc.).

✔ **Design:** Page creator sites offer lots of standard designs. See whether any sites have a design you like.

✔ **Special features:** Some sites let you include message boards, guest books, blogs, calendars, photo galleries, and video on your site. Some help you sell items on your site, with connections to PayPal for checkout.

✔ **Size:** The amount of information you can store on your website varies, along with the maximum number of pages.

Here are some page creator sites we know about:

✔ **Google Sites,** at `sites.google.com`, is a free page creator site run by (who else?) Google. It isn't hugely flexible, but it's easy to use.

✔ **Homestead,** at `www.homestead.com`, is for small businesses and lets you start from more than 2,000 business templates.

✔ **Jigsy,** at `www.jigsy.com`, is free for one small, personal website, but charges a modest fee for a larger or commercial site. You can include Twitter messages, Google maps, and other fancy components on your pages.

✔ **uCoz,** at `www.ucoz.com`, hosts websites for free and lets you include photos, videos, photo albums, polls, guest books, and forms that email you the information that people fill in. It's one of the most popular sites in Russia.

✔ **Weebly,** at `www.weebly.com`, has a nice drag-and-drop system for setting up your site — and no ads.

✔ **Webs,** at `www.webs.com`, has lots of design templates and can host photos, videos, blogs, and message forums.

✔ **Yola,** at `www.yola.com`, is another well-regarded page creator site.

All these sites make creating your own website incredibly easy — for free. You can add pages, add text and pictures to the pages, and create links in the text. Most page creator sites provide a bunch of other items you can add to your pages, such as a calendar, a weather report, a Google map, a blog, an MP3 music player, and videos. For example, you can include a map to your church's or club's meeting location.

What do you say?

Creating a web page is easy. Choosing what to put on your page, however, is harder. What is the page for? What kind of person do you want to see it? Is it for you and your family and friends and potential friends across the world, or are you advertising your business online?

Consider which information you want the entire world to know, because a website is potentially visible to absolutely anyone, including that guy who has hated you ever since fifth grade. If your page is a personal page, don't include your home address or phone number unless you want random people who see the page potentially calling you up. If it's a business page, include your address, phone number, and any other information that potential customers might want.

Why you don't care (much) about HTML

Just so you know what *HTML* is, in case someone asks, it stands for *HyperText Markup Language,* the language used for formatting web pages. Web pages are made up of text and pictures that are stuck together and formatted with HTML codes. In ye olden days of the past millennium (1999), you had to write the HTML yourself. Fortunately, you have waited until now to start creating a web page: Clever page-creator websites and programs are available that let you create your pages by writing the HTML codes for you automatically.

If you want to write a lot of web pages, you should eventually master some HTML.

Although complex, interactive pages require a fair amount of programming, the basics aren't all that complicated. The HTML for **complicated** is `<b>complicated</b>` (that's `<b>` for bold type). In case you decide that you want to be in the web-page creation business, entire books have been written about how to do it. We recommend *HTML, XHTML & CSS For Dummies,* 7th Edition, written by Ed Tittel and Jeff Noble (John Wiley & Sons, Inc.) for the basics, and *Web Design in a Nutshell,* 3rd Edition, written by Jennifer Niederst (O'Reilly Media) for more advanced information.

Setting Up an Online Shop

Selling stuff on the Internet used to take hundreds of thousands of dollars' worth of software and programming talent. A number of sites now let you create web stores for modest fees. Here are a few:

- ✔ **Amazon.com Marketplace,** at `sellercentral.amazon.com`, is easy to set up. Sign in with an Amazon.com account (the same account you use if you buy books or other items on the site), click Your Account, and click Your Seller Account to find out how to set up a seller account. Or, search Amazon.com for the item you want to sell and click the Sell Yours Here button. The site even processes credit card sales for you, eliminating what was once a horrible pain in the neck.

- ✔ **eBay.com Stores,** at `pages.ebay.com/sellerinformation`, enables you to sell items in auctions (for which eBay is famous) or at fixed prices (using the Buy It Now option). Your store can have its own name and logo, and items in your store show up when people search eBay for merchandise.

- ✔ **Craigslist,** at `www.craiglist.com`, is a huge online local classified ads site. You can list almost anything for sale. The site has separate sections for every major city and every U.S. state and they strongly encourage people to meet in person for the transaction; if your browser displays the wrong site, click links in the righthand column to find the site for your area.

- ✔ **Etsy,** at `www.etsy.com`, lets you sell crafts, including clothing, jewelry, ceramics, and anything else you can make by hand.

- ✔ **Yahoo,** at `smallbusiness.yahoo.com`, lets you create a storefront for a monthly fee.

To set up a store, you sign up for a free account at the website and then click the link to create the store. You provide information about the items you sell, including descriptions, prices, and shipping costs. On eBay, you're usually paid by PayPal; on Craigslist, buyer and seller usually meet in person and pay in cash or with a local check; for everyone else, the site typically accepts credit cards and deposits your share to your own bank account.

If you don't want to set up a whole store, you can still sell individual items either on consignment at sites such as `www.half.com` or at auction at sites such as `www.ebay.com`. eBay owns Half.com, so when you set up an account to buy or sell items on one, you're ready to buy or sell on the other, too.

To sell an item on `Half.com` (or any other consignment site), first find the item you want to sell. Half specializes in books, movies, and music, and it has almost everything in print in its database. When you find your item, click the Sell My Copy link, specify the condition of the item, add a description, and state your asking price. When you click the List Item link, your listing goes into the Half.com database and appears on the site within an hour. When you sell your item — which can be minutes, hours, or months later — Half.com keeps a commission.

Selling an item on eBay is similar for books, CDs, and DVDs, but for other items it can be a little more complicated. You write a description for the item and take or scan a digital picture of it. Start at `www.ebay.com`, click the Sell tab or link, and follow the directions. Auctions can last as long as seven days, or you can set up a fixed-price offer with no end date. eBay charges you a listing fee, although if your item doesn't sell, you can usually relist it (try again, perhaps with a lower starting price) for free. Click Customer Support in the upper-right corner of any eBay page, and then click Selling & Seller Fees for instructions and hints for selling.

Search completed eBay listings to get ideas for effective titles and descriptions, along with prices at which similar items have sold. And be sure to include a good photo of the item. For most of these sites, you need a PayPal account (described in Chapter 16) to accept payments.

Chapter 18

Blogging: The World Reads Your Diary

In This Chapter

▶ Reading other people's blogs, or online diaries

▶ Commenting on other people's blogs (politely, we hope)

▶ Subscribing to a blog so that you know when it has a new posting

▶ Making your own blog

▶ Posting to your blog

Diaries are as old as writing. (We made up that statement, but it may well be true. Perhaps you can do some Internet research and let us know whether it is.) However, diaries that every single person on the entire Internet can read are a more recent invention. Not many people have always dreamed of publishing their diaries, but lots of people want to write regular columns where they can express their opinion, tell stories, or post pictures. Blogs have made that expression possible, easy, and free.

If you want to look at or post photos or video instead of prose, you can use a website like Tumblr.

If you're not an enthusiastic and voluminous writer and you want to post tiny articles or journal entries, microblogs were invented for you – Twitter is the best-known microblog. See Chapter 11 for how to read and post on Twitter.

What's in a Blog?

A *weblog*, usually abbreviated as *blog*, is a public online diary where someone posts more or less regular updates. A blog uses software that lets you easily post entries by using your web browser — no additional software is needed. You can even post updates by email or from your cellphone.

Most blogs are updated frequently by one author and contain short, dated entries, as in a diary, with the newest ones at the top. Other blogs are more complex, with multiple topics or pictures as well as or instead of words, but they retain the idea of relatively short entries, updated relatively often. Figure 18-1 shows the political blog of a friend of ours, Doug Muder, who posts once a week at `weeklysift.blogspot.com`.

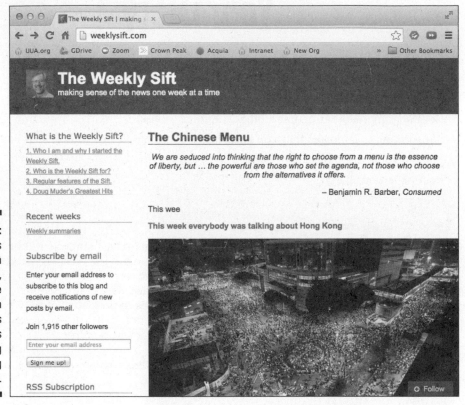

Figure 18-1:
A blog is sort of an online diary, and its value depends on whether its author has anything interesting to say.

The best blogs offer cutting-edge journalism and commentary and brilliant, witty, sparkling writing, whereas the worst disprove the old cliché that a million monkeys at a million typewriters would eventually produce the works of Shakespeare. If you search Google (`google.com`) for the word *blog* or *weblog* and some topic words that are of interest to you, you'll invariably find someone blogging away at it. But keep reading to find out better ways to discover and organize the blogs you read.

As blogs have become more popular, many websites have added blogs to post news, gossip, or behind-the-scenes stories. Every _New York Times_ columnist (at `www.nytimes.com`) has a blog — go to `nytimes.com/blogs` to see a list. Some sites show the latest blog posting or two in a prominent spot, and you can click a link to see older posts.

How to read a blog

Reading a blog is easy because blogs are just web pages. Point your browser at the home page of the one you're interested in and read it. (Bet you thought it would be more complicated than that.) If you want to see more information about a particular story, click the link in the story. Scroll down to read older stories.

Reading one blog is like eating only one potato chip, which never happens. When you find one blog, it usually has links to other blogs. If you search for one blog on a particular topic, you find a dozen blogs on that subject, and before you know it, you're mired deep in the swamps of Blogistan, with far too many interesting blogs to keep track of.

Which blogs should you read? It depends on what you are interested in. Try using Google or another search website to search for a topic that interests you plus the word "blogs" and see what comes up. Here are few blogs we like:

✔ Cool Tools, at `kk.org.cooltools`, posts a description of one useful or intriguing tool each day.

✔ Love and Lemons, at `loveandlemons.com`, about cooking with seasonal produce, by a couple in Austin, Texas

✔ PostSecret, at `postsecret.com`, where people mail postcards (or virtual postcards) with their darkest secrets

✔ Sportsologist, at `sportsologist.com`, about the business and statistics of U.S. sports

✔ The Weekly Sift (`weeklysift.com`) is a weekly round-up of news analysis from a thoughtful liberal perspective.

Because blogs change frequently (at least they're supposed to), you might want to bookmark your favorite ones in your browser so that you can find them again. As you find more blogs, you soon find your bookmark folder and your brain exploding from trying to keep track of them.

More photos than text

If you are looking for photos and videos rather than text, Tumblr.com is worth looking at. Go to `tumblr.com` and enter a topic into the search box.

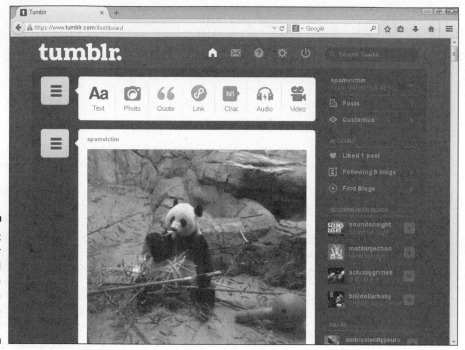

Figure 18-2:
Tumblr blogs tend to include more images than writing.

Lots of blogs, on and off of Tumblr, are mainly photos or videos. For a laugh, check out these sites:

- FailBlog, at `www.failblog.org`, with videos of epic failures (a favorite of teenagers everywhere)
- Cheezburger, at `www.cheezburger.com`, with silly photos, comics, and videos.

Commenting on blogs

Many blogs allow comments, so you can read what other people thought about the post you just read, and you can post your own thoughts. If a blog allows comments, they usually appear below the blog. To post a comment, you may need to create an account and log in. Some blogs don't display comments until the blog owner reads and approves them. Sometimes the comments are the most interesting part of a blog!

Curated super-blogs

There are so many blogs with so much content that sites arose to collect the best material in one place. Some of the *curated sites* have stables of authors to write for them, like these super-blogs:

- ✔ Boing Boing, at www.boingboing.net, for eclectic technogossip
- ✔ Business Insider, at www.businessinsider.com
- ✔ Engadget, at www.engadget.com, for news about cool gadgets
- ✔ *The Huffington Post,* at www.huffingtonpost.com or www.huffpost.com, which expanded to become AOL's online newspaper
- ✔ Mashable, at www.mashable.com, with news about technology, media, and web culture
- ✔ TMZ, at www.tmz.com, for celebrity gossip
- ✔ Wonkette, at www.wonkette.com, for Washington, DC, political gossip

Subscribing to blogs

Luckily, you can subscribe to blogs so that you don't have to remember to return to each blog website to read the latest postings. When you subscribe to a blog, the new entries arrive on your computer automatically, so you don't have to check the blog website. You can find two kinds of blog subscriptions: RSS and email.

RSS blog subscriptions

An RSS feed is one way to subscribe to a blog and receive new postings automagically. (*RSS* stands for Really Simple Syndication.) An *RSS feed* is a special web address (URL) that usually ends with .rss. When you're reading a blog in your browser, look for a Subscribe link or RSS link, which should display information about the site's RSS feed. Some blogs use a URL at feedburner.google.com for their feeds. *Atom* is the successor to RSS; any Atom feed works like an RSS feed.

The system you use to read your RSS subscriptions is an *aggregator*, although almost no one uses the term. Look for web-based *aggregators,* or websites that track and show you all your favorite blogs. You can go to Feedly (`feedly.com`), create an account, and read your blog subscriptions there. If you use My Yahoo! (`my.yahoo.com`) to create your own web start page, you can add your subscriptions to the page. On the blog website, click the Subscribe or RSS link, choose My Yahoo!, and click Add to My to confirm. (Not all blogs work with My Yahoo!.)

Aggregators in your browser

You can install aggregator add-ins to most web browsers which create pseudo-web pages that show you what's new in your RSS feeds. We like Slick RSS for Chrome (do a Google search for "Slick RSS" to find it.) There are dozens of aggregators for Firefox with different usage styles; visit `addons.mozilla.org` and search for "RSS".

Email blog subscriptions

We use a system that alerts us to new information — it's called email. Rather than bother with RSS feeds and aggregator sites, we'd rather just get an email message when our favorite blogs have a new posting. Many, but not all, blogs enable you to subscribe to receive email notifications. If yours don't, you can go to BlogTrottr (`www.blogtrottr.com`) and sign up to receive email notifications for as many blogs as you want for free, accompanied by ads. You cut and paste the RSS feed address and your email address, and you're all set.

Can I make big buck$ with my blog?

Probably not. The alleged path to blog riches is that you start a blog, fill it with fabulous writing, and add some ads down the side and then millions of people flock to your blog and click the ads, and your share of the advertising income buys a tropical island where you retire.

A few famous blogs have succeeded with this plan, but you can probably count them on your fingers, and running each one is a full-time job. We've experimented with ads on some of our bloggish websites, such as John's airline information site at `airinfo.travel` or his blog about Internet and email policy, at `jl.ly`, and we've never seen more than a few dollars a day, which means that our tropical island will be limited to about four square inches.

You can put up a blog with ads for free at Blogger (`www.blogger.com`), so you have nothing to lose other than your time and perhaps your self-esteem. Don't quit your day job quite yet.

Writing Your Own Blog

After you're comfortable reading other people's blogs, how about starting your own? People read blogs for their brilliant, witty, sparkling content. Sparkling is hard, and sparkling regularly is exhausting. If you start your own blog, try blogging for a while on your own before telling all your friends about it. Otherwise: "It was okay at the beginning, but now, big yawn."

Many blogging sites accept text, photos, and even video as part of your blog. You don't have to decide in advance what kind of material you'll include. If you lead an interesting life and want a way to let your friends and family know what's up, a blog may be perfect for you.

Finding a place for your blog

Many big blog sites let you blog away without having to install anything. These sites offer a basic usable blog for free. Some also have extra-cost add-ons that they hope you'll use. For reasons that will shortly become apparent if you read this entire section, we suggest that most of our users try Blogger.

Here are the two most popular blog-hosting sites:

Blogger

```
www.blogger.com
```

Also known as Blogspot, Blogger is part of the Google empire. After you create an account, you can add and edit blog entries at the website, customize it in any of a zillion ways, and publish your blog. Blog entries can include photos and videos. You can even post text and pictures from your mobile phone.

Blogger is remarkably uninterested in asking for your money. As far as we can figure out, its reason for existence is mostly to be a place for people to display Google ads. That's fine — it's a nice site, and the ads are entirely optional.

WordPress

```
www.wordpress.com
```

WordPress can provide you with a customizable blog for free. Because its software is widely used, lots of plug-ins allow you to mix photos from Flickr, posts from Twitter, and other kinds of information directly into your blog. You can also create nonjournal pages, such as an About Me page. WordPress can do more than just blogs; it's become a full-fledged *content management system* (CMS) capable of displaying all kinds of websites. Refer to *WordPress For Dummies*, by Lisa Sabin-Wilson (John Wiley & Sons, Inc.), for more information, or go to www.wordpress.org.

The top five reasons not to start your own blog

Blog entries are usually short, so in that spirit, we offer you a short list:

5. You work on your blog when you should be working on your day job, annoying your co-workers and boss, and you spend hours reading *other* blogs, looking for topics to comment on or borrow.

4. Every conversation or experience becomes a potential blog entry rather than part of your life (also known as novelist's syndrome).

3. You try to have strange conversations and experiences in order to have something to blog (bad novelist's syndrome).

2. Everything, no matter how trivial, takes on a deep bloggable meaning. ("Did you ever notice all the different ways that rain streaks the dirt on the side of a city bus?")

1. You realize that you have nothing to say.

We practice what we preach here. Neither of us has a personal blog, just work-related ones.

Going postal

When you're ready to post to your blog an article, a diary entry, a story, or a rant, you have a number of options:

- **Use your web browser.** Go to the blog's website in your browser and click the Create Post or New Post link. Type your article, or cut and paste it from your word processor. Most blog sites allow you to preview your posting before publishing for the world to see.

- **Use your smartphone.** You can install an app on your iPhone or Android or other type of smartphone that enables you to post on your blog. WordPress, Blogger, and Tumblr all have apps that enable you to post directly from your phone or tablet.

- **Mail it in.** At some blog sites in this list, you can email articles to a special address. In Blogger, you click Settings and then Email to set up the address. On WordPress, go to Dashboard > My Blogs, choose Screen Options, and enable the Post by Email option.

For more ways to blog, get *Blogging For Dummies* (written by Amy Lupold Bair and Susannah Gardner; John Wiley & Sons, Inc.).

Illustrating your blog

Text is so 20th century. (Actually, it's more 15th century, but who's counting?) If you find text constraining, just about every blog site, including the ones we describe in the preceding section, lets you include pictures as part of your blog, often uploaded directly from your mobile phone.

For example, when you're creating a new post on Blogger or WordPress, you can add a picture or video to your post. You upload it and there it is, in your blog! You may need to use photo editing software to crop or resize your photo, or reduce its size if it's enormous.

Blogging in song

If you're a storyteller or musician, or you just have a lot to say, you can post your digital recording on the web as a *podcast*, which is an audio blog. You can upload any audio file you created yourself, containing music, speech, or any sounds you like, and other people can subscribe to it, just like on a blog. Chapter 14 describes how to find and subscribe to podcasts.

One way to set up a podcast is to make a blog and post audio files on it. Several websites will host your podcast for free or for a small monthly fee. Here are two:

- ✔ **PodBean,** at www.podbean.com, is free for personal podcasting, for the first 100MB of audio files. To store more files, you need to pay a modest monthly fee.
- ✔ **Liberated Syndication,** at www.libsyn.com, offers accounts starting at $5 per month.

After you have a podcast, be sure to submit it to the iTunes Store so that people who use iTunes can easily subscribe: Run the free iTunes program (which is useful even if you don't own an i-Anything), click iTunes Store, click Podcasts, and click Submit a Podcast. (See Chapter 14 to find out how to use iTunes.)

For details on creating and maintaining a podcast, read *Podcasting For Dummies* (written by Tee Morris, Chuck Tomasi, Evo Terra, and Kreg Steppe; John Wiley & Sons, Inc.).

Another possibility is to upload your videos to YouTube, and then blog about them, with a text description and a link to the video. (See "Putting the 'You' in YouTube" in Chapter 14.) Or to be even slicker, you can "embed" the YouTube video as a sub-window in your blog post. To do that, visit the YouTube page for your video, click the "Share" icon under the video, then the Embed link that appears. It will show you a box containing a line of web HTML code. Copy and paste that code into your blog post, and your video will appear there.

Part VI

The Part of Tens

Visit www.dummies.com for more great *For Dummies* content online.

In this part . . .

- ✔ Internet problems and how to solve them
- ✔ Some fun things you can do online
- ✔ Ways you can use the Internet to make a difference in the world

Chapter 19

Ten Fun Things You Can Do Online

Y̲ou can use the Internet in hundreds of ways for work and profit. In this chapter, we focus on fun. When you find new and fun things to do on the Net, let us know by sending us an email at internet14@gurus.org. If you want to spend your time online doing something more worthwhile — we're sure you do! — take a look at Chapter 20, too.

Share Pictures and Videos with Your Friends and Family

Email attachments (see Chapter 9) are an excellent way to ship snapshots anywhere in the world for free. You don't even need a digital camera; your phone can probably take stills and maybe even video.

If you have more than one or two pictures or videos and you want to share them with more than one or two people, making an online photo album is the convenient way to go. If you use Facebook you can upload photos to your account and share them with your friends. Or, create an account at Flickr (at www.flickr.com) or Picasa Web Albums (at picasaweb.google.

com), upload your photo and video files, and tell the site who else can see them. You can point your friends to your album by giving them the URL, and they can view the pictures online. You can also use Instagram (owned by Facebook) and Snapchat (which displays your photo for 10 seconds and then deletes it). Chapters 10 and 12 explain it all.

Watch Movies, TV, and Ads

The Internet has created a new way for makers of short and experimental movies to find an audience. Many sites feature miniflicks that you can watch for free. The most popular is Google's YouTube at youtube.com, whose users upload vast amounts of video, from the profound to the inane. Try looking for *airplane landings*. You can upload your own videos, too, as long as you made them yourself, they're no more than ten minutes long, and they follow other YouTube guidelines. TED Talks, at www.ted.com, are short lectures about Technology, Education, and Design, and are almost always interesting.

Hulu, at www.hulu.com, puts television on the web, so you can watch early episodes of shows that you tuned in partway through. The site is supported by ABC, Fox, NBC, and others, so you see the real shows, not chopped-up pirated recordings of shows, although shows are prefaced with advertisements because they're TV and someone has to pay the bills. Blip.tv (at blip.tv — no *.com* at the end) hosts shows you may never have heard of because they're made by independent creators. If you belong to Netflix (www.netflix.com), you can stream videos from its website and watch them on your computer, tablet, or phone. If you have a box that connects your television to the Internet (like a Roku, Amazon Fire TV, or a Blu-Ray player), you can watch Netflix on your TV, too. Chapter 14 lists other ways to watch movies and TV online.

ISpot.tv (www.ispot.tv/browse) features the best current ads and classics. Either way, now you can catch those humorous Super Bowl ads without having to watch the tedious football.

Listen to Current and Classic Radio Programs

Have you ever turned on your radio, found yourself in the middle of a fascinating story, and wished you could have heard the beginning? National Public Radio and Public Radio International in the United States keep many of their past programs available online. If you want to hear the whole program, visit www.npr.org and www.pri.org. You can also use the sites' search features to browse for stories you missed completely. Some radio shows have their own websites, such as *Car Talk* and *This American Life,* shown in Figure 19-1.

Figure 19-1:
The "This American Life" podcast provides stories and insight into the weirdness of daily life.

Many NPR affiliates and other radio stations have live streaming audio of their programs, so you can listen, live, to stations all over the country — go to Google or your favorite search engine and search for the station's call letters or the program name. (John recommends his local station at wrvo.org, especially the old shows from the 1930s through 1950s, which they play in the late evening.) Many other radio stations now let you listen to their live programs over the Internet, which is particularly handy in large office buildings with poor radio reception. You can listen to stations from around the world and get a taste of world music firsthand or hear the news from different perspectives.

If you have an iPod or another type of MP3 player, you can download audio files and listen to many radio shows at any time. See Chapter 14 to find out how to subscribe to podcasts.

Play Checkers or Bridge

Or play chess, poker, hearts, backgammon, cribbage, go, or any other board game or card game. The classic games hold up well against the ever-more-bloody electronic games. If you used to play *Diplomacy,* our favorite board game, back in the 1970s, try `playdiplomacy.com`. Bring out your fiendishly scheming side.

True bridge aficionados like to think of bridge not as a card game but, rather, as a way of life. You can round up a bridge foursome at `bridgebase.com` (for free) and `okbridge.com` ($99 per year after a free trial period). Many free and fee sites are listed at `greatbridgelinks.com`.

Play Lots More Online Games

Now you don't need to round up live friends to play with you — you can find willing partners at any time of the day or night at sites such as `games.yahoo.com`, `www.games.com`, and Microsoft's `zone.msn.com`.

Other good sites for both single-person and multiplayer games are `www.addictinggames.com` and `www.virtualnes.com` for re-created classic Nintendo games.

Words with Friends (`zynga.com/games/words-friends`) enables you to play a Scrabble-like word game with friends and strangers. Download the app for your smartphone or tablet (from the App Store or Google Play Store).

Find Out What Your Stuff Is Worth

You may already know about eBay, the online auction site where you can buy and sell almost anything. (If not, flip to Chapter 15 to read about it.) But you may not know that you can use eBay to find out the value of almost anything — at least, anything that has sold on eBay in the past 90 days — by searching completed eBay auctions.

You need an eBay account in order to search completed auctions, so start at `www.ebay.com` and register for a free account if you don't already have one. Then click the Advanced Search link (we can't tell you exactly where it is, because website designs change often, but it's probably next to the Search bar or the Search button). Type key words about your priceless treasure into the Search bar and select the Completed Listings check box. When you click the Search button, you see all auctions with those keywords and the item's final selling price. If any of the merchandise is similar to your fabulous object, you can see what people are paying for it.

(We're warning all you Beanie Babies speculators: You may be depressed to find out the current price of your vintage, rare, one-of-a-kind, limited-edition, collectible, new-in-box Beanie Babies.)

Build Your Own Jumbo Jet

Even staid corporate sites have the occasional goodies tucked away. Airbus builds airplanes, including the very, very, *very* large A380 superjumbo. Normally, an A380 lists for $300 million, but if that number is a little out of your price range, or you don't have space for one in your garage, Airbus Goodies has some paper versions you can print, cut out, fold, and fly, at www. airbus.com/galleries/goodies/index-cut-outs. It also has some nice screen wallpaper pictures.

Visit Art Museums around the World

Art museums are interesting places to spend rainy afternoons. Now you can visit museums and galleries all over the world by using your browser. Not all museum websites have online artwork, but many do. Our favorites include the Louvre in Paris (at www.louvre.fr; click English in the upper-right corner if you don't read French), Boston's Museum of Fine Arts (www.mfa. org), Metropolitan Museum of Art in New York (www.metmuseum.org), Rijksmuseum in Amsterdam (www.rijksmuseum.nl), and State Hermitage Museum in Russia (www.hermitagemuseum.org/html_En). Check out the spectacular color photographs from Tsarist Russia by Sergei Prokudin-Gorskii, digitally reconstructed by the Library of Congress, at www.loc.gov/exhibits/empire, and the amazing American Memory collection of historical photos at memory.loc.gov/ammem (shown in Figure 19-2).

Figure 19-2:
The
American
Memory
collection at
the Library
of Congress.

Tour the Earth

The modestly named Google Earth downloadable program (at `earth.google.com`) lets you fly around the earth and zoom in and out. After you get fairly close to the ground, you find links to pictures contributed by users (including some impressively remote places — try looking for South Georgia), Wikipedia links, and enough to keep you busy for hours, days, or even months, if you aren't careful.

Or, check out Google Maps Street View: Start at `maps.google.com`, visit an urban area (try *15th Avenue, New York, NY 10011*), and click Street View. You can make a 360-degree pan of the spot to see what it looked like the last time a Google employee was there with a camera.

Lots of other interesting maps are on the web. Watch the "walmartization" of the United States at `projects.flowingdata.com/walmart`. A wonderful analysis of the red-state-versus-blue-state political landscape is at `www-personal.umich.edu/~mejn/election`.

Tour the Solar System

The last half of the 20th century will go down in history as the time when humans began to explore outer space. Probes visited several comets and asteroids and every planet except Pluto. The probes sent back amazing pictures: storms on Jupiter, oceans on Europa, mudslides on Mars, and the Earth at night.

Which generation will get to play tourist in the solar system remains to be seen; here are some fascinating space sites:

- ✔ `apod.nasa.gov/apod`: Be sure to bookmark the astronomy picture of the day.
- ✔ `antwrp.gsfc.nasa.gov/apod/image/0011/earthlights_dmsp_big.jpg`: Above all, don't miss the incredible NASA montage of human civilization.

Build Your Own World

Virtual worlds are electronic places you can visit on the Web — kind of like 3D chat rooms. Rather than create a screen name, you create a personal action figure, or *avatar,* that walks, talks, and emotes (but doesn't make a mess on your floor). When you're in one of these worlds, your avatar interacts with the avatars of other people who are logged on in surroundings that range from quite realistic to truly fantastic. In some virtual worlds, you can even build your own places: a room, a house, a park, a city — whatever you can imagine. Other worlds let you make money, gain status, and battle complete strangers. People who enjoy role-playing games can disappear into online games for hours, days, or months at a time. The biggest, most successful online worlds are *World of Warcraft,* which costs money, at `us.battle.net/wow`, and *RuneScape,* which is free, at `www.runescape.com`.

Most virtual worlds require you to download a plug-in or special software. Some are free, whereas others require monthly or annual subscriptions. For example, *Second Life,* at `secondlife.com`, lets you create your own part of a shared online world, including spending real-world money.

Web-based online worlds are an outgrowth of MUDs (which stands for Multi-User Dimensions or Multi-User Dungeons or various other names, depending on whom you ask), which were text-based virtual online worlds long before there was a web.

Read the Comics

Why get newsprint ink on your hands just to read your favorite comic strip? Ours are

- *Dilbert,* at `dilbert.com` (Okay, you knew we were geeks!)
- *Doonesbury,* at `doonesbury.washingtonpost.com`
- *Foxtrot,* at `foxtrot.com`

GoComics (at `www.gocomics.com` has lots of other comic strips, including vintage *Peanuts* strips.

We also like web-only comics, such as `xkcd.com` (three comics a week, occasionally PG-13; we frequently resort to `explainxkcd.com` to understand the humor). You can find thousands more; the best way to find good ones is to follow links from comics you like and check out the comics they like.

Share Your Screen with a Friend

If you're doing something interesting on your computer, or if you need a friend's help to make your computer cooperate, you can allow your friend to see your screen. Many video chat programs also provide screen sharing, including Google Hangouts (`plus.google.com`), Skype (`www.skype.com`), and Zoom (`www.zoom.us`).

For example, if you sign up for a free Zoom account (which limits you to 40 minutes, but that's long enough for most meetings anyway!), click the Share Screen icon at the bottom of the screen to allow the other people in your video conference to see your whole screen or a specific window.

Chapter 20

Ten Worthwhile Things to Do Online

*T*he Internet lets you make the world a better place, by working directly on projects or making it possible for other people to do so. Whenever you find other ways to improve the world, send email to us at internet14@ gurus.org.

Feed the Hungry

On the web, you can donate money to fight world hunger while improving your vocabulary — what more could you ask of one website? Free Rice (www. freerice.com) asks you to match words with their meanings. For every correct answer you give, the site donates ten grains of rice to an international food relief organization. You start with easy words at Level 1 and work your way up; the challenge can become addictive (we tend to get stuck at level 50). If you know a teenager who is studying for a standardized college entrance test, this site is a helpful way for them to learn some new, fancy words.

Support a Charity While You Shop

If you buy on the eBay online auction site (described in Chapter 15), look for charities selling things or people selling things and donating part or all of their proceeds to charity. A little blue-and-yellow ribbon icon indicates charitable listings. If you want to see only charitable listings, visit eBay Giving Works, at `givingworks.ebay.com`, where you can search, buy, or sell on behalf of charities.

Find Charities That Don't Waste Money

When you choose to give money to a charitable organization, you want the money to go to the organization's mission, not to their management, marketing, or overhead. Charity Navigator at `www.charitynavigator.org` helps you evaluate how efficiently your favorite charities spend their (or your) money. For more detailed information on individual charities, Guidestar at `www.guidestar.org` has details about every charity in the country.

Become a Microfinancier or a Philanthropist

Microfinance pioneer Muhammad Yunus won a Nobel Peace Prize for starting the Grameen Bank, which makes tiny loans to people in Bangladesh and other developing countries to start small rural businesses. Kiva (`www.kiva.org`) lets you become your own microfinance lender to groups of people in Latin America, Africa, and Asia for projects such as starting a sewing business, delivery service, or fish market. Loans start at $25.

Heifer International (`www.heifer.org`) provides livestock and other resources to poor farmers for both food security and income. A *heifer* (that's a young cow, for you city folk) costs $500, and a share of a goat or pig starts at $10.

Educate Yourself

Thomas Jefferson said, "If a nation expects to be ignorant and free, in a state of civilization, it expects what never was and never will be." Keeping up with national, international, political, and economic news is your responsibility as a citizen. Try searching the web for newspapers; almost all have websites. Some prominent newspapers charge if you want to read more than a few articles a month, such as the *New York Times* (www.nytimes.com), but most online newspapers are free. At election time, go to Project Vote Smart (www.votesmart.org) to find unbiased information about issues and candidates.

If you need background information, you can take a course at the Ivy League level on almost any subject at MIT OpenCourseWare (ocw.mit.edu). Videos of lectures, lecture notes, and exams are all posted online. You receive no credit, but you can get educated for free!

Edit an Encyclopedia

Wikis were designed to enable groups of people to work together to make and maintain websites. A wiki (named for the interterminal bus at Honolulu International Airport, which is in turn named for the Hawaiian word *wiki-wiki*, which literally means "in a hurry" — no, really) can have an unlimited number of authors, all of whom can add and change pages within the wiki website. Unlike a blog, it doesn't have to be a sequence of journal entries. Instead, you can organize your text any way you like, including making as many new, interlinked pages as you like.

If this process sounds potentially chaotic when you have more than one author, it is, but most wikis have ground rules that keep the group moving in more or less the same direction. A wiki can work well if it has a single author or if it has a group of people who trust each other to edit each other's writing. For example, a group of co-workers can make a wiki that contains information about a project they're working on. A church or club can make a wiki with committee meeting minutes, mission statements, plans, and schedules.

The biggest wiki of them all is *Wikipedia,* at en.wikipedia.org, a collaborative encyclopedia that is, with more than 4 million entries (in English, plus millions in other languages), well on its way to including all human knowledge.

Not only is Wikipedia a free encyclopedia, but it also lets you edit its articles. If you feel knowledgeable about a topic, look it up in Wikipedia. Most pages have an Edit link so that you can add what you know. If you find mistakes or have more to say, just set up a free account and then click the Edit tab. If no article exists, Wikipedia offers to let you create one. Read en.wikipedia.org/wiki/Help:Editing for how to edit existing articles and write new ones, following the rules of Neutral Point of View. A page might have a sidebar with complaints about the article from the Wikipedia editors, begging you to help improve it.

Digitize Old Books

Many websites require that you decode some blurry text known as a CAPTCHA (which allegedly stands for Completely Automated Public Turing test to tell Computers and Humans Apart) before it will let you set up an account or post a message. The reCAPTCHA project at Carnegie-Mellon University (now owned by Google) uses CAPTCHAs to help digitize old books and newspapers. The scanning process first makes a photographic image of a page and then tries to identify the words in the text. It can recognize most words, but some are just too blurry or obscure for automatic identification. That's where you come in. Every reCAPTCHA challenge shows you two words: one that's already been decoded and one that hasn't, as shown in Figure 20-1. When you type the two words, reCAPTCHA checks the one it knows, and if you get that one right, it assumes that you probably got the other one right, too. Just to make sure, the unknown words are shown to several different people, and if they all agree, the word is considered decoded. ReCAPTCHA is used by thousands of websites all over the world, showing about 30 million CAPTCHAs per day. Not all of them are solved, of course, but that's still a lot of decoded words.

You're helping the reCAPTCHA project every time you solve a two-word reCAPTCHA challenge. For more information, see its website at www. google.com/recaptcha.

Figure 20-1:
Are you a
person or a
program?

Search for Extraterrestrial Life or Cure Cancer

The SETI@home (setiathome.ssl.berkeley.edu) scientific experiment uses Internet-connected home and office computers to search for extraterrestrial intelligence (SETI). The idea is to have thousands of otherwise idle PCs and Macs perform the massive calculations needed to extract the radio signals of other civilizations from intergalactic noise. You can participate by running a free program that downloads and analyzes data collected at the Arecibo radio telescope in Puerto Rico.

If eavesdropping on space aliens seems a bit far out, you may enjoy lending your computer's idle time to solving problems in cryptography and mathematics. Distributed.net (`www.distributed.net`) manages several projects. (Feel free to join the Internet Gurus team there.) When you sign up to help a project, you can set up its program on your computer to run when the computer isn't otherwise occupied, and your donation of computer time helps achieve the goal of the project.

If math and cryptography don't ring your chimes, consider joining the Folding at Home project at `folding.stanford.edu`. This project studies how proteins acquire their three-dimensional shapes, an important question in medical research. By signing up to run its program, you're helping with basic research that may help find a cure for "Alzheimer's, Mad Cow (BSE), CJD, ALS, Huntington's, Parkinson's disease, and many cancers and cancer-related syndromes."

You can find other ways to volunteer to help with scientific research at `crowdcrafting.org`.

Mentor a Teenager or Young Adult Online

An adult mentor can make all the difference to a young person struggling with life. Several online mentoring websites match adults with youth. `Icouldbe.org` serves 2,300 underprivileged junior high, high school, and college students every year. Sign up to share your career expertise — or your life experience — with the next generation. iMentor (`www.imentor.org`) concentrates on the New York City area.

Adopt a Kid

Do you surf the web for hours each day? Maybe your life needs more meaning. Adopting a child is more of a commitment than upgrading to the latest Microsoft operating system, but at least kids grow up eventually and you don't have to reinstall them to get rid of viruses. These two excellent websites list special children in need of homes: `rainbowkids.com` and `capbook.org`. It can't hurt to look.

Index

• ⅅ •

About the Authors

John R. Levine was a member of a computer club in high school — before high school students, or even high schools, had computers — where he met Theodor H. Nelson, the author of *Computer Lib/Dream Machines* and the inventor of hypertext, who reminded us that computers should not be taken seriously and that everyone can and should understand and use computers.

John wrote his first program in 1967 on an IBM 1130 (a computer somewhat less powerful than your typical modern digital wristwatch, only more difficult to use). He became an official system administrator of a networked computer at Yale in 1975. He began working part-time — for a computer company, of course — in 1977 and has been in and out of the computer and network biz ever since. He got his company on Usenet (the Internet's worldwide bulletin board system) early enough that it appears in a 1982 *Byte* magazine article on a map of Usenet, which then was so small that the map fit on half a page.

Although John used to spend most of his time writing software, now he mostly writes books (including *UNIX For Dummies* and technical books such as *Linkers and Loaders* and *qmail*) because it's more fun and he can do so at home in the tiny village of Trumansburg, New York, where in his spare time he was the mayor for several years and can hang around with his daughter when he's supposed to be writing. John also does a fair amount of public speaking. (Go to www.johnlevine.com to see where he'll be.) He holds a BA degree and a PhD in computer science from Yale University, but please don't hold that against him.

In high school, **Margaret Levine Young** was in the same computer club as her big brother, John. She stayed in the field throughout college against her better judgment and despite John's presence as a graduate student in the computer science department. Margy graduated from Yale and went on to become one of the first PC managers in the early 1980s at Columbia Pictures, where she rode the elevator with big stars whose names she wouldn't dream of dropping here.

Since then, Margy has co-authored more than 25 computer books about topics that include the Internet, UNIX, WordPerfect, Microsoft Access, and (stab from the past) PC-File and Javelin, including *The Internet For Dummies Quick Reference* and *UNIX For Dummies,* and *Windows Vista: The Complete Reference* and *Internet: The Complete Reference* (both from Osborne/McGraw-Hill). She met her future husband, Jordan, in the R.E.S.I.S.T.O.R.S. (the computer club we mentioned).

Her other passion is her children, along with music, Unitarian Universalism, reading, knitting, gardening (you can never grow too much garlic), and anything to do with eating. She lives in Vermont (see `www.gurus.org/margy` for some scenery) and works as the Web Team Manager for the Unitarian Universalist Association (`www.uua.org`).

Please visit both authors online at `net.gurus.org`.

Dedication

John and Margy dedicate this book to their father, Bob Levine, who after 93 years is still working hard to make the world a better place, and to the memory of Dionir de Souza Gomes Young.